CHASTE VALUE

EDINBURGH CRITICAL STUDIES IN SHAKESPEARE AND PHILOSOPHY
Series Editor: Kevin Curran

Edinburgh Critical Studies in Shakespeare and Philosophy takes seriously the speculative and world-making properties of Shakespeare's art. Maintaining a broad view of 'philosophy' that accommodates first-order questions of metaphysics, ethics, politics and aesthetics, the series also expands our understanding of philosophy to include the unique kinds of theoretical work carried out by performance and poetry itself. These scholarly monographs will reinvigorate Shakespeare studies by opening new interdisciplinary conversations among scholars, artists and students.

Editorial Board Members

Ewan Fernie, Shakespeare Institute, University of Birmingham
James Kearney, University of California, Santa Barbara
Julia Reinhard Lupton, University of California, Irvine
Madhavi Menon, American University
Simon Palfrey, Oxford University
Tiffany Stern, Oxford University
Henry Turner, Rutgers University
Michael Witmore, The Folger Shakespeare Library
Paul Yachnin, McGill University

Published Titles

Rethinking Shakespeare's Political Philosophy: From Lear to Leviathan
Alex Schulman
Shakespeare in Hindsight: Counterfactual Thinking and Shakespearean Tragedy
Amir Khan
Second Death: Theatricalities of the Soul in Shakespeare's Drama
Donovan Sherman
Shakespeare's Fugitive Politics
Thomas P. Anderson
Is Shylock Jewish?: Citing Scripture and the Moral Agency of Shakespeare's Jews
Sara Coodin
Chaste Value: Economic Crisis, Female Chastity and the Production of Social Difference on Shakespeare's Stage
Katherine Gillen

Forthcoming Titles

Making Publics in Shakespeare's Playhouse
Paul Yachnin
Derrida Reads Shakespeare
Chiara Alfano
The Play and the Thing: A Phenomenology of Shakespearean Theatre
Matthew Wagner
Shakespearean Melancholy: Philosophy, Form, and the Transformation of Comedy
J. F. Bernard
Shakespeare and the Fall of the Roman Republic: Selfhood, Stoicism, and Civil War in Julius Caesar and Antony and Cleopatra
Patrick Gray
Conceiving Desire: Metaphor, Cognition, and Eros in Lyly and Shakespeare
Gillian Knoll

For further information please visit our website at edinburghuniversitypress.com/series/ecsst

CHASTE VALUE

Economic Crisis, Female Chastity and the Production of Social Difference on Shakespeare's Stage

◆ ◆ ◆

KATHERINE GILLEN

EDINBURGH
University Press

Edinburgh University Press is one of the leading university presses in the UK. We publish academic books and journals in our selected subject areas across the humanities and social sciences, combining cutting-edge scholarship with high editorial and production values to produce academic works of lasting importance. For more information visit our website: edinburghuniversitypress.com

© Katherine Gillen, 2017

Edinburgh University Press Ltd
The Tun – Holyrood Road, 12(2f) Jackson's Entry, Edinburgh EH8 8PJ

Typeset in 12/15 Adobe Sabon by
IDSUK (DataConnection) Ltd

A CIP record for this book is available from the British Library

ISBN 978 1 4744 1771 6 (hardback)
ISBN 978 1 4744 1772 3 (webready PDF)
ISBN 978 1 4744 1773 0 (epub)

The right of Katherine Gillen to be identified as the author of this work has been asserted in accordance with the Copyright, Designs and Patents Act 1988, and the Copyright and Related Rights Regulations 2003 (SI No. 2498).

CONTENTS

Acknowledgements vi
Series Editor's Preface viii

Introduction: Chastity and the Question of Value 1

1. Chastity and the Ethics of Commercial Theatre in *Measure for Measure*, *Pericles* and *The Revenger's Tragedy* 33

2. Commercial Chastity and Aristocratic Value in *Troilus and Cressida*, *The White Devil* and *The Changeling* 87

3. Chaste Selfhood: Ben Jonson's Critique of Urban Chastity Tropes 127

4. Chastity and Blackness: Racial Value and Commodity Potential in *The Fair Maid of the West, Part I* and *Othello* 168

5. Mediterranean Markets, Commoditised Masculinity and the Whitening of Christian Chastity in *The Merchant of Venice* and *The Renegado* 205

6. Chaste Treasure and National Identity in *The Rape of Lucrece* and *Cymbeline* 254

Coda: Approaching Capitalist Modernity 297

Index 301

ACKNOWLEDGEMENTS

This project would not have been possible without the support of many friends, mentors, colleagues and institutions. It began as a dissertation at the University of New Hampshire, where Douglas Lanier introduced me to the rigours and joys of early modern scholarship. Doug's guidance was – and still is – invaluable. While at UNH, I had the privilege of working with Cristy Beemer, Dennis Britton, Elizabeth Hageman and Sean Moore, all of whom provided incisive feedback on drafts and, more broadly, fostered a rich intellectual environment. A special thanks to Coppélia Kahn for her generosity as an outside reader and to Dennis for his continued support as the project evolved from a dissertation to a book. My time at UNH was also enriched by the camaraderie and acumen of fellow early modernists Nicola Imbracsio and Jay Zysk.

This book has benefited from the archives and the vibrant scholarly community at the Folger Shakespeare Library and from the expertise of the Folger staff, particularly Georgianna Zeigler. I thank the Folger for a research fellowship in 2013. I have presented several pieces of the project at symposia and conferences. I am particularly indebted to the Shakespeare Association of American, as this project is stronger for having been shared in seminars and on the 2015 Next Generation Plenary. For their encouragement and intellectual generosity, I thank Mark Bayer, Keith Botelho, Arthur Little, James Mardock, Patricia Parker and Bradley Ryner.

Acknowledgements

It has been a great pleasure to work with the talented team at Edinburgh University Press and to be included in the Edinburgh Critical Studies in Shakespeare and Philosophy series. My thanks to Kevin Curran for his masterful editorial guidance and to Michelle Houston, Adela Rauchova and the anonymous readers whose insights strengthened the project.

A warm thank you to my marvellous colleagues at Texas A&M University-San Antonio: Jackson Ayres, Ann Bliss, Katherine Bridgman, Scott Gage, Lisa Jennings, Adrianna Santos, William Bush, Vicky Elias, Amy Porter and Edward Westermann. Working at a start-up institution is not for the faint of heart, and your solidarity, dedication and humour have made the adventure worth it. I am also indebted to our wonderful library staff, especially Stefanie Wittenbach, Sarah Timm, Bryant Moore and Emily Bliss-Zaks.

My community has sustained me as I've worked on this book. My dear friends Cathryn Merla-Watson, Claire Price, Jim Webber, Rose Whitmore and Katie Wiskoski have provided intellectual and emotional support (and lots of phone calls). The San Antonio yogis have deepened my practice, on the mat and at my desk. Heartfelt thanks to my family: the Finley-Stillmans, Michael and Margo Gillen, the Upstate Gillen crew (especially Joan for the babysitting!), and in particular my parents John and Mary Kay who provide unending support and keep my writing honest. Owen, who showed up as this project was nearing completion, lights up my life. I reserve my deepest love and gratitude for James Finley. He has read every word of this book, talked over every idea, and made the last nine years a joy.

A section of Chapter 3 appeared as 'Female Chastity and Commoditized Selfhood in *Bartholomew Fair*', *Studies in English Literature* 55.2 (Spring 2015): 309–26, and an early version of Chapter 6 was published as 'Chaste Treasure: Protestant Chastity and the Creation of a National Economic Sphere in *The Rape of Lucrece* and *Cymbeline*', *Early English Studies* 4 (November 2011): 1–38. Both are reprinted with permission.

SERIES EDITOR'S PREFACE

Picture Macbeth alone on stage, staring intently into empty space. 'Is this a dagger which I see before me?' he asks, grasping decisively at the air. On one hand, this is a quintessentially theatrical question. At once an object and a vector, the dagger describes the possibility of knowledge ('Is this a dagger') in specifically visual and spatial terms ('which I see before me'). At the same time, Macbeth is posing a quintessentially philosophical question, one that assumes knowledge to be both conditional and experiential, and that probes the relationship between certainty and perception as well as intention and action. It is from this shared ground of art and inquiry, of theatre and theory, that this series advances its basic premise: Shakespeare is philosophical.

It seems like a simple enough claim. But what does it mean exactly, beyond the parameters of this specific moment in Macbeth? Does it mean that Shakespeare had something we could think of as his own philosophy? Does it mean that he was influenced by particular philosophical schools, texts and thinkers? Does it mean, conversely, that modern philosophers have been influenced by him, that Shakespeare's plays and poems have been, and continue to be, resources for philosophical thought and speculation?

The answer is yes all around. These are all useful ways of conceiving a philosophical Shakespeare and all point to lines of inquiry that this series welcomes. But Shakespeare is philosophical in a much more fundamental way as well. Shakespeare is philosophical because the plays and poems actively create new worlds of knowledge and new scenes of ethical encounter. They ask big questions, make bold arguments, and develop new vocabularies in order to think what might otherwise be unthinkable. Through both their scenarios and their imagery, the plays and poems engage the qualities of consciousness, the consequences of human action, the phenomenology of motive and attention, the conditions of personhood, and the relationship among different orders of reality and experience. This is writing and dramaturgy, moreover, that consistently experiments with a broad range of conceptual crossings, between love and subjectivity, nature and politics, and temporality and form.

Edinburgh Critical Studies in Shakespeare and Philosophy takes seriously these speculative and world-making dimensions of Shakespeare's work. The series proceeds from a core conviction that art's capacity to think – to formulate, not just reflect, ideas – is what makes it urgent and valuable. Art matters because unlike other human activities it establishes its own frame of reference, reminding us that all acts of creation – biological, political, intellectual and amorous – are grounded in imagination. This is a far cry from business-as-usual in Shakespeare studies. Because historicism remains the methodological gold standard of the field, far more energy has been invested in exploring what Shakespeare once meant than in thinking rigorously about what Shakespeare continues to make possible. In response, Edinburgh Critical Studies in Shakespeare and Philosophy pushes back against the critical orthodoxies of historicism and cultural studies to clear a space for scholarship that confronts aspects of literature that can neither be reduced to nor adequately explained by particular historical contexts.

Shakespeare's creations are not just inheritances of a past culture, frozen artifacts whose original settings must be expertly reconstructed in order to be understood. The plays and poems are also living art, vital thought-worlds that struggle, across time, with foundational questions of metaphysics, ethics, politics and aesthetics. With this orientation in mind, Edinburgh Critical Studies in Shakespeare and Philosophy offers a series of scholarly monographs that will reinvigorate Shakespeare studies by opening new interdisciplinary conversations among scholars, artists and students.

Kevin Curran

INTRODUCTION: CHASTITY AND THE QUESTION OF VALUE

The early modern English stage frequently renders female chastity, virginity as well as married fidelity, in economic terms. Images of jewels, pearls and treasure abound, indicating chastity's immeasurable worth. Leontio in Thomas Middleton's *Women Beware Women*, for example, refers to his chaste wife Brancha as a 'most matchless jewel' and sequesters her, believing that ''tis great policy / To keep choice treasures in obscurest places'.[1] In many instances, this conventional imagery is replaced with the more overtly commercial terms of commodity, usury and currency. Paroles in William Shakespeare's *All's Well That Ends Well*, for example, calls virginity a 'commodity will lose the gloss with lying; the longer kept, the less worth'.[2] Monticelso in John Webster's *The White Devil* compares unchaste women to 'the guilty counterfeited coin / Which whosoe'er first stamps it brings in trouble / All that receive it', and in Middleton's *The Revenger's Tragedy*, Lussurioso hopes that Castiza's chastity will be 'br[ought] . . . into expense, for honesty / Is like a stock of money laid to sleep / Which ne'er so little broke, does never keep'.[3] This economic discourse is as common as it is imprecise, often conflating the woman, her spiritual essence and her genitalia in its attempt to identify the source of chastity's value. In each case, the drama calls attention to chastity's interpolation into, or its resistance to, economic forces.

Chaste Value: Economic Crisis, Female Chastity and the Production of Social Difference on Shakespeare's Stage considers chastity's significance in light of this ubiquitous economic imagery, situating dramatic representations of chastity within broader anxieties about the social, ethical and epistemological effects of early capitalism. As I will demonstrate, many plays by Shakespeare and his contemporaries invoke chastity – itself a virtue, a symbol of stability, a quasi-commodity and a mode of selfhood – to interrogate competing understandings of personal value and to explore the ramifications of incorporating people, their labour and their productions into commercial exchange. As such, I argue, chastity informs the theatre's staging of subjectivities born of commoditisation as well as its articulation of emerging distinctions between human and economic value.[4] Chastity, moreover, figures centrally in the process whereby the stage disrupts pre-capitalist understandings of intrinsic personal value and, in response to this disruption, reallocates personal value according to hierarchies of gender, race, class and nationality. Ultimately, *Chaste Value* aims to show that chastity functions not simply as an ideal of female conduct but as an ideological category that was integral to dramatic interrogations of value, subjectivity and even humanity at a moment of profound economic upheaval.

In many ways, the commercial imagery surrounding chastity reflects the theatre's intense concern with economic signification. The sixteenth century witnessed the unprecedented growth of commodity exchange, wage labour, conspicuous consumption, credit systems and overseas trade.[5] 'What marks the sixteenth century from preceding centuries', Craig Muldrew contends, 'was that the scale of marketing expanded over such a short period of time, propelled by increasing demand and competition for the profits generated by higher prices'.[6] As Sandra Fischer argues in her foundational study *Econolingua*, a new language develops in the sixteenth century as economics 'begins to penetrate all human relations' and 'money becomes the only way of assessing value, profit the only impetus for human action'.⁷ To early moderns the market seemed to encroach upon all aspects of life, infusing daily transactions and transfiguring interpersonal relationships. As Karl Polanyi states, under capitalism, 'Instead of economy being embedded in social relations, social relations are embedded in the economic system.'⁸ Market logics threatened the landed aristocracy and its worldview, instantiating new modes of thinking that considered objects, actions, ideas and people in terms of the money they could garner. The drama's 'econolingua', to borrow Fischer's term, seeks to make sense of these broad capitalist transformations, interrogating the market's influence on social, ethical and aesthetic realms. Ultimately, Fischer argues, this economic imagery 'illuminate[s] the transition from medieval economy to mercantilist ethics'.⁹

Female chastity, *Chaste Value* contends, occupies a privileged place within the drama's investigation of economic language, ideologies and practices. It does so in part because of chastity's role in protecting aristocratic class structures that were threatened by capitalist transformations. As Lawrence Stone explains, virginity acquires value 'in the marriage market of a hierarchical and propertied society [assuring] that there should be no legal doubts about the legitimacy of the heirs to property and title'.¹⁰ Married chastity extends this function to ensure that a woman engages in sexual relations exclusively with her husband and that her children belong to him. The early modern obsession with female sexuality, therefore, often reflects anxieties about shifting class structures, with the figure of the bastard embodying the chaos that presumably results from uncontrolled female appetites.¹¹ Though chastity was held up as a political, social and religious ideal, it was in perpetual danger of unravelling, as the female body was imagined as unruly and open, in need of constant surveillance.¹²

Given the family's status as a microcosm for the state in early modern England, chastity functioned as a symbol of political stability and, more broadly, in Mark Breitenberg's words, 'as the linchpin of every other aspect of the social network'.¹³ This ideological significance was heightened in Elizabethan England, as royal iconography relied on associations of virginity with bodily and national integrity. As Mary Douglas argues, 'the body is a model which can stand for any bounded system. Its boundaries can represent any boundaries which are threatened or precarious.'¹⁴ With Elizabeth I's body representing the contained yet vulnerable borders of the English nation, her chastity metonymically extended to the state.¹⁵ Stephanie H. Jed points out that the word *chastity*, stemming from the Latin *carere*, 'to be cut off from or lack', connotes the condition of being protected from contact or contamination.¹⁶ The nation thus becomes ideologically purified – a purity represented in the queen's physical body. This ideological formulation remains resonant in England after the death of Elizabeth I, though it is complicated by the ascendance of James I to the throne.

Chastity's national significance coexisted with its function within England's patriarchal familial arrangements, as the need to positively identify offspring led to a social and legal system that considered women's sexuality an element of male property.¹⁷ Chastity was exchanged from a father to a husband in marriage, constituting the traffic in women that Gayle Rubin identifies as the defining element of patriarchy.¹⁸ Rubin's paradigm, which revises Claude Lévi-Strauss's, points toward chastity's structural significance, suggesting that women and their chastity function as symbolic currency used to cement male relationships. Because of its status as property – both as an attribute belonging to a woman and as the possession of a man – chastity raises vexing questions regarding the relationship between property and personhood.

In the early capitalist economy, this form of property was often conceived as a commodity, an entity defined primarily by its exchange value. Luce Irigaray argues that the virginal woman is figured as 'pure exchange value', as 'nothing but the possibility, the place, the sign of relations among men. In and of herself, she does not exist: she is a simple envelope veiling what is really at stake in social exchange.'[19] In early modern England, this commodity status extended to married chastity, which presumes that a virgin's chaste value could be transferred to her husband in marriage. Protestant moralists such as William Perkins considered companionate marriage 'a state in it selfe, farre more excellent, then the condition of single life'.[20] Rejecting the Catholic valorisation of physical virginity, Protestants instead emphasised chastity's spiritual elements to suggest that chastity could maintain its essential character even after a woman had engaged in sexual intercourse. This formulation underscores chastity's commodity properties, as its physical essence is sublimated in favour of its exchange value and the conditions of its circulation are obscured. Despite this spiritualisation, chastity's physical dimension persists, attested to by its lasting connection to the female body and by the continued use of material objects such as jewels to represent it. Accordingly, chastity is rendered as what Polanyi terms a *fictitious commodity*, an entity that is 'obviously *not* [a] commodit[y]' but is treated as one.[21]

The commoditisation of chastity, *Chaste Value* argues, raises questions about personal value. Early moderns considered chastity, in both its virginal and married forms, to constitute the entirety of a woman's value; as Ruth Kelso memorably states, 'let a woman have chastity, she has all. Let her lack chastity and she has nothing.'[22] Chastity, therefore, often represents personal value writ large, analogous to a range of male virtues, including honour, courage and temperance. When chastity is commoditised, as it is so easily within patriarchal sex-gender systems, it raises the possibility that men and their attributes may be similarly commoditised. The transformations attending early capitalism heightened this concern. The early modern stage, *Chaste Value* demonstrates, repeatedly invokes commoditised chastity as a means of interrogating capitalism's disruption of the aristocratic order and of exploring the potential effects of commoditising people, their labour and their attributes.

In its focus on issues of value, exchange and representation, *Chaste Value* draws on a body of new economic criticism that traces formal relationships between money and language, viewing both as systems of representation. Economics, as Marc Shell argues, is fundamentally semiotic and, like language, is a mode of conveying meaning.[23] For this reason, economic discourse is often invoked to explore questions of value and representation more broadly. Literary texts, in particular, Shell observes, are 'composed of small tropic exchanges or metaphors, some of which can be analyzed in terms of signified economic content and all of which can be analyzed in terms of economic form'.[24] Following this line of inquiry, *Chaste Value* considers the discursive significance of the economic language surrounding chastity, particularly as it relates to the drama's presentation of personal value and its reflexive exploration of theatrical representation.[25]

Recent scholarship has broadened the scope of early modern economic criticism by recovering a materialist interest in the social and political implications of economic discourse. John Guillory has warned against the tendency of literary critics to view the appearance of economic language in the cultural and social realms as merely metaphoric. Instead, he suggests that we understand social space as 'non-Euclidean':

> The difference between the cultural and the economic is not analogous, then, to a kind of territorial distinction, where everything occurring within the one field is simply autonomous in relation to anything occurring within the other. Rather, the non-Euclidean character of social space means that all fields are *present* in any given social action, and that the identity of any particular field is defined in part by the *mode of presence* of other fields within it.[26]

As such, the theatre does not simply apply economic tropes to social contexts; instead, theatrical moments are infused simultaneously with both economic and social import. Both the economy and the theatre, moreover, are situated within systems of power. Critiquing what she calls Shell's 'restrictive formalism or systematicity', Barbara Correll calls on early modernists to engage with 'a more politically invested post-structuralism', which she associates with the work of Jean-Joseph Goux, 'that does not lose sight of the relations between signifying practices and social relations, or between structures of power and manifestations of resistance'.[27] This goal is shared by much recent economic criticism that draws variously from the traditions of cultural materialism, material culture studies, legal studies and object oriented ontology to elucidate the precise relationships of economic discourse to material, embodied history and to the ideologies that shape it. Natasha Korda, for instance, blends linguistic and materialist approaches in her investigation of the ways in which female subjectivity is forged in relation to moveable property.[28] Like Korda, Amanda Bailey raises questions of economic subjectivity as she examines the influence of debt bondage on understandings of possessive individualism and property in person.[29] Through concerned with the more traditional new economic critical topic of money, Stephen Deng and David Landreth employ new materialism and object oriented ontology to consider money's physical, social and political aspects.[30] In a different vein, Deng and Barbara Sebek's collection *Global Traffic: Discourses and Practices of Trade in English Literature and Culture from 1550 to 1700* expands the scope of new economic criticism to explore the global aspects of trade, including questions of religion, race and imperialism.[31]

Chaste Value joins these studies by connecting its investigation of economic discourse to questions of power, culture, subjectivity and social difference. In particular, I return to Fischer's observation that 'the understanding, appraisal, and use of human value are at the core of much Renaissance drama and logically assume an economic context – as well as adopting economic language'.[32] *Chaste Value* reveals chastity's central place within this theatrical exploration of human value, as it is mobilised both to conceptualise capitalist subjectivity and to interrogate the interpolation of people, their bodies and their labour into systems of exchange. Though expressed frequently at the level of metaphor, economic chastity possesses material, sociopolitical consequences. I endeavour, therefore, to identify the operations of power referenced in and mobilised by the theatre's interweaving of discourses of chastity and economics and to demonstrate how these discourses work on and through bodies, the bodies of male actors as well as those of women and men beyond the stage. Economic chastity discourse, I hope to show, is never exclusively about questions of currency, credit, debt and exchange, but also informs articulations of personal value and, by extension, sociopolitical questions of gender, race, class and nationality.

Critics have long noted discursive connections between sexual and economic intercourse in early modern drama. Douglas Bruster, for example, emphasises links between sexual and economic possession, while David Hawkes observes the ways in which sodomitical sexuality was depicted through the language of usury.[33] Prostitution provides the most obvious analogue to commercial exchange. Jean Howard contends that early modern drama invokes prostitution as a means of delimiting appropriate commercial behaviour.[34] Within this context, the prostitute is depicted as fully commoditised, subjected to the laws of the marketplace and therefore devoid of intrinsic personal value. As David Hawkes points out, the word commodity also referred to a prostitute, a congruence that points to the ways in which prostitution was used to encapsulate human commodification.[35] In this sense, prostitution also functioned as a stand-in for wage labour, and many early moderns took the view later expressed by Karl Marx that 'Prostitution is only a *particular* expression of the *general* prostitution of the *labourer*.'[36] The figures of the prostitute, the pander and the bawd provided a means of approaching capitalist labour relations more generally. Prostitution tropes are ubiquitous on the stage, moreover, because the commercial theatre was itself associated with the institution, an accusation that, as Joseph Lenz contends, underscores the degraded nature of all exchange.[37]

Chaste Value demonstrates that, like prostitution, female chastity figures centrally within the theatre's investigation of capitalist practices, epistemologies and ethics. Because of its status as the lynchpin of the social and metaphysical order, chastity often stands in opposition to prostitution, signifying an inherently valuable entity that resists commoditisation and whose essence, therefore, needs no representational augmentation. As Goux contends, chastity signifies stability not only in the sexual, economic and political realms but also in the realm of linguistic representation. In his discussion of Vesta, the Roman goddess of hearth, home and family, Goux emphasises the link between virginity and unrepresentability:

> Vesta's virginity and her unrepresentability are both protected at once. A man (*vir*) should neither penetrate, nor see, nor imagine. The inviolable virginity and the strict unrepresentability are identical, as if there were a complicity, on some opposing plane, between 'rape' by manly sexual desire (the Priapic appetite) and the visualization, which would be a phantasm and an impious fraud.[38]

For this reason, early modern drama repeatedly invokes virginity to connote authenticity. Whereas the prostitute is characterised by artifice, the virgin is ideally as pure as she looks, leaving no mimetic gap between her reality and her representation. This representational authenticity, therefore, is often counterpoised to the sense of fungibility that arises from exchange, whether sexual, economic or representational. Married chastity is a vexed concept therefore precisely because it merges stability and exchange: in maintaining that virgin purity could persist into marriage, Protestant marriage ideologies suggest that exchange is compatible with, rather than antithetical to, sexual and representational authenticity. Theatrical portrayals of chastity, in addition, raise the conundrum of how an essentially unrepresentable characteristic can be presented on the stage.

Mercantile tracts often invoke chastity to describe the ideal of sound currency, drawing on chastity's association with representational stability to indicate that English coins possess intrinsic value matching their nominal inscriptions. Perhaps the most extended of these images is found in Gerard de Malynes's 1601 tract *Saint George for England, Allegorically Described*, which warns of the manifold dangers of international usury, most specifically the manipulation of exchange rates by foreign powers without the permission of the English monarch. Using the conventions of chivalric romance, Malynes depicts an Edenic kingdom beset by the dangerous Dragon of International Usury who threatens the National Treasure, which is allegorically figured as the King's Virgin Daughter. Here, virginity marks the social, representational and economic stability that is threatened by usury, a term Malynes employs to signify a broad spectrum of capitalist practices and epistemologies. For Malynes, international usury upsets equilibrium across all levels of society, 'tending to the ouerthrow of equality & concord'; that is, by disrupting measures of value and communication, usury undermines the social hierarchy as well as the sovereignty of the English nation.[39] Political equilibrium depends upon the purity of the nation's currency, which 'remaineth still a Virgin immaculate, though all the world seemeth to be contaminated by her, for her constancy is singular, she is bright shining as the Moone'.[40] Invoking the logic of Protestant chastity, English coinage remains pure despite passing through multiple exchanges. In this, the paradox of chastity mirrors the paradox of coinage expressed by Marx in *A Contribution to Political Economy* that 'Despite the coin's wear and tear in each individual purchase or sale it still passes for the original quantity of gold.'[41] For Marx, money becomes increasingly symbolic as its value detaches from its specie content; so too with chastity, which grows increasingly – though not fully – detached from the female body. Malynes's tract, however, like much mercantilist writing, reflects the anxiety that currency's value may in fact be neither stable nor intrinsic. Despite its purity, the virgin treasure ultimately proves defenceless against the developments of international commerce and must be protected by royal policy makers, allegorised as St George. Although Malynes's chaste coinage maintains representational legitimacy despite constant circulation, it – like chastity – remains eternally vulnerable.[42]

Mercantilists such as Malynes and his contemporaries Edward Misselden and Thomas Mun explored the function of money as both the object and measure of exchange, considering the effects of trade, credit mechanisms and state policy on understandings of monetary value. Their considerations of these topics hinged on the question of whether money contained or simply represented wealth, an ambiguity inherent to the nature of coinage. As David Landreth explains, 'Physically [the coin] is unitary and discrete, easily encompassed by a hand, while conceptually it is a specific combination of two different things – it is the coordination of extrinsic and intrinsic value, through the material imprinting of stamp upon bullion.'[43] The sense that monetary value was unstable was heightened in the period not only because currency could be clipped or otherwise damaged and because foreign coins circulated throughout the English economy, but also because increased trade, developing credit markets, widespread inflation and royal recoinages increased the rate of currency fluctuation.[44] Although intended to increase royal revenue and to restore faith in the currency, recoinages such as Henry VIII's Great Debasement in 1542 and Elizabeth I's Great Recoinage in 1560 threw the intrinsic value of currency into question, showing it to be subject to state power.[45] Rising inflation, caused primarily by an influx of gold and silver from the Americas and exacerbated by national debt, had a similar effect, as the value of coins depreciated each year.[46] At the same time, the international specie market revealed gold and silver to be commodities in their own right, shaking the collective belief that bullion served as a neutral and stable arbiter of value. These combined factors led to a disconcerting sense among early moderns that external markers of value may bear no essential relation to intrinsic value and that money might simply act as a signifier – rather than as an embodiment – of value.

Concerns about the disjuncture between a coin's nominal and intrinsic value were driven by the sense that specie might itself be a commodity, as commodities are defined by the subordination of use value to externally imposed exchange value.[47] As Hawkes states, early moderns 'were the first Western Europeans since ancient times to be exposed to the effects of a large-scale market economy, so they were unavoidably struck by the divergence it instituted between real use-value and symbolic exchange-value'.[48] Early modern mercantile tracts, conduct books and imaginative literature dissect the relationship between use value and exchange value.

These texts often caste this distinction as a conflict between intrinsic value and value constituted externally, either through appearance, public opinion or the laws of supply and demand. As Hawkes states, capitalism involved a shift in perspective 'away from an essentially qualitative outlook, which sees things in terms of their essences, and toward a quantitative approach, which evaluates things by their relations to other things'.[49] In practical terms, the market causes people to wonder if the prices and appearance of goods accurately reflect their substance, or if consumers are being cozened by swindlers or seduced by popular opinion. Intrinsic value, in this context, becomes increasingly hard to pin down.

When chastity is presented as a commodity – often a sign of the market's destabilising effects – its essence becomes similarly difficult to identify. Chastity's commodity status, combined with the Protestant emphasis on chastity as an interior virtue, renders its essence inscrutable. Tracts such as Barnabe Rich's *The Excellency of Good Women* (1613), Alexander Nicolas's *A Discourse of Marriage and Wiving*

(1615), and Nicholas Brenton's *The Good and the Badde* (1616) all address this conundrum, instructing men to differentiate chaste from unchaste women. In a move characteristic of the genre, Rich laments that 'It is a hard matter . . . in this age to distinguish betweene the good woman and the bad', and he endeavours to uncover not only 'what she is but also where unto she is like'.[50] Like the commodity, chastity inspires interrogations into the relationship between external appearance and interior essence, what Katharine Eisaman Maus calls 'the difference between an unexpressed interior and a theatricalized exterior'.[51] The performance of chastity, therefore, provokes particular scrutiny, making explicit the gap between essence and representation. Considered in relation to commodities, then, chastity no longer signifies representational stability but rather raises epistemological quandaries about competing theories of value.

Comparisons between people and commodities intensified as early modern life became increasingly mediated by acts of buying and selling, raising concerns about the role and reach of markets and the effects of commoditising people, their attributes and their labour. Early moderns worried about the potential of early capitalism to transform their society and its values – one of which was the primacy of women's chastity – and they were especially concerned about the extent to which people could be subjected to commodity exchange. Behind this concern lurked anxieties about both slavery and wage labour, institutions that put a price on humans' bodies and productive capacity. John Wheeler, for instance, contends in his 1601 *A Treatise of Commerce* that trade can become threatening if left unregulated: according to him, 'all the world choppeth and changeth, runneth & raveth after Marts, Markets and Merchandising, so that all things come into Comerce, and pass into traffique'.[52] This accelerated traffic includes human as well as natural resources, threatening to reduce people to their commodity potential as labourers or even as slaves. In the expanding economy, Wheeler contends, 'one selleth words, another maketh traffike of the skins & blood of other men; yea there are some found so subtill and cunning merchants, that they perswade and induce men to suffer themselves to bee bought and sold'. When all is said and done, these traffickers 'have made merchandise of mens soules'.[53] Although Wheeler regards commerce as natural, he suggests that unchecked traffic can result in physical and spiritual subjugation, with men's bodies and souls turned to commodities.

Such commoditisation threatens to drain people of their intrinsic value, making them interchangeable as they are reduced to the common denominator of the cash nexus. As Ian Moulton explains, 'If everything can be changed into anything else, nothing has any real identity beyond an abstract (and fluctuating) exchange value. If anything has a price, nothing is unique; nothing has a fixed identity.'[54] Through the process of commoditisation, essence is largely replaced by exchange value. 'To the degree that anything is regarded as a commodity', Hawkes maintains, 'its nature is obliterated. To the degree that a human being is commodified, it follows, his or her essential identity is occluded.'[55] A commoditised person, for early moderns, is defined by exteriors, not simply their price but also their appearance and reputations. As such, concerns about commoditisation influence the belief that identity was fashioned or performed. If people, their bodies and their production function as commodities, their value becomes similarly difficult to locate, assess and represent.

Questions of value, commoditisation and capitalist subjectivity were of particular concern in the public theatre, where actors' bodies and creative productions were interpolated into systems of credit, debt bondage and profit creation. Emphasising its commercial aspects, Thomas Dekker famously described the theatre as

> your poets' Royal Exchange upon which their Muses – that are now turned to merchants – meeting, barter away that light commodity of words for a lighter ware than words – plaudits and the breath of the great beast which, like the

threatenings of two cowards, vanish all into air. Players are their factors who put away the stuff and make the best of it they possibly can, as indeed 'tis their parts to do so.[56]

In Dekker's formulation, the theatre's commercial productions render it insubstantial, with players peddling words in exchange for applause in the manner of merchants selling their wares.

Jean-Christophe Agnew, in his influential account of the theatre's mediation of capitalist developments, contends that this attentiveness to exchange was fundamental to the theatre's cultural role, as it 'furnished a laboratory of representational possibilities for a society perplexed by the cultural consequences of its own liquidity'.[57] Through its ongoing interrogation of the relationship between exterior appearance and interior essence, 'The theatre bestowed an intelligible albeit Protean human shape on the very *formlessness* that money values were introducing into exchange.'[58] In so doing, for Agnew, the stage modelled the malleable selves necessary to navigate early capitalist environments. These theatrical subjects combine an acute awareness of performativity with a relatively stable sense of self, balancing public exchange value with private intrinsic value. In this sense, the theatre contributes to the production of *homo economicus*, bringing forth '"another nature" – a new world of "artificial persons" – the features of which audiences were just beginning to make out in the similarly new and enigmatic exchange relations developing outside the theatre'.[59] The early modern theatre thus reflects the dynamics of the emerging commercial world, not only thematically but also through its mode of representation, which relies on embodied acting, spectacle and mimetic exchange.

These explorations were often reflexive, with actors and playwrights examining their own positions as businesspeople and labourers in early capitalist London and interrogating changing dynamics of aesthetic value and representation. Douglas Bruster contends that 'London's playhouses can best be understood in terms of commerce, as centres for the production and consumption of an aesthetic product.'⁶⁰ Modifying this thesis, Paul Yachnin underscores the largely artisanal nature of the early modern theatre in which actors and playwrights 'made their living primarily from labor'.⁶¹ Yachnin's emphasis on theatrical labour broadens our understanding of the early modern theatre's treatment of issues surrounding commoditisation, value and representation, showing that early modern drama comments on competing methods of evaluating theatrical labour and its aesthetic products. As an artisanal as well as a commercial institution, the theatre was uniquely positioned to interrogate shifting modes of assessing and representing value – economic, artistic and personal – in London's early capitalist marketplace. Plays often pit different methods of valuation against one another within specific dramatic contexts, resulting in what Lars Engle describes as a pragmatic mode of theatrical thinking in which meaning and value are continually negotiated within specific dramatic contexts rather than established as absolutes.[62] As such, the stage's interpretations of early capitalism rivalled those of more explicitly economic texts. According to Bradley Ryner, 'the stage offered a space for conceptualizing different economic models', and its acknowledgment of the fictive nature of these models facilitated more nuanced analyses than those found in mercantile tracts, which claimed to encapsulate economic reality.[63] Viewed in this light, the theatre reflects its material underpinnings not only by 'respond[ing] with a felt, if complicit, urgency . . . to the ability of economic forces to shape urban society', as Bruster contends, but also by becoming a public site in which truth and value are constructed and assessed.[64] The theatre concerns itself with modes of assessing human value and with the sorts of subjects produced within the early capitalist economy.

The theatre's preoccupation with early capitalist subjectivity often registers in terms of the status of women and more specifically in relation to female chastity. Kathryn

Schwarz identifies female will, manifested in obedient as much as transgressive women, as central to articulations of the subject, who expresses agency largely by submitting to state authority.[65] Amy Greenstadt and Christina Luckyj similarly elucidate questions of agency and subjectivity arising from early modern treatments of rape and feminine silence, respectively.[66] Taken together, these studies show that, in addition to reflecting cultural expectations for and anxieties about women, chastity discourse also reflects more expansive concerns about the early modern subject. *Chaste Value* builds on this body of work to show that because of its broad economic significance – its commodity status as well as its function as a sign of integrated selfhood and a symbol of stability – chastity figures centrally within theatrical interrogations of *homo economicus*, the early capitalist subject. *Chaste Value* fills a gap in the previous scholarship by tracing the manifold ways in which dramatists invoke chastity to negotiate questions of commoditised selfhood and to define the relationship between personal and economic value.

Reckoning with chastity's broad economic significance does not obviate its gendered dimensions, but rather suggests that the early modern stage's mediation of questions of value, representation, commoditisation and selfhood is itself complexly gendered. Called into being in part through the performance of female chastity, the early capitalist subject emerges on the all-male stage not solely as masculine but often as queer. Although many early modern plays posit binary gender categories, with representations of women reflecting male fantasies and fears, the stage's embodied mode of representation destabilises these binaries in a manner illuminated by Judith Butler's insight that 'Gender ought not to be constructed as a stable identity or locus of agency from which various acts follow; rather, gender is an identity tenuously constituted in time, instituted in an exterior space through a *stylized repetition of acts.*'[67] The representational strategies of the cross-dressed theatre call attention to the stylised nature of gender. Woman, and by extension man, emerges as a deeply unstable category, produced through the mechanisms of the theatre. By arguing that the public theatre produces early capitalist subjectivity in part through tropes of female chastity, *Chaste Value* contributes to our understanding of the subject's ambiguous gendering: it is purportedly male, but queered, defined through the denaturalising conventions of the cross-dressed theatre, and, more specifically, through the performance of chaste and unchaste women.

Reframing the common assumption that interiority arises with the development of Protestantism and capitalism, and therefore achieves ontological reality, Butler asks, 'From what strategic position in public discourse and for what reasons has the trope of interiority and the disjunctive binary of inner/outer taken hold? In what language is "inner space" figured?'[68] These questions are particularly well suited to the early modern theatre, which performs interiority and, despite the absence of female bodies on the stage, often asserts essential gendered value. Interior essence, as *Chaste Value* demonstrates, is constituted through embodied speech acts that repeatedly examine personal value in relation to economic value, which – mirroring the conditions of the theatre itself – appears malleable, defined through exchange and dependent upon context. With its multiple valences, the construct of chastity proves central to the stage's negotiation of intrinsic versus extrinsic conceptions of identity, informing not only the stage's presentation of gender but also its presentation of race, nationality and class.

The stage's responses to personal commoditisation vary according to dramatic genre. Broadly speaking, tragedy explores the more degrading, objectifying aspects of personal commoditisation and depicts performative subjectivity as a symptom of general social decline, in which aristocratic values – chastity first among them – have been eroded and in which aristocratic selfhood has been drained of its superior essence.

City comedy, despite its critique of urban commerce, largely embraces aspects of commoditised selfhood and invokes chastity as a means of conceptualising such a mode of being. International romances (some of which, like *Othello*, turn tragic) often apply concepts of personal commoditisation to questions of race and nationality in order to delineate between performative selfhood and the objectified commoditisation associated with slavery. Tragicomedy, a genre that overlaps with romance, often seeks to recuperate intrinsic value through recourse to Christian spirituality and to a domestic sphere associated with intrinsic female chastity.

While economic treatments of chastity often undergird articulations of contingent, performative selfhood shaped by the exigencies of exchange value, they also figure in the ideological processes by which intrinsic value is recovered, reconfigured and redistributed among different sorts of subjects. In response to anxieties about commoditisation, many of the plays discussed in *Chaste Value* attribute intrinsic value to specific sorts of subjects, often those who are white, English and middle to upper class. By addressing the theatre's recuperation of intrinsic value, *Chaste Value* adds nuance to Agnew's contention that the early modern stage created the protean selves needed to navigate early capitalism. Such protean selfhood was available only to certain sorts of people. The stage, these plays indicate, also participated in reallocating intrinsic personal value and commodity potential according to emerging modern hierarchies of gender, race, class and nationality.

With its intimate connection to personal value, theatrical chastity informs emerging definitions of the human. During the late sixteenth and early seventeenth centuries, the stage begins to define the human against the economic and to delineate gradations of humanity according to the ease and acceptability with which one could be incorporated into commercial exchange. As Butler reminds us, the 'exclusionary matrix by which subjects are formed . . . requires the simultaneous production of a domain of abject beings, those who are not yet "subjects," but who form the constitutive outside of the domain of the subject'.[69] In the plays discussed throughout *Chaste Value*, this abject realm is populated by those racialised, classed and gendered bodies whose commodity potential is especially evident. Those who are figured as readily commoditisable are regarded as somewhat less than human and are ultimately deemed unsuitable for full civic subjecthood. At the same time, ideological mechanisms develop so as to elide the commodity potential of white, middle and upper class English subjects. Theatrical explorations of chastity – with its gendered, racial and class dimensions – prove integral to this process and shape its social ramifications, as the reallocation of intrinsic value shields some people from the vicissitudes of the market while simultaneously subjecting others to the institutions of wage labour, prostitution and slavery.

Chaste Value traces chastity's deployment within varied generic and geographical contexts so as to uncover its broader significance within dramatic explorations of economic and personal value. The book begins by addressing chastity's role within the theatre's reflexive interrogation of its own representational strategies and commercial underpinnings. The first chapter, 'Chastity and the Ethics of Commercial Theatre in *Measure for Measure*, *Pericles* and *The Revenger's Tragedy*', explores the ways in which chastity is invoked to designate representational, economic and ethical legitimacy. Antitheatrical tracts often depict the theatre as a brothel that commoditises people and as a deceptive seller of cheap, corrupt wares. William Shakespeare's *Measure For Measure*, Shakespeare and George Wilkins's *Pericles*, and Thomas Middleton's *The Revenger's Tragedy* engage with these antitheatrical arguments, presenting prostitution as a synecdoche for economic exchange that commoditises bodies and sells them using theatrical artifice. Each play invokes the figure of a chaste woman, however, to trouble this association between the theatre and the brothel, interrogating the imputation that the theatre, like the brothel, traffics in human bodies and in excessive, supplemental, and therefore disingenuous forms of representation. Although the plays reach disparate conclusions about the possibility of creating an ethical commercial theatre, they collectively illuminate the problematics of theatrical chastity, as it is used to interrogate the theatre's commercial and representational investments.

Chaste Value then turns to the theatre's invocation of chastity to assess the personal value of English men, both aristocratic and bourgeois. The second chapter, 'Commercial Chastity and Aristocratic Value in *Troilus and Cressida*, *The White Devil* and *The Changeling*', focuses on the significance of intrinsic chastity to aristocratic selfhood and to the social and metaphysical hierarchies that support it. Whereas *Measure*, *Pericles* and *Revenger's* present chastity as an intrinsic good, characterised by an identity of essence and representation, Shakespeare's *Troilus and Cressida*, John Webster's *The White Devil*, and Middleton and William Rowley's *The Changeling* deploy economic discourses to dismantle ideologies of intrinsic chastity, revealing chastity to be a social construct whose worth is determined by outside forces. Conclusions reached about chastity ultimately influence the plays' presentations of aristocratic men, suggesting that their personal worth may rest not in class-based virtue but rather in the more relativistic dynamics of the marketplace. In these plays, performative identity arises through resistance to discourses of intrinsic chastity.

The third chapter, 'Chaste Selfhood: Ben Jonson's Critique of Urban Chastity Tropes', considers the bourgeois subjectivity articulated in city comedy. This chapter begins by addressing the tendency of city comedies such as Middleton and Thomas Dekker's *The Roaring Girl*, Middleton's *A Chaste Maid in Cheapside*, and the anonymous *The Fair Maid of the Exchange* to juxtapose chaste women with desiring, fragmented male characters so as to critique an ineffectual masculinity that flounders in the urban marketplace. The chapter then turns to Ben Jonson, whose treatment of chastity – and the intersection of gender, sexuality and commerce more generally – has been underexplored. Jonson satirises conventional deployments of chastity in *Epicoene*, rendering chaste integrity impossible in early capitalist environments and rejecting the queer implications of a model of male subjectivity that defines itself through theatrical chastity. *Bartholomew Fair*, by contrast, invokes chastity's commodity status in order to present – and largely embrace – a queer, contingent form of early capitalist subjectivity. Furthermore, Jonson applies this model of commoditised subjectivity to the condition of the commercial playwright, indicating that his own agency as an author lies in the ability to negotiate the strictures of the commodity markets to which he is subjected.

The next two chapters treat international, proto-colonial spaces in which chastity acquires additional resonance as a marker of racial purity. The fourth chapter, 'Chastity and Blackness: Racial Value and Commodity Potential in *The Fair Maid of West, Part I* and *Othello*', addresses the role of economic chastity discourse in determining the value and subject potential of racial others. Thomas Heywood's *Fair Maid of the West, Part I* draws out the racial implications of city comedy's invocation of chastity to articulate subject status. Although foreign men are judged unfavourably against the virtue of the heroine Bess, her mode of chaste agency – grounded as it is in her negotiation of market forces – is ostensibly available to Moors such as Mullisheg who regard her as a model for moral rehabilitation. Shakespeare's *Othello* supplants *Fair Maid*'s assimilationist paradigm with an alternate discourse, expounded by Iago, that asserts chastity's commodity value and then assesses racialised men in similar terms. In this way, *Othello* dramatises the logic by which commercial ideologies disrupt claims to intrinsic moral virtue and by which external traits – not only blackness but also whiteness – are transformed into signifiers of essential personal value. In contrast to *Fair Maid*, which tests the city comedy's model of subject formation in multiracial contexts, *Othello* invokes chastity discourse to address the status of people who may, quite literally, be regarded as commodities. Reading *Othello* in conjunction with *Fair Maid*, therefore, illuminates how conceptions of *chastity-as-subject* and *chastity-as-object* converge in English assessments of racial value, and how a prevailing emphasis on commodity status proves central to the development of white supremacism.

The fifth chapter, 'Mediterranean Markets, Commoditised Masculinity and the Whitening of Christian Chastity in *The Merchant of Venice* and *The Renegado*', turns from the commoditisation of black foreigners to the commodity potential of white Europeans in multiracial trading environments. Shakespeare's *The Merchant of Venice* and Philip Massinger's *The Renegado; or The Gentleman of Venice* register anxieties about Eastern trade, invoking the spectre of captivity to explore the racial, religious and sexual effects of commoditising Christian bodies. Both *Merchant* and *Renegado*, I argue, resolve crises of personal commoditisation by discursively removing chastity from the commercial realm, a development that mitigates the potentially miscegenational circulation of Christian women and works to reclaim the intrinsic personal value of Christian men. The tragicomic trajectory of each play depends upon transforming chastity from a potential commodity into an inherently Christian – and increasingly white – virtue. As such, the plays' redefinitions of chastity inform their articulations of racial whiteness, a category which emerges as a repository of intrinsic personal value that exempts certain subjects from the most objectifying aspects of the market, leaving others even more vulnerable to its commoditising energies.

The final chapter, 'Chaste Treasure and National Identity in *The Rape of Lucrece* and *Cymbeline*', addresses chastity's role in English – and an emerging British – national identity. Building on Stephanie Jed's analysis of the Lucretia myth as a means of producing purified national origins, I argue that

Shakespeare's *The Rape of Lucrece* and *Cymbeline* question the Roman myth's applicability to early capitalist England. In particular, both works employ chastity-as-treasure tropes to interrogate the ways in which commercial models disrupt national ideologies that aligned Elizabeth I's virgin body with the integrity of the state. *The Rape of Lucrece* exposes the ways in which mercantile treasure discourse invites sexual violence, compromising a woman who metonymically symbolises the state. In the Jacobean tragicomedy *Cymbeline*, Shakespeare reconfigures the Lucretia myth so as to articulate a revised mode of chaste thinking suited to a nation headed by a male monarch and aspiring to become an imperial mercantile power. By transforming Innogen's jewellery into currency that circulates in her name, Shakespeare infuses Britain's expanding mercantile sphere – and its imperial projects – with chaste, white legitimacy while simultaneously removing the female body from its once central place in the national imaginary.

Notes

1. Thomas Middleton, *Women Beware Women*, ed. William C. Carroll, New Mermaids, 2nd edn (London: Methuen, 1994; reprint 2002), I, i, 162, 165–6.
2. William Shakespeare, *All's Well That Ends Well*, ed. G. K. Hunter, The Arden Shakespeare, Second Series (London: Methuen, 1959; reprint 2013), I, i, 149–50.
3. John Webster, *The White Devil*, ed. Christina Luckyj, New Mermaids (London: Methuen, 2008), III, ii, 100–2; Thomas Middleton, *The Revenger's Tragedy*, ed. Brian Gibbons, New Mermaids (London: A & C Black Publishers, 2008), I, iii, 116–19.
4. I use Arjun Appadurai's term 'commoditisation', meaning a process by which something becomes a commodity, rather than the more general term 'commodification', indicating that something is being treated as a commodity. See Appadurai,

'Introduction: Commodities and the Politics of Value', in *The Social Life of Things*, ed. Arjun Appadurai (New York: Cambridge University Press, 1996), 3–63.

5. For the development of capitalism in England, see Maurice Dobb, *Studies in the Development of Capitalism* (London: G. Routledge and K. Paul, 1946); R. H. Tawney, *Religion and the Rise of Capitalism* (Gloucester, MA: P. Smith, 1962); Immanuel Wallerstein, *The Modern World-System: Capitalist Agriculture and the Origins of the European World-Economy in the Sixteenth Century* (New York: Academic Press, 1976) and *Historical Capitalism* (London: Verso, 1983); Jan de Vries, *Economy of Europe in an Age of Crisis: 1600–1750* (New York: Cambridge University Press, 1976); David McNally, *Political Economy and the Rise of Capitalism: A Reinterpretation* (Berkeley: University of California Press, 1988); Michael Perelman, *The Invention of Capitalism: Classical Political Economy and the Secret History of Primitive Accumulation* (Durham, NC: Duke University Press, 2000); Ellen Meiksins Wood, *The Origins of Capitalism: A Longer View* (New York: Verso, 2002); and Robert Brenner, *Merchants and Revolution: Commercial Change, Political Conflict, and London's Overseas Traders, 1550–1653* (New York: Verso, 2002).

6. Craig Muldrew, *The Economy of Obligation: The Culture of Credit and Social Relations in Early Modern England* (New York: St. Martin's Press, 1998), 37.

7. Sandra Fischer, *Econolingua: A Glossary of Coins and Economic Language in Renaissance Drama* (Newark: University of Delaware Press, 1985), 16.

8. Karl Polanyi, *The Great Transformation: The Political and Economic Origins of Our Time*, 2nd edn (1944; repr., Boston: Beacon Press, 2001), 60.

9. Fischer, *Econolingua*, 18.

10. Lawrence Stone, *The Family, Sex and Marriage in England, 1500–1800* (New York: Harper & Row, 1977), 502. Friedrich Engels makes essentially this argument in his 1884 *The Origin of the Family* where he claims that the family is 'based on the supremacy of the man, the express purpose being to

produce children of undisputed paternity; such paternity is demanded because these children are later to come into their father's property as his natural heirs' (*The Origin of the Family, Private Property and the State*, ed. Eleanor Burke Leacock [New York: International Publishing, 1972], 125). Because of this exigency, men are afforded 'the right of conjugal infidelity' while female chastity is enforced (125).

11. For the figuring of social change in gendered terms, see Karen Newman, Fashioning Femininity and *English Renaissance Drama* (Chicago: University of Chicago Press, 1991). For the economic implications of the bastard, see Michael Neill, 'Bastardy, Counterfeiting, and Misogyny in *The Revenger's Tragedy*', *Studies in English Literature* 36.2 (1996): 397–416.

12. For this contradictions inherent in early modern representations of women, see Peter Stallybrass, 'Patriarchal Territories: The Body Enclosed', in *Rewriting the Renaissance: The Discourse of Sexual Difference in Early Modern Europe*, ed. Margaret W. Ferguson, Maureen Quilligan and Nancy J. Vickers (Chicago: University of Chicago Press, 1986), 123–42.

13. Mark Breitenberg, *Anxious Masculinity in Early Modern England* (New York: Cambridge University Press, 1996), 24. For a study of the increasing political importance of the household, which informs the homological relationship of the family to the state, see Lena Cowen Orlin, *Private Matters and Public Culture in Post Reformation England* (Ithaca, NY: Cornell University Press, 1994).

14. Mary Douglas, *Purity and Danger: An Analysis of the Concepts of Pollution and Taboo* (London: Routledge, 1966), 115.

15. For discussions of Elizabeth I's conflation of bodily and national boundaries, see Susanne Scholz, 'Textualizing the Body Politic: National Identity and the Female Body in *The Rape of Lucrece*', *Shakespeare-Jahrbuch* 132 (1996): 103–43, and Susan Frye, 'The Myth of Elizabeth at Tilbury', *Sixteenth Century Journal* 23.1 (1992): 95–114.

16. Stephanie H. Jed, *Chaste Thinking: The Rape of Lucrece and the Birth of Humanism* (Bloomington: Indiana University Press, 1989), 8.

17. Keith Thomas makes this argument in his essay 'The Double Standard', *Journal of the History of Ideas* 20 (1959): 195–216.
18. Gayle Rubin, 'The Traffic in Women: Notes Toward a Political Economy of Sex', in *Toward an Anthropology of Women*, ed. Rayna Reiter (New York: Monthly Review Press, 1975): 157–210.
19. Luce Irigaray, *This Sex Which is Not One*, trans. Catherine Porter with Carolyn Burke (Ithaca, NY: Cornell University Press, 1985), 186.
20. William Perkins, *Christian Oeconomie: or a Short Survey of the Right Manner of Erecting and Ordering a Familie, According to the Scriptures*, trans. Tho[mas] Picering (London: Felix Kyngston, 1609), 11–12. For Protestantism's revision of chastity, see Stone, *The Family, Sex, and Marriage*; Anthony Fletcher, 'The Protestant Idea of Marriage in Early Modern England', in *Religion, Culture, and Society in Early Modern Britain: Essays in Honour of Patrick Collinson*, ed. Anthony Fletcher and Peter Roberts (Cambridge: Cambridge University Press, 1994), 161–81; John Rogers, 'The Enclosure of Virginity: The Poetics of Sexual Abstinence in the English Revolution', in *Enclosure Acts: Sexuality, Property, and Culture in Early Modern England*, ed. Richard Burt and John Michael Archer (Ithaca, NY: Cornell University Press, 1994), 229–50; Patricia Crawford, *Women and Religion in England: 1500–1720* (New York: Routledge, 1996), 25–39; and Kathleen Coyne Kelly, *Performing Virginity and Testing Chastity in the Middle Ages* (New York: Routledge, 2000).
21. Polanyi, *The Great Transformation*, 75.
22. Ruth Kelso, *Doctrine for the Lady of the Renaissance* (Urbana: University of Illinois Press, 1956), 24.
23. See Marc Shell, *The Economy of Literature* (Baltimore: Johns Hopkins University Press, 1978) and *Money, Language, and Thought: Literary and Philosophical Economies from the Medieval to the Modern Era* (Berkeley: University of California Press, 1982).
24. Shell, *The Economy of Literature*, 7.
25. In this respect, *Chaste Value* shares methodological similarities with works of new economic criticism such as David Hawkes,

Idols of the Marketplace: Idolatry and Commodity Fetishism in English Literature: 1580–1680 (New York: Palgrave, 2001); Jonathan Gil Harris, Sick Economies: *Drama, Mercantilism, and Disease in Shakespeare's England* (Philadelphia: University of Pennsylvania Press, 2004); and Valerie Forman, *Tragicomic Redemptions: Global Economics and the Early Modern Stage* (Philadelphia: University of Pennsylvania Press, 2008). For an overview of the expansive body of early modern scholarship that falls under the rubric of new economic criticism, see Peter Grav, 'Taking Stock of Shakespeare and the New Economic Criticism', *Shakespeare* 8 (2012): 111–36.

26. John Guillory, 'A New Subject for Criticism', in *The Culture of Capital: Properties, Cities, and Knowledge in Early Modern England*, ed. Henry S. Turner (New York: Routledge, 2002), 223–30, esp. 227.

27. Barbara Correll, 'Scene Stealers: Autolycus, *The Winter's Tale*, and Economic Criticism', in *Money and the Age of Shakespeare: Essays in New Economic Criticism*, ed. Linda Woodbridge (New York: Palgrave, 2003), 53–66, esp. 61. See Jean-Joseph Goux, *Symbolic Economies: After Marx and Freud*, trans. Jennifer Curtiss Gage (Ithaca, NY: Cornell University Press, 1990).

28. Natasha Korda, *Shakespeare's Domestic Economies: Gender and Property in Early Modern England* (Philadelphia: University of Pennsylvania Press, 2002).

29. Amanda Bailey, *Of Bondage: Debt, Property, and Personhood in Early Modern England* (Philadelphia: University of Pennsylvania Press, 2013).

30. Stephen Deng, *Coinage and State Formation in Early Modern English Literature* (New York: Palgrave, 2008); David Landreth, *The Face of Mammon: The Matter of Money in English Renaissance Literature* (New York: Oxford University Press, 2012).

31. Barbara Sebek and Stephen Deng, eds, *Global Traffic: Discourses and Practices of Trade in English Literature and Culture from 1550 to 1700* (New York: Palgrave, 2008).

32. Fischer, *Econolingua*, 28.

33. Douglas Bruster, *Drama and the Market in the Age of Shakespeare* (New York: Cambridge University Press, 1992); David

Hawkes, 'Sodomy, Usury, and the Narrative of Shakespeare's Sonnets', *Renaissance Studies* 14.3 (2000): 344–61.

34. Jean E. Howard, '(W)holesaling: Bawdy Houses and Whore Plots in the Drama's Staging of London', in *Theater of a City: The Places of London Comedy, 1598–1642* (Philadelphia: University of Pennsylvania Press, 2007), 114–61.
35. David Hawkes, *The Culture of Usury in Renaissance England* (New York: Palgrave, 2010), 129.
36. Karl Marx, *Selected Writings*, ed. Lawrence H. Simon (Indianapolis: Hackett Publishing, 1994), 72.
37. Joseph Lenz, 'Base Trade: Theater as Prostitution', *English Literary History* 60.4 (1993): 833–55, esp. 834.
38. Jean-Joseph Goux, 'Vesta, or the Place of Being', *Representations* 1 (1983): 91–107, esp. 94.
39. Gerard de Malynes, *Saint George for England, Allegorically Described* (London: Richard Field for William Tymme, 1601), A4v, EEBO.
40. Malynes, *Saint George for England*, E1v–E2r.
41. Karl Marx, *A Contribution to Political Economy*, ed. Maurice Dobb (New York: International Publishers, 1970), 109. Stephen Deng calls attention to this passage, contending that this shift to symbolic money was by no means complete in the early modern period (*Coinage and State Formation*, 12–13).
42. Jonathan Gil Harris has noted this paradox in much of Malynes's writing about currency: that currency's value is intrinsic, yet this intrinsic value must be ensured through policy decisions ('"The Enterprise is Sick": Pathologies of Value and Transnationality in *Troilus and Cressida*', *Renaissance Drama* 29 [1998]: 3–37, esp. 20).
43. Landreth, *The Face of Mammon*, 7.
44. For an overview of this volatile history of English currency, see Fischer, *Econolingua*, 23–7.
45. For the relationship of coinage to state power, see Deng, *Coinage and State Formation*.
46. For the effects of American bullion on European markets, see Glyn Davies, *A History of Money from Ancient Times to the Present Day* (Cardiff: University of Wales Press, 1994), esp. 87. For discussions of inflation as well as the effects of recoinages,

see McNally, *Political Economy and the Rise of Capitalism*. For an overview of mercantilist attempts to discern the causes of rising inflation and thus the source of monetary and commodity value, see M. Beer, 'Sixteenth Century Economics', in *Early British Economics from the XIIIth to the Middle of the XVIIIth Century* (1938), Reprints of Economic Classics (New York: Augustus M. Kelly, 1967), 82–129.

47. See Karl Marx, 'Two Factors of a Commodity: Use Value and Value', in *Capital: A Critique of Political Economy* (New York: Penguin Putnam, 1976, rpt. 1990), 125–30.
48. David Hawkes, *Shakespeare and Economic Theory*, The Arden Shakespeare (New York: Bloomsbury, 2015), 12.
49. Hawkes, *Shakespeare and Economic Theory*, 16.
50. Barnabe Rich, *The Excellency of Good Women. The Honour and Estimation that Belongeth unto Them. The Infallible Markes Whereby to Know Them* (London: 1613), B2r, B3r, reproduction of the Huntington Copy, EEBO.
51. Katharine Eisaman Maus, *Inwardness and Theater in the English Renaissance* (Chicago: University of Chicago Press, 1995), 2.
52. John Wheeler, *A Treatise on Commerce* (London, 1601; repr., New York: Columbia University Press, 1931), 6.
53. Wheeler, *A Treatise*, 6.
54. Ian Moulton, 'Whores as Shopkeepers: Money and Sexuality in Aretino's *Ragionamenti*', in *Money, Morality, and Culture in Late Medieval and Early Modern Europe*, ed. Juliann Vitullo and Diane Wolfthal (Burlington, VT: Ashgate, 2010), 71–86, esp. 81.
55. Hawkes, *Shakespeare and Economic Theory*, 132.
56. Thomas Dekker, *The Gull's Horn-Book*, in *The Non-Dramatic Works of Thomas Dekker*, vol. 2, ed. Alexander B. Grosart (London, 1885; repr., New York: Russell and Russell, 1963), 246–7.
57. Jean-Christophe Agnew, *Worlds Apart: The Market and the Theater in Anglo-American Thought, 1550–1750* (New York: Cambridge University Press, 1986), 54.
58. Agnew, *Worlds Apart*, xi.

59. Agnew, *Worlds Apart*, xi.
60. Bruster, *Drama and the Market*, 3.
61. Paul Yachnin, '"The Perfection of Ten": Populuxe Art and Artisanal Value in *Troilus and Cressida*', *Shakespeare Quarterly* 56.3 (2005): 306–27, esp. 311. See also Paul Yachnin, *Stage-wrights: Shakespeare, Jonson, Middleton, and the Making of Theatrical Value* (Philadelphia: University of Pennsylvania Press, 1997). Matthew Kendrick builds on Yachnin's thesis to argue that the category of labour is particularly important in the early modern theatre, as 'The stage offered a space in which to negotiate the value and meaning of labour in an increasingly exploitative society' (*At Work in the Early Modern English Theater: Valuing Labor* [Madison, NJ: Fairleigh Dickinson University Press, 2015], xiii).
62. Lars Engle, *Shakespearean Pragmatism: Market of His Time* (Chicago: University of Chicago Press, 1993).
63. Bradley Ryner, *Performing Economic Thought: English Drama and Mercantile Writing 1600–1642* (Edinburgh: Edinburgh University Press, 2014), 5.
64. Bruster, *Drama and the Market*, 10.
65. Kathryn Schwarz, *What You Will: Gender, Contract, and Shakespearean Social Space* (Philadelphia: University of Pennsylvania Press, 2011). Schwarz builds on considerations of marriage and erotic love in constituting the political subject. For this topic, see also Victoria Kahn, *Wayward Contracts: The Crisis of Political Obligation in England, 1640–1674* (Princeton: Princeton University Press, 2004); Frances E. Dolan, *Marriage and Violence: The Early Modern Legacy* (Philadelphia: University of Pennsylvania Press, 2008); and Melissa E. Sanchez, *Erotic Subjects: The Sexuality of Politics in Early Modern English Literature* (New York: Oxford University Press, 2011).
66. Amy Greenstadt, *Rape and the Rise of the Author: Gendering Intention in Early Modern England* (Burlington, VT: Ashgate, 2009) and Christina Luckyj, *A Moving Rhetoricke: Gender and Silence in Early Modern England* (Manchester: Manchester University Press, 2011).

67. Judith Butler, *Gender Trouble: Feminism and the Subversion of Identity* (New York: Routledge, 1990; reprint 2006), 191. Although Butler nuances this position in *Bodies that Matter*, clarifying that gender performance is not agential or even properly theatrical, but is instead a process by which regulatory power materialises identity, the framework laid out in *Gender Trouble* resonates with the conditions of the all-male stage, in which the work of articulating gendered subjectivity is self-consciously performed. See Butler, *Bodies that Matter: On the Discursive Limits of Sex* (New York: Routledge, 1993).
68. Butler, *Gender Trouble*, 183.
69. Butler, *Bodies that Matter*, xiii.

CHAPTER 1

CHASTITY AND THE ETHICS OF COMMERCIAL THEATRE IN *MEASURE FOR MEASURE, PERICLES* AND *THE REVENGER'S TRAGEDY*

Antitheatrical tracts often depict the theatre as a brothel that commoditises people and sells a debased product. By extension, the playwright is figured as a bawd and the player as a prostitute, selling his body for money and enticing audiences with deceptive artifice. Like the brothels neighbouring the public theatres, theatrical displays are cast as dangerously seductive, both in Puritan antitheatrical literature and in policy documents aimed at mitigating the theatre's potential threat to public health and morality.[1] As Stephen Gosson writes in *The Schoole of Abuse* (1579), plays feature 'melody to tickle the eare; costly apparel, to flatter the sight; effeminate gesture, to ravish the sence; and wanton speache, to whet desire too inordinate lust'.[2] The theatre assaults audience members with, in the language of the Lord Mayor's 1597 petition to suppress the theatre, its 'unchaste matters, lascivious devices, shiftes of cozenage, & other lewd & ungodly practices'.[3] As John Rainolds further asks, 'who can deny that men are made adulterers and enemies of chastitie by coming to such plaies?'[4]

For Gosson and his fellow antitheatricalists, the theatre not only caters to prostitutes and other sexual reprobates, but its very medium resembles the prostitute's self-presentation, with its appealing exterior belying a corrupt interior. Dramatists, Gosson alleges in *Plays Confuted in Five Actions* (1582), 'falsifie, forge, and adulterate' reality, weaving elaborate lies by presenting things 'otherwise than they are'.[5] Beneath these lies, one finds only corruption and degradation. In *The Schoole of Abuse*, Gosson warns,

> [If you] pul off the visard that Poets maske in, you shall disclose their reproach, bewray their vanitie, loth their wantonnesse, lament their follie, and perceive their sharpe sayings to be placed as Pearles in Dunghils, fresh pictures on rotten walles, chaste Matrons apparel on common Curtesans.[6]

Altering this chestnut slightly, Donald Lupton contends in *London and the Country carbonadoed* (1632) that actors 'are as crafty with an old play, as Bauds with olde faces; the one puts on a new fresh colour, the other a new face and Name'.[7]

Compounding the actor's troubling exchange of personae was discomfort with the commercial exchange underlying both theatre and prostitution. Whereas antitheatricalists often conceded that select plays possessed educative content, they felt that producing plays 'for profit and gaine of money' caused playwrights and actors to pander to the lowest common denominator.[8] This pandering, they alleged, led to bawdy, sexual content and to the creation of outrageous spectacles with little relation to reality and no moral content. The association of the theatre with prostitution solidified in the late sixteenth century, as theatre owners such as Philip Henslowe became involved in the brothel business and, more generally, as concerns about commercialisation intensified. As Joseph Lenz explains, 'Prostitution emblematizes, all too vividly, the worldliness of trade, the mercenary nature of all commerce', and depictions of the theatre as a brothel reflect 'the "base" nature of any exchange or transaction, whether sexual, economic, or aesthetic'.[9] Aligned with early modern homologies linking the economic, sexual and representational realms, the conceptual framework evoked by theatre-as-prostitution tropes links commercialism, inappropriate sexuality and mimetic representation.[10] The theatre combines these transgressions, coming to be seen, in Gosson's epithet, as a 'generall Market of Bawdrie'.[11]

Early modern dramatists engage with these antitheatrical accusations in order to delineate the proper form and function of drama in a culture that both desired spectacle and viewed it with suspicion. As Huston Diehl contends, 'Elizabethan and Jacobean drama reflexively addresses the reformers' inquiry into the legitimacy of the theatre, exploring Protestant-induced fears that plays seduce and corrupt their audiences.'[12] This theatrical inquiry, like that of the reformers, concerns the infusion of commerce into daily life, a trend epitomised by prostitution's incorporation of bodies and affective relations into economic exchange. A quasi-artisanal institution in a proto-capitalist marketplace, the theatre was well poised to interrogate shifting economic dynamics as well as modes of representing labour and value in commercial societies. As Paul Yachnin argues, 'The theatre's position between the court and the culture market aroused within the drama itself a critical self-description focused on the de-authenticating effects of theatrical mimesis within a commercial domain.'[13] The theatre therefore may have been 'less given over to commodifying what we imagine as older, more authentic and communitarian forms of cultural expression and more involved with developing new ways of forging communities and workable values within the complex conditions of a changing world'.[14] Early modern plays, therefore, often interrogate their own commercial nature, reflexively questioning the theatre's 'exchange' of people as it occurred mimetically within the drama and as it incorporated actors' bodies into early capitalist networks of labour, debt and profit.

Both antitheatricalists and theatre practitioners noted in early modern society a connection between the predominance of exchange and questions of representational reliability. As theorists such as Jacques Derrida, Jean-Joseph Goux and Marc

Shell have noted, words have a close relationship to money, as both function as media of exchange and raise questions of value and representation.[15] Verbal exchange is most evident in metaphor, where the tenor is replaced by the vehicle, but it is also present in all language because linguistic meaning consists of a series of substitutions and because words are used to exchange ideas and conduct business transactions. As with coins, the truth content of words and their relationship to their referents is subject to debate. Early moderns suspected that, like coins, words could be counterfeit. Additionally, debates about usury, which commoditised money and seemed to make it reproduce of its own volition, raised questions about the commoditisation of representation more generally – a dynamic of great interest to the early modern theatre, which in a larger sense commoditised representation.[16]

Tropes of female chastity figure centrally within the theatre's response to antitheatrical attacks that associate plays with prostitution.[17] Operating as a kind of currency within patriarchal transactions, chastity functions as a sexual analogue to both coins and words, signifying integrity of self as well as representational authenticity. In contrast to the prostitute, the chaste woman's representational stability matches her sexual purity; as Richard Brathwaite writes in *The English Gentlewoman*, 'Outwardly, therefore, shee expresseth what she inwardly professeth.'[18] Yet, like any coin, chastity contained within it the possibility of corruption, often as a result of debasement but also from commoditisation. Paradoxically, the chaste woman's commodity status is foregrounded as she moves from maid to wife, revealing her uncanny similarity to the prostitute. This commoditisation threatens to dismantle her representational purity, prying open a division between her interior essence and external appearance and revealing chastity to be a performance. As such, dynamics of chastity provide a means by which playwrights approach the ethics of exchange, both representational and commercial as well as sexual.

This chapter treats three plays that situate female chastity within the antitheatrical framework that associates the theatre with prostitution: William Shakespeare's *Measure for Measure* (1604), Shakespeare and George Wilkins's *Pericles* (1607), and Thomas Middleton's *The Revenger's Tragedy* (1606/7). Each of these plays invokes the figure of the chaste woman – Isabella in *Measure*, Marina in *Pericles*, and Castiza in *Revenger's* – to interrogate this framework and to explore the possibility that the theatre might achieve representational authenticity and moral respectability. However, these plays reflect radically different possibilities for the jointure of chastity and theatre: *Measure*'s treatment of militant virginity exposes the violence of exchange but also gestures toward a more redemptive theatrical ethic; *Pericles* invokes ideologies of artisanal labour and companionate marriage to authorise the exchanges of the theatre; and *Revenger's* addresses a fallen capitalist world in which chastity fails to provide catharsis, ultimately embracing the perverse power of an unchaste, usurious metatheatricality. Taken together, these plays suggest that chastity provided a powerful lens – perhaps even more powerful than that of the prostitute – through which dramatists could explore the theatre's commercial investments and its modes of embodied, mimetic representation.

Chastity and the Perils of Exchange in Measure for Measure

Measure for Measure presents a society beset by syphilis and pestilence, diseases attributed to prostitution and also associated with London's public theatres, which were closed during the plague years.[19] Within this context, *Measure* interrogates the interrelated ethics of theatricality and sexuality as well as the countervailing impulses of the Puritans, represented in the play by the 'precise' Angelo.[20] Perhaps most overtly of all early modern plays, *Measure* dramatises a dialectic between prostitution and chastity to explore the nature of early capitalist exchange and its effects on English subjects. More specifically, *Measure* situates chastity within a matrix of exchanges, emphasising its problematic status as a sign of absolute purity as well as a commodity. Isabella's fate as a novice displaced from the convent and forced to enter a complex sexual marketplace reflects the broader Protestant shift away from considering chastity an absolute virtue.[21] Isabella initially presents herself as a self-sufficient virgin, an 'enskied' (I, iv, 34) saint resistant to sexual exchange. Her militant virginity is associated with representational purity, a union of external beauty and inner virtue manifested in her desire for transparency and her dislike of theatrical spectacle. Chastity thus operates as a site of resistance in *Measure*, calling attention to the reductive and potentially dehumanising effects of exchange – that is, until the Duke forces Isabella to comply with his theatrics and subsequent marriage proposal, harnessing her chastity in the interests of state power.

Isabella's purity is contrasted with Angelo's hypocrisy, which is articulated in terms of counterfeit currency, an image often used to describe unchaste women.[22] Angelo – whose name recalls the English coin – requests that his worth be tested before assuming the office of deputy, asking, 'Let there be some more test made of my metal' (I, i, 48). Though approved or 'stamp'd' (I, i, 50) by the Duke, Angelo quickly proves counterfeit, a status he acknowledges when, lusting after Isabella, he laments a system of authority that permits a disjuncture between his outward office and inner worth:

> O place, O form,
> How often dost thou with thy case, thy habit,
> Wrench awe from fools, and tie the wiser souls
> To thy false seeming!   (II, iv, 12–15).

This emphasis on false appearances, echoed in Isabella's 'Seeming, seeming!' (II, iv, 149), characterises Angelo's falsehood in terms generally reserved for women, a connection also present in Angelo's association of counterfeit masculinity with bastards whose parents 'do coin heaven's image / In stamps that are forbid' (II, iv, 45–6). The bastards, like Angelo, are 'false' (II, iv, 49), lacking legitimacy passed through the name of the father.[23]

In contrast to Angelo, Isabella is legitimately pure, her outward performance of chastity mirroring her chaste interior. Despite this authenticity, however, Isabella refuses to circulate sexually, and her militant chastity is depicted as uncomfortably sterile in comparison with the fecundity of Claudio's fiancée Juliet.[24] Lucio, the play's spokesperson for sexual liberality, depicts Juliet and Claudio's sexual relationship and the resulting pregnancy in agricultural terms:

> As those that feed grow full, as blossoming time
> That from the seedness the bare fallow brings
> To teeming foison, even so her plenteous womb
> Expresseth his full tilth and husbandry.   (I, iv, 41–4)

In his idyllic vision, the couple's alleged transgression instead accords with the natural order, and Juliet's womb reflects Claudio's sexual husbandry, soon to result in the plenty of generation. Isabella repudiates this reproductive ideal, nearly aligning herself with Angelo's Puritanical prohibitions against extramarital sex, strictures that Lucio claims will 'unpeople the province with continency' (III, ii, 168–9). To Lucio, Angelo's zealous rejection of sexuality is nearly inhuman; he calls the deputy 'a man whose blood / Is very snow-broth' (I, iv, 57–8) and speculates that 'Angelo was not made by man and woman, after this downright way of creation' (III, ii, 100–1), but rather that 'a sea-maid spawned him' (III, ii, 104) leaving him a 'motion ungenerative' (III, ii, 108). Though less hypocritical than Angelo, Isabella's virginity is similarly ungenerative and privileges death over life, a sensibility best articulated in her fantasies of martyrdom, in which she insists that, were she

> under the terms of death
> Th'impression of keen whips I'd wear as rubies,
> And strip myself to death as to a bed
> That longing have been sick for. (II, iv, 100–3)

Isabella relishes the idea of dying for her honour and considers this fate preferable to sexual submission. She thus encapsulates the tensions inherent in virgin chastity: it resists commoditising, subjugating exchanges that threaten personal integrity, but it simultaneously disavows the social and sexual intercourse necessary to sustain the social order. Moreover, Isabella's eroticisation of martyrdom, in which whipping replaces sexual penetration, indicates that passion for virginity can undo itself.

In contrast to Isabella's idealisation of virginity as an absolute virtue, Angelo embraces a generalised ethic of exchange exemplified in the legal system over which he has jurisdiction. He considers the law to reflect a transcendental system of justice in which punishments compensate for crimes and in which the lives of criminals are exchanged for the lives of victims. To him, the law is all encompassing and abstract, disregarding the particularity of either judge or criminal.[25] Angelo thus distances himself from his decision to execute Claudio, asserting, 'What's open made to justice, / That justice seizes' (II, i, 21–2), and telling Isabella, 'It is the law, not I, condemn your brother; / Were he my kinsman, brother, or my son, / It should be thus with him' (II, ii, 80–2). In rendering human particularity insubstantial, the legal system enhances the sense, already common in the early modern economy, that actions, losses and lives can be quantified and are therefore fungible, subject to principles of exchange.

As a counterfeit duke, however, Angelo embraces this ethic of exchange while simultaneously positioning himself above the law – a combination that leads him to demand Isabella's chastity in exchange for saving Claudio's life. Doing so both forges an equivalence between Isabella's chastity and Claudio's life and situates Angelo himself, rather than the law, as the arbiter of social exchange.[26] Angelo proposes the sexual rendezvous as an extralegal exchange, asking Isabella what she would do if the only way to 'fetch [her] brother from the manacles / Of the all-binding law' (II, iv, 93–4) were to 'lay down the treasures of [her] body' (II, iv, 96). Angelo manipulates the law, even as he projects it as an abstract system over which he has no control, a manoeuvre Isabella identifies with tyrants who 'Bid[] the law make curtsey to their will' (II, iv, 174). Attempting to transcend the law, Angelo shifts from a legal index to a religious one as he suggests that Isabella could redeem Claudio by 'Give[ing] up [her] body to such sweet uncleanness / As she that [Claudio] hath stain'd' (II, iv, 54–5). Here, Angelo posits exchange as a mechanism of cosmic justice in which sins cancel one another out, with Isabella's sexual submission obviating Juliet's. Angelo's toggling among legal, sexual and religious registers reflects the interpenetration of systems of exchange, and projects a series of substitutions in which all entities can, in some way, be adequated to all others. The tenuous logic of his proposition, however, depends upon his ostensibly transcendent power to administer this system of exchange and therefore to determine value.

Isabella initially opposes this system of exchange in which all human attributes – and transgressions – are made commensurate with one another. Preferring a more absolute value system, Isabella refuses to separate her body from her soul and insists that her chastity cannot be submitted to exchange, as its loss will damn her eternally. To her, Angelo's proposed solution constitutes 'Ignomy in ransom' (II, iv, 111) and 'foul redemption' (II, iv, 113), a perverse exchange sharing nothing in common with the 'free pardon' (II, iv, 111) and 'lawful mercy' (II, iv, 112) that Antonio should exert as a Christian ruler. To counter Angelo's emphasis on earthly traffic, Isabella appeals to the unequal exchange of Christian salvation in which Christ died to redeem humanity, reminding Angelo that 'all the souls that were, were forfeit once, / And He that might the vantage best have took / Found out the remedy' (II, ii, 73–5). Isabella not only promotes Christ-like mercy in dealing with prisoners such as Claudio who should be 'forfeit', but also gestures toward a higher law that, while based in exchange, does not level particularity to the common denominator of either the law or the market. In keeping with this principle, she refuses to bribe Angelo with 'fond sickles of the tested gold, / Or stones' (II, ii, 150–1) because the worth of these items is determined through arbitrary exchange, their 'rate . . . either rich or poor / As fancy values them' (II, ii, 151–2). Instead she bribes him 'with such gifts that heaven shall share with you' (II, ii, 148):

> true prayers,
> That shall be up at heaven and enter there
> Ere sunrise: prayers from preserved souls,
> From fasting maids, whose minds are dedicate
> To nothing temporal. (II, ii, 152–6)

These gifts, associated with fasting virgins, are valuable in a more absolute sense than the aforementioned treasure and are not subject to the laws of supply and demand that determine the price of jewels. Isabella regards her own chaste value in a similar manner, as operating in a realm outside of temporal evaluation and exchange, and she seeks to preserve this absolute value.

Isabella's Christian stance is compromised, however, by her fetishisation of her chastity as the sole entity that should remain exempt from exchange. As a result, she considers sacrificing her life, which she would 'throw . . . down for [Claudio's] deliverance / As frankly as a pin' (III, i, 103–5), but not her chastity, deciding, 'Better it were a brother died at once, / Than that a sister, by redeeming him, / Should die for ever' (II, iv, 106–8). Isabella's conclusion indicates that she does not oppose all legalistic exchanges, only those that would compromise her chastity. Angelo exposes this tendency through his rhetorical gymnastics, forcing her into the admission: 'I something do excuse the thing I hate / For his advantage that I dearly love' (II, iv, 119–20). With this concession, Isabella acquiesces to Angelo's quantifying logic. Rather than accepting his premise that her chastity equals Claudio's life, however, she concludes that it is of greater value, proclaiming, 'More than our brother is our chastity' (II, iv, 184). She hopes, moreover, that her brother will agree, and predicts

> That had he twenty heads to tender down
> On twenty bloody blocks, he'd yield them up
> Before his sister should her body stoop
> To such abhorr'd pollution. (II, iv, 179–82)

While Claudio's willing death is imagined as an extravagant act of sacrifice, similar to the martyrdom Isabella had earlier imagined for herself, her statement hints at a logic of equivalence, as it imagines her chastity to be worth twenty of Claudio's heads.

When Claudio refocuses Isabella's attention on the exchange of chastity, she rekindles her antipathy toward exchange, adopting Angelo's discourse of bastardy and prostitution. When Claudio asks her to submit to Angelo's demand, she echoes Angelo's view that death is preferable to bastardy in her assertion that she 'had rather [her] brother die by the law, than [her] son should be unlawfully born' (III, i, 188–90). She depicts the proposed transaction as unnatural perversion, a 'kind of incest' (III, i, 138) in which Claudio is 'made a man out of [her] vice' (III, i, 137), 'tak[ing] life from [his] own sister's shame' (III, i, 138–9).[27] Like the bawd, Claudio seeks to profit from illicit sexual commerce, a parallel Isabella draws in her claim that his 'sin's not accidental, but a trade' (III, i, 148). She thus condemns

Claudio in the same terms the Duke uses to condemn Pompey when he forces him to admit that, 'From their abominable and beastly touches / I drink, I eat, array myself, and live' (III, ii, 23–4). Conceptually linking bawds with bastards as creatures constituted through sexual sin, Isabella questions Claudio's legitimacy, wondering whether her mother 'play'd [her] father fair: / For such a warped slip of wilderness / Ne'er issued from his blood' (III, i, 140–2). As in the image of Angelo as a false coin, the bastard's production and subsequent reproduction are 'usurious', created unnaturally through what Pompey calls the 'merriest' of the 'two usuries' (III, ii, 6–7). Sexual traffic, in *Measure*, threatens not only patriarchal legitimacy but also racial identity and personal subjectivity. As Elbow contends, prostitution 'needs buy and sell men and women like beasts', creating a world of 'brown and white bastards' (III, ii, 2–4). Such commerce encourages sexual exchange with outsiders, compromising Vienna's racial purity, and its commoditising force dehumanises men and women, turning them into beasts with no particular intrinsic value of their own.

This emphasis on exchange informs the play's discussion of theatricality. Theatrical exchange is highlighted in the bed trick, in which Angelo's abandoned fiancée Mariana substitutes for Isabella, and in the 'head trick', in which the head of a prisoner is swapped for Claudio's.[28] Although they facilitate the plot's comic resolution, these exchanges remain uncomfortably similar to those advocated by Angelo, and the bed trick recalls the human traffic of prostitution and raises questions about the equivalence of the two women. The levelling, even dehumanising, aspects of such exchanges are intensified when the Duke suggests that the prisoner Barnardine might die in Claudio's stead. Emphasising the fungibility of the heads, the Duke instructs the provost, 'O death's a great disguiser; and you may add to it. Shave [Barnardine's] head, and tie the beard, and say it was the desire of the penitent to be so bared before his death; you know the course is common' (IV, ii, 174–7). The Duke's instructions highlight the fabrications of the theatre, calling attention to the way in which the stage exchanges actors for characters, creating artificial personae in the process.[29] Though this literal substitution of life is avoided when the pirate Ragozine dies in prison of natural causes, conveniently providing a head adorned with the same colour hair and beard as Claudio's, the resulting exchange of heads literalises eye-for-an-eye justice, substantiating Isabella's concerns about the morality of earthly justice systems. As John C. Higgins suggests, the inherent implausibility of the bed trick may be intensified in the theatre, where the bodies of the actors are present, and it seems that the same may hold true for the head trick.[30] Presenting audiences with distinct actors or with a prop head, these theatrical conventions call attention to the personal particularity that is effaced by – or that sometimes disrupts – mechanisms of exchange that aim toward commensurability.

The Duke, however, seeks to recuperate sexual and theatrical exchange in the interests of state power, averring that 'disguise shall by th'disguised / Pay with falsehood false exacting, / And perform an old contracting' (III, ii, 273–5), and he marshals Isabella's chastity so as to validate these exchanges. Left with few options, Isabella facilitates the bed trick and agrees to accuse Angelo publicly of taking her virginity. Although she chafes against any misrepresentation of the truth, she turns to the language of the theatre to justify her role in revealing Angelo's crimes. Of their respective roles in the spectacle, she tells Mariana,

> To speak so indirectly I am loth;
> I would say the truth, but to accuse him so
> That is your part; yet I am advis'd to do it,
> He says, to veil full purpose.   (IV, vi, 1–4)

Though she would rather Mariana be the one to accuse Angelo of seducing her, she accepts that each woman has a different 'part' to play in order for the Duke's plan to succeed. Despite her willingness to temporarily 'veil full purpose', however,

Isabella adheres to her faith in absolute truth, attesting that, in a larger sense, her claim 'is ten times true, for truth is truth / To th'end of reck'ning' (V, i, 48–9). For Isabella, truth, like chastity, cannot be reckoned or exchanged, even if its representation is slightly unreliable. Isabella's vision of truth resembles the theological and philosophical truth that 'only doth judge itself', which Francis Bacon lauds in 'Of Truth' (1623), but it also begins to incorporate aspects of what Bacon calls the 'truth of civil business', which accommodates itself to early capitalist contingency.[31]

Because she begins to accommodate contingency, Isabella offers the play's most convincing vision of ethical theatricality by affirming the audience's interpretive abilities, asking them to 'let your reason serve / To make the truth appear where it seems hid, / And hide the false seems true' (V, i, 68–70). Like the theatrical practitioner, Isabella relies on the audience to discern truth from the mimetic exchanges they see before them and, in the process, suggests that theatricality can serve an ameliorative social function. The vexed exchanges of the theatre, heretofore associated with the artifice and commoditisation of prostitution, are thus partially redeemed by Isabella's chaste presence.[32] This shift registers in Isabella's discourse of gifts, as she claims that Angelo asked her to submit the 'gift of my chaste body / To his concupiscible intemperate lust' (V, i, 100–1). Though her wording does little to mitigate the nature of the proposition, it gestures toward an alternate paradigm in which exchange, theatrical as well as sexual, can be understood in terms of gift giving rather than dehumanising transactions.[33]

The Duke appropriates Isabella's emphasis on the gift in his efforts to validate the multiple marriages he arranges at the end of the play and to reassert authority over his subjects. In his insistence that Angelo marry Mariana, the Duke emphasises his power to determine the relative value of his subjects by arranging exchanges, contrasting his legitimate power with that which Angelo has usurped as deputy. He asserts that Mariana is now Angelo's equal, telling Angelo that, even without a substantial dowry, 'her worth' is now, 'worth yours' (V, i, 495) because Angelo's value has been debased by his misconduct. Even as he validates exchange, the Duke demonstrates that his ultimate power rests in his ability to transcend legal principles by granting mercy.[34] Still behaving as though Claudio has been executed, he tests the legal logic that would demand Angelo's death in exchange for Claudio's:

> An Angelo for Claudio; death for death.
> Haste still pays haste, and leisure answers leisure;
> Like doth quit like, and Measure still for Measure.
> (V, i, 407–9)

Articulating the play's titular theme, the Duke suggests that he will exact the harshest of judgements in which one man's life is repaid by another's, condemning Angelo 'to the very block / Where Claudio stoop'd to death, and with like haste' (V, i, 412–13). With this threat, the Duke returns to the unsettling aspects of human commensurability raised earlier in the bed trick and the exchange of heads. After forcing Isabella to grant Angelo clemency, he affirms his ducal power by revealing that he has preserved Claudio and pardoned Barnardine. The Duke's authority, the final act indicates, arises both from his mastery of theatrical and juridical exchange and from his willingness to transcend the logic of exchange through the power of the gift, a power intimately associated with Isabella's chastity.

The troubled jointure of exchange and gift in *Measure* is nowhere more apparent than in the Duke's concluding marriage proposal to Isabella. As Barbara Sebek contends, marriage 'incorporate[s] elements of the symbolic economies of both gift and commodity for its conceptual articulation', and the Duke invokes the institution as a means of reconciling the two economies.[35] Reconfiguring the proposition that set the plot in motion, the Duke offers to pardon Claudio in exchange for Isabella's sexual submission in his syllogistic proposal, 'If he [the newly revealed Claudio] be like your brother, for his sake / Is [Angelo] pardon'd; and for your lovely sake / Give me your hand and say you will be mine' (V, i, 488–90). Despite his discourse of merciful pardoning, the Duke emphasises a dynamic of substitution: Angelo is pardoned for Claudio's sake, and the Duke takes Isabella in marriage, ostensibly for her own benefit. Though the Duke appropriates the discourse of the gift, the scene exposes the exchange principles underlying the traffic in women. The upshot remains that Isabella's chastity is, in a sense, traded for her brother's life. The Duke himself underscores this exchange in his chiastic statement, 'What's mine is yours, and what is yours is mine' (V, i, 533), suggesting that Isabella, who was prepared to relinquish her possessions as a novice in the Poor Clares, will gain materially from the transaction.

By joining himself to Isabella, the Duke, whom many critics have read as resembling James I, not only buttresses his patriarchal authority but also infuses his state with the chaste purity of Elizabeth I, suggesting that his rule will be temperate as well as judicious.[36] Chastity is transformed, however, as it is incorporated into marriage, with Isabella losing her Elizabethan autonomy. Yet despite the Duke's best efforts, chastity retains a resistant quality in *Measure* that contributes to the play's unsatisfying ending. Isabella's silent response to the Duke's proposal reflects the play's residual discomfort with early capitalist systems of exchange, including the mimetic exchanges of the theatre, which the Duke uses to buttress the biopolitical power of the state to control sexuality, reproduction and death.[37] Although *Measure* never fully abandons the image of the actor/playwright/theatre as prostitute/bawd/brothel, Isabella's participation in the final scene gestures toward a redemptive, socially ameliorative theatrical ethic. Whereas the Duke seeks to mystify his power, the play as a whole calls attention to the objectifying commerce underlying the Duke's rule, and

Isabella's plea to 'let your reason serve / To make the truth appear where it seems hid, / And hide the false seems true' (V, i, 68–70) alerts audiences to the social violence undergirding the play's superficially comic ending. Her appeal, however, conjures an alternate understanding of theatrical exchange – one modelled on the shared consensual intercourse of companionate marriage – that is more fully developed in Shakespeare and Wilkins's *Pericles*.

Marina's Chaste Theatre: Antitheatrical Anxieties and Economic Redemption in Pericles

Anxieties about theatrical representation are particularly prevalent in Shakespeare and Wilkins's *Pericles*, a play that translates prose romance to the stage. As Shakespeare and Wilkins tackle this aesthetic challenge, they weigh the merits and weaknesses of dramatic representation and wrestle with methods of stabilising the unruly signs of the theatre.[38] Critics have long focused on the antitheatrical nature of *Pericles*, with particular attention given to its episodic nature.[39] In addition to narrative speeches by the choric Gower, whose 1393 *Confessio Amantis* serves as a source for the play, *Pericles* contains other forms of nondramatic representation, including dumb shows and divine, masque-like spectacles. Contributing to this nondramatic sensibility, scenes set in aristocratic spaces feature morally fixed characters whose typological representation narrows the gap between signs and referents that characterises mimetic representation. As in *Measure for Measure*, this antitheatricality dovetails with concerns about disease, syphilis as well as the plague, and about commerce, with the homologous matrix of commercial, sexual and theatrical exchange converging in the brothel to which Marina is sent. By transforming the brothel, as I will argue, Marina's powerful chastity redeems principles of exchange, legitimating exogamous marriage and profitable labour while also proffering a morally and mimetically reliable drama grounded in the contractual nature of the commercial theatre.

The seductive dangers of theatre are highlighted in the play's opening scene, in which Pericles attempts to win the hand of the daughter of the tyrannous King of Antioch, who is embroiled in an incestuous relationship with her father. To preserve this illicit relationship, King Antiochus has devised a spectacular ritual in which he invites his daughter's suitors to answer a riddle. Designed to 'to keep [the daughter] still and men in awe', the riddle contravenes expectations by readily disclosing the incestuous secret yet prohibiting suitors from revealing what they have discerned.[40] At the heart of the deceptive spectacle is the misleading beauty of Antiochus' daughter. Like an actor in a stage play, the daughter presents a disingenuous persona to the outside world. She arrives 'clothed like a bride' (I, i, 7), eliciting Pericles' misguided remarks about her natural beauty and unparalleled virtue:

> See where she comes, apparelled like the spring,
> Graces her subjects, and her thoughts the king
> Of every virtue gives renown to men;
> Her face the book of praises, where is read
> Nothing but curious pleasures.   (I, i, 13–17)

Presuming the daughter to conform to romance conventions, Pericles understands her appearance to signify the purity of spring. He presumes to read her face like a book, but proves incapable of the task. Although his glimpse of 'curious pleasures' hints at her incestuous history, he does not consider the secret that underlies her beauty. As such, the daughter of Antioch embodies a range of concerns surrounding mimetic representation, particularly the charge that acting disguises corruption and that artifice may be mistaken for reality. Like Gosson's actors, who resemble 'common Curtisans' wearing 'chaste Matrons apparel', the daughter hides her true identity and circumstances with an alluring exterior that seduces viewers.[41] Even after comprehending the riddle, Pericles calls the daughter a 'Fair glass of light' (I, i, 77), remarking that he might still love her 'were not this glorious casket stored with ill' (I, i, 78). Taken in by the daughter's acting ability, Pericles has difficulty reconciling his knowledge of her secret with her external persona, even though he knows from the riddle that her appearance misleads.

In his choric interludes Gower instructs the audience how to interpret the scene at Antioch, ensuring that they are not seduced by the spectacle as Pericles is. Even before Pericles' experience is dramatised, Gower explains the purpose of the riddle and the history of the 'Bad child' (I, o, 27), whose beauty 'Made many princes thither frame / To seek her as a bedfellow' (I, o, 32–3). Although Gower often indicates that dramatisation will augment or 'justify' (I, o, 42) his narrative, his speeches distance audiences from the dramatic scenes, protecting them from the theatre's power to entice and mislead.[42] As Gower later explains when Queen Dionyza pretends to mourn for Marina's supposed death, artifice can disguise reality: 'See how belief may suffer by foul show. / This borrowed passion stands for true-owed woe' (IV, iv, 23–4). Gower teaches the audience how to root out hypocrisy, a trait associated most closely with unchaste women, and he does so in large part by warning of the dangers and limitations of theatrical spectacle.

Despite the indictment of theatricality at Antioch, Pericles' landing on Pentapolis reveals that some forms of theatrical – and economic – exchange can be beneficial. As in the later brothel scenes, the fishermen who rescue Pericles from his shipwreck reflect the commercial dynamics of early seventeenth-century England. Whereas economic exchange signifies corruption in the brothel and perfidy in the aristocratic scenes, as when Dionyza pays to have Marina killed, the fishermen offer a vision of honest labour in a rustic setting. As they nurse Pericles, the fishermen provide witty commentary about the kingdom's social divisions and the plight of the poor, comparing oppressive social hierarchies to ocean life. Fish live as men do, the First Fisherman explains:

> the great ones eat up the little ones. I can compare our rich misers to nothing so fitly as to a whale: 'a plays and tumbles, driving the poor fry before him, and at last devours them all at a mouthful. Such whales have I heard on o'th' land, who never leave gaping till they swallowed the whole parish, church, steeple, bells and all.   (II, i, 28–34)

In their oppositional critique, the fishermen offer an alternate economic vision to that seen in the aristocratic scenes. Demonstrating that aristocrats rely on unidirectional consumption, as does the whale, they suggest that more egalitarian exchange would be advantageous to social health. Much like Isabella's discourse of the gift in *Measure*, artisanal labour functions in *Pericles* as an ameliorative force, mediating emerging capitalist logics by emphasising an unalienated connection between the labourer and his productions.[43] As Julia Reinhard Lupton argues, *Pericles* emphasises the power of artisanal labour in its varied forms, acknowledging 'the collaborative, creaturely, and networked character of all forms of action and authorship, including their always only partial release from capture in structures of alienation and exploitation'.[44] The fishermen's artisanal labour – later replicated in Marina's work educating women in the arts – functions as a middle ground between the aristocratic rejection of exchange and capitalist traffic, ostensibly facilitating exchange without exploitation and alienation. As Matthew Kendrick contends, the theatre often defends the worth of labour, particularly theatrical labour, in an economy that sought to commoditise and debase it.[45] In *Pericles*, those who labour and sell their wares are depicted as reforming oppressive, exploitative societies.

The artisanal world of the fishermen, furthermore, like that of the theatre, is characterised by representational signification. When Pericles washes ashore, 'bereft . . . of all his fortunes' (II, i, 9) and stripped of signs of rank, the fishermen refute the generic convention of self-evident nobility by refusing to believe that Pericles is a prince until they retrieve his armour from the sea. In this more dramatic, commercial realm, Pericles' identity must be fashioned and signalled though external representation. With his status affirmed, the fishermen then procure him a horse and construct leg protection for him out of the Second Fishermen's 'best gown' (II, i, 159), thus providing the castaway with the accoutrements he needs to appear as noble at the Court of Pentapolis, where he wins the tournament as well as Thaisa's hand. Pericles' triumph would have been impossible without the aid of the fishermen, whose presence attests to the labour and commercial exchange that support aristocratic life as well as to the performance of self undergirding seemingly natural aristocratic identity. Noting his debt, Pericles promises the fishermen that if his fortunes improve, he will 'pay [their] bounties, till then rest [their] debtor' (II, i, 139). Although nothing in the play suggests that Pericles keeps this promise, the fishermen scene highlights the debt that the romance plot owes to dramatic and commercial forms of exchange. It is this sort of ameliorative exchange – contrasted with the incestuous insularity at Antioch – that Marina more fully affirms in her purification of the brothel.

The brothel to which Marina is sent occupies a more commercial space than did the fishermen's rustic enclave, and its denizens traffic in human bodies rather than in the natural abundance of the earth. In contrast to the fishermen's artisanal labour, the brothel commoditises women, who are referred to as 'creatures' (IV, ii, 6) and are discussed in terms of their market value. Marina becomes a precious commodity, a 'prize' (IV, i, 89) who is sold to the brothel for the sizable price of one thousand pieces. The Bawd considers this purchase a wise investment, noting that she will profit handsomely from selling Marina's virginity, as 'Such a maidenhead were no cheap thing' (IV, ii, 54). Even more explicitly than in *Measure*, the brothel in *Pericles* is associated with the theatre, not only through its traffic in human bodies but also through its emphasis on acting and artifice. Successful prostitution, the Bawd instructs Marina, requires convincing acting ability, as a prostitute must be able to manipulate the desires of the men she services: 'Mark me, you must seem to do that fearfully which you commit willingly, despise profit where you have most gain. To weep that you live as ye do makes pity in your lovers. Seldom but that pity begets you a good opinion, and that opinion a mere profit' (IV, ii, 108–13). A prostitute, in the Bawd's view, makes money by acting as though she is virginal when she is not and by pretending that she wishes to escape her situation. Here the Bawd suggests that, like the theatre audience, the early capitalist sexual consumer willingly suspends disbelief in order to have his desires piqued. The prostitute's job is to manipulate these consumer desires by offering the fantasy of a pure, nearly unattainable woman who then submits to her john's entreaties.

Rejecting prostitution, the symbol of commoditised, idle and debased labour, Marina reclaims theatrical work, and she counters the Bawd's emphasis on artifice with her authentic purity. In contrast to the antitheatrical tracts' depiction of the theatres as 'plain devourers of maidenly virginity and chastity', the Bawd's corrupting theatricality proves no match for Marina's purity, which ultimately brings about the theatre's redemption.[46] By transforming the bawdy house into an 'honest house' (V, o, 2) where she teaches the artisanal arts of singing, dancing and needlework, Marina redeems the dramatic aspects of theatre, aiding in what Richard Finkelstein calls *Pericles*' '*apologia* for theatre'.[47] Reading Marina in terms of Protestant representation, Finkelstein argues that she is a 'miraculously fixed natural object, with her meaning equal to her appearance', who possesses the power to secure the potentially idolatrous signs of the theatre by imbuing them with grace.[48] This power is intimately linked to her chaste essence, which, like that of many romance virgins, aligns unstable representation. With beauty that corresponds to her virtue, Marina is presented as the antithesis of the daughter of Antioch, signifying both sexual purity and transparent value. In the brothel, Marina's chastity shows itself to be an exceptionally powerful force, buttressed by the powers of Diana, to whom Marina appeals, pledging, 'If fires be hot, knives sharp or waters deep, / Untried I still my virgin knot will keep. / Diana, aid my purpose!' (IV, ii, 138–40). The brothel is both counterpoised to this principled chastity – the Bawd dismisses Marina's pleas, asking, 'What have we to do with Diana?' (IV, ii, 141) – and threatened by it. In response to this threat, the Bawd commands Bolt to 'have [her] maidenhead taken off' (IV, v, 132), explaining that 'She's able to freeze the god Priapus and undo a whole generation. We must either get her ravished or be rid of her' (IV, v, 12–14).

Intensifying the audience's appreciation of Marina's power, the conversion of the brothel's patrons is depicted as almost miraculous. Before the audience witnesses Marina's rhetorically sophisticated conversion of Lysimachus, the Governor of Mytilene, they see converted gentlemen vowing to behave piously and chastely, with one of them improbably proclaiming, 'I am no more for bawdy houses. Shall's go hear the vestals sing?' (IV, v, 6–7). The immediacy of their transformation creates the impression that Marina's very essence encourages conversion. This sense of the miraculous is tempered, however, when the audience watches Marina convert Lysimachus, not through her divinely chaste essence but through rhetorical appeals and emotional displays of the sort associated with the theatre. Whereas the Bawd recommends feigning innocence as a means of enhancing one's desirability, Marina asserts her innocence in passionate emotional appeals designed to convey the truth of her situation.

She weeps in an attempt to convince Lysimachus that she is a virgin and should not be abused, insisting that she is 'a maid, though most ungentle Fortune / Have placed me in this sty' (IV, v, 100–1). Furthermore, she appeals to his sense of nobility, demanding, 'If you were born to honour, show it now' (IV, v, 96). Here, Marina adopts strategies advocated by the Bawd, such as crying and pleading, to express her own personal truth and to encourage moral behaviour. Lysimachus is moved by her performance, stating 'Had I brought hither a corrupted mind / Thy speech had altered it' (IV, v, 108–9) and giving her gold to free herself from the brothel. In this scene, Marina not only transforms Lysimachus, who had indeed possessed a 'corrupted mind', but also begins to redeem the dramatic arts, using them for morally sound purposes. Marina's appeal to Lysimachus models the kind of drama the play ultimately promotes, drama that uses the strategies of the theatre not to artificially distort reality but to convey truth. Theatricality, Marina suggests, in not itself immoral; rather its morality depends upon the ends to which it is put and the authenticity of the spirit animating it. Her brothel performance does not distort reality in the manner expected of a prostitute but rather heightens it, creating a theatrical hyperreality that serves virtuous ends.

Combining the miraculous powers of a Catholic virgin with a Protestant willingness to engage in chaste exchange, Marina reforms but does not reject the dramatic and commercial exchange underlying theatrical production. As with her cooption of the brothel's arts of persuasion, Marina does not disavow the brothel's economic underpinnings but transforms them through artisanal labour for productive, virtuous ends. Marina uses Lysimachus' gold to convince Bolt to accompany her in finding honourable work, admonishing him that 'Empty[ing] / Old receptacles or common stores of filth' would be 'better than this' (IV, v, 177–80). Marina herself takes up a trade, teaching 'pupils . . . of noble race / Who pour their bounty on her' (V, o, 9–10) to sing, weave, sew and dance. Whereas monetary exchanges were regarded with suspicion earlier in the play, Marina shows that money, here understood as a bountiful gift, can be used productively. She adopts an attitude toward labour that is similar to that espoused by the fishermen, who accept the necessity of economic exchange but do not allow the pursuit of profit to compromise their moral sensibilities. Although Marina continues to use her body and her performance skills to make a living, and must relinquish her profits to her overseers, her labour is largely free of the objectifying commercialism of the brothel, and her services are valuable to her society.

Marina's decision to transform the brothel into a school resonates with language from the antitheatrical tracts, which often referred to the theatre as a school of corruption, or in Gosson's case, of 'abuse'. In a 1577 treatise, for example, John Northbrooke called the theatre a 'schoole' in which Satan brought 'men and women into his snare of concupiscence and filthie lustes'.[49] In *Pericles*, though, Marina's affective and material labour transforms this lustful school into a chaste school, where students are educated in the pious as well as the domestic and creative arts. Marina's redemption of the brothel space suggests that the theatre, despite being embedded in capitalist structures, might similarly house forms of labour and representation that are 'honest', a word Marina uses to connote both morality and authenticity.

Because of Marina's redemptive presence, the final act of *Pericles* is more traditionally dramatic than previous acts and displays little of the antitheatrical anxiety noted earlier in the play. Marina herself employs dramatic techniques to revive Pericles from his depressed lethargy when she encounters him on board a ship docked at Mytilene. Because the father and daughter do not immediately recognise each other, their reunion unfolds slowly and dramatically. As the two converse, Marina exhibits glimmers of recognition, turning to the audience in one of the play's few dramatic asides to say 'I will desist, / But there is something glows upon my cheek

/ And whispers in mine ear, "Go not till he speak"' (V, i, 85–7). Marina gently manipulates Pericles as an actor might his audience, yet she does it for his own wellbeing and edification. When Pericles rebukes her, thinking himself mocked, Marina admonishes him, twice threatening to stop telling her story with statements such as 'Patience, good sir, / Or here I'll cease' (V, i, 135–6). The audience knows at this point that Marina is invested in discovering the king's identity and reviving him from his psychological slumber, but her threats succeed in calming Pericles and heightening his (and the audience's) interest in her story. Her approach succeeds, so much so that Pericles remarks that she 'starves the ears she feeds and makes them hungry / The more she gives them speech' (V, i, 103–4). At this point, Marina, rather than Gower, controls the audience's reactions, using her own dramatic sensibility to reveal the truth.

Because of this dramatic tension, some fear remains that the familial revelations will be thwarted, or, even more disastrously, that the incest of Antioch may be repeated. Marina's honest presence, though, assures both Pericles and the audience that the reunion will unfold as it should. As Pericles tells her, 'Falseness cannot come from thee, for thou look'st / Modest as Justice, and thou seem'st a palace / For the crowned Truth to dwell in' (V, i, 111–13). In contrast to his experience at Antioch, Pericles' assumptions based on Marina's appearance are proven true, validated both by Marina's semi-divine essence and by her resemblance to her mother, whom Pericles associates with fidelity. Moreover, the veracity of the scene has been facilitated on a structural level by Marina's transformation of the brothel from a bawdy house to an honest house. The theatre, like the honest house, has become a space where one's body can be used for worthwhile labour and where representation, though not transparent, is nonetheless reliable. Marina's chastity has enabled this transformation, ensuring that the dramatic ending does not repeat the unchaste spectacle with which the play began.

Pericles and Marina's reunion is further authorised as chaste by the captivating music of the spheres and by the entrance of Diana, who descends to the stage in Pericles' dream, instructing him to travel to her temple at Ephesus where he will discover his wife. Following the traditional pattern of the court masque, authority in *Pericles* descends from above and imposes divine order on the tumultuous world below. The ending of *Pericles* reflects the triumph of Diana's spiritual order, but also signals the reincorporation of dramatic representation and economic exchange, aspects of theatrical romance that were not generally permitted in the largely symbolic mode of the masque. After Marina recuperates the space of the theatre from below, Diana blesses the resulting dramatic production from above, aligning it with her divine chastity and with faithful rather than duplicitous representation. Because of Marina's authorising presence, the drama of the final scenes – including the discovery that Thaisa is alive as well as the familial reunion – overshadows Gower's authorial apparatus, and Gower's final speech takes the form of a conventional epilogue that merely summarises the action rather than validating it. In place of Gower's aesthetic theorising, Shakespeare – working through Marina – suggests that drama can be mimetically sound as long as the players' intentions are pure and audiences are properly poised to receive their productions. As in *Measure*, *Pericles*' conclusion emphasises audience reception, appealing to the contractual, communal nature of the public theatre.

The play's final scenes, therefore, reincorporate an ethic of commercial and sexual exchange that is absent from much of the play. Associated with both virginity and maternal fertility in early modern England, Diana's spirit links Marina's magical purity with the play's overall trajectory toward familial reunion and reproduction.[50] As Marina's transformation of the brothel shows, not all exchanges are equal: some, like the exchange of female bodies in prostitution, are degrading, while others, like the exchange of money for education, may be acceptable and even edifying. Alleviating some of *Measure*'s anxieties surrounding commensurability, *Pericles* presents exchange not as a levelling out of difference but as a system that can exist within a moral framework and that remains beholden to social hierarchies.

The play's gradual reframing of exchange is evident when Pericles' liege Helicanus lands in Mytilene and asks Lysimachus and his men for provisions in exchange for gold (V, i, 47–9). Rather than simply giving them the supplies, Lysimachus agrees to his offer, saying that accepting the exchange is 'a courtesy / Which, if we should deny, the most just gods / For every graft would send a caterpillar / And so inflict our province' (V, i, 50–3). Earlier in the play, such exchanges were regarded with suspicion, but now they are accepted as courteous acts that create social bonds. Marina is exchanged in a similar transaction. In return for facilitating the reunion of Pericles' family, and for thwarting the threat of father-daughter incest, Lysimachus is granted Marina's hand in marriage as well as sovereignty over the kingdom of Tyrus. Marina is therefore reincorporated into the commodity exchange of marriage, her chaste behaviour having facilitated the 'legitimate' exchange of women as an alternative both to prostitution and to the incestuous insularity with which the play began. This sanctioned traffic in women, by extension, serves as the mechanism through which other forms of exchange, both commercial and mimetic, are legitimised.

Pericles thus works to articulate a vision of a chaste public theatre, undergirded by unalienated artisanal labour and exchanges figured as gifts. As Suzanne Gossett observes, Marina's marriage is framed within the discourse of gift giving, which 'in the ethical and allegorical registers that tend to predominate in romance . . . is always a sign of virtue' and which in *Pericles* is contrasted with the commercial exchange of the brothel.[51] *Pericles*, even more so than *Measure*, works not to repel the discourse of exchange but to recuperate it by associating it with gift giving and with the chaste maiden's grace.[52] In contrast to *Measure*, the miraculous power of the virgin is presented as consistent with the exchange of marriage, which, though it might hinder Marina's autonomy, presumably leaves her chastity uncompromised. By reforming exchange, *Pericles* redeems the commercial basis of the public theatre, raising the possibility of a collective theatrical enterprise in which unstable signs are given value through the consensus of players and audiences who join in the process of meaning making. In a sense, *Pericles* articulates what Lars Engle terms the pragmatic vision which 'substitute[s] a mutable economy of value, action, and belief for what the philosophic tradition has tried to establish as a fixed structure of fact, truth, and knowledge'.[53] Even though theatrical signs lack intrinsic, absolute meaning, however, *Pericles* suggests that they are not ultimately arbitrary, as they are grounded in artisanal labour and a communitarian ethos. In this way *Pericles* confirms Yachnin's contention that the artisanal theatre explored 'new ways of forging communities and workable values within the complex conditions of a changing world'.[54] In contrast to the antitheatrical tracts, then, *Pericles* suggests that the commercial theatre might serve as a site of productive exchange, envisioned more as gift giving and artisanal production than as the traffic in bodies or commodities. In this dramatic model, the audience adopts the interpretive function earlier occupied by Gower, filling in the gaps in mimetic representation with their own discerning intellects. Set in this light, the theatre does not resemble the brothel so much as Marina's educative school, where the role of pupil is as central as the role of teacher.

This redemption of the theatre, however, is inseparable from the play's recuperation of patriarchal sexual exchange. Despite her efforts to transform the objectifying labour of the brothel, Marina falls victim to the commodity exchange of marriage when she is betrothed without her consent.

Her reformation of dramatic and economic exchange therefore does not transcend the traffic in women, but instead – as in *Measure* – facilitates it. Chastity's symbolic function as a sign of representative stability, then, is ultimately inseparable from its centrality to patriarchal kinship structures, shaping gender ideologies and representations of women. In both *Measure* and *Pericles*, the discourse of chastity-as-gift functions not only to recuperate the manifold exchanges of the market and the theatre but also to elide the commoditising aspects of patriarchal marriage.

Necrophilic Chastity, Usurious Representation and the Ethics of Metatheatre in The Revenger's Tragedy

Although chastity is idealised in Middleton's *The Revenger's Tragedy*, it nonetheless proves incapable of restoring a decaying aristocratic culture.[55] As in *Measure* and *Pericles*, *Revenger's* proposes the idea that militant virginity may serve as an antidote to the corrupting exchanges and excessive supplementarity of prostitution, usury and theatrical representation. *Revenger's* diverges from Shakespeare's plays, however, both by critiquing this idealisation of virginity as inappropriately nostalgic and even necrophilic and by rejecting marriage as a means of legitimating either the exchange of women or the homologous exchanges of the theatre and commerce. Refusing to 'chasten' the commercial theatre, *Revenger's* revels in the perverse joy of supplemental exchange, embracing its own usurious metatheatricality, its production of theatrical signs with no immediate relationship to reality. Such exchanges, the play suggests, may never achieve the edifying standard of the moralists but instead prove profitable and pleasurable. In contrast to Shakespeare's efforts to demonstrate the commercial theatre's morality, Middleton's *Revenger's* ultimately preserves the dichotomies of the antitheatricalists but perversely celebrates the excess that they demonise.

Revenger's dramatises a fall into a capitalist society marked by sexual depravity as well as duplicitous and excessive representation. This supplementarity is rooted in new forms of usurious exchange, which produce seemingly unnatural surpluses in the economic, sexual and semiotic realms. In this, Middleton adapts the Aristotelian dictum, still dominant in the early modern period, that coins must serve as stable signs of value in order to facilitate exchange.[56] Usury disrupts this ideal function; as Thomas Wilson laments in his 1572 *Discourse Upon Usury*, 'moneye was not first devised for thys ende, to bee merchaundize, but to bee a measure and a beem betwixt man and man, for the buying and selling of wears'.[57] Usury, Wilson recognises, commoditises money and divorces it from the material value it was assumed to signify. Within the Aristotelian framework, usury unnaturally causes money to multiply, making it breed as though it were an animate being. Analogously, the concept of verbal usury referred to supplemental forms of language such as punning and flattery. As Marc Shell explains, 'theorists since the medieval era have argued that punning is [usury's] linguistic counterpart, since punning makes an unnatural, even a diabolical, supplement to meaning from a sound that is properly attached on to one (if any) meaning'.[58] The danger of verbal usury, like the supplemental spectacle of theatre, is not only that it reproduces representation unnaturally, but that this supplemental language has no clear referent in the material world and therefore contains within it the potential for misrepresentation. As Aristotle's reproductive idiom suggests, these economic and linguistic concerns are homologically related to discourses of sexuality, with sexual reproduction functioning variously as a sign of usury or as the natural antithesis of usury's sterile generation.[59] In addition, as David Hawkes maintains, both usury and prostitution were compared as 'forms of concupiscence, diverting money and sex from their natural purpose and "taking advantage" of people's desire for both'.[60]

Throughout *Revenger's*, Middleton engages with discourses of usury and sexuality – the same discourses used by antitheatricalists to condemn the theatre – to interrogate the nature of theatrical spectacle and commercial exchange.

Sexuality, in *Revenger's*, serves as both a cause and a sign of social and economic decline. For Vindice, the play's principal social commentator, the social hierarchy is disintegrating because of aristocrats' depraved sexuality and their lust for money and commodities: 'Were't not for gold and women', Vindice declares, 'there would be no damnation'.[61] Aristocrats' lust, in particular, depletes their financial reserves and destroys their estates. According to Vindice, they must sell their land to buy clothing for their mistresses; loose women, he comments, 'Walk with a hundred acres on their backs – / Fair meadows cut into green foreparts' (II, i, 213–14). Aristocratic lands, once the basis of national stability, have become commoditised, alienated by the impecunious sexual impulses of their owners. In his disguise as the bawd Piato, Vindice brags,

> I have been witness
> To the surrenders of a thousand virgins,
> And not so little;
> I have seen patrimonies washed apieces,
> Fruit fields turned into bastards.   (I, iii, 49–53)

Sold to facilitate adulterous exchanges, the fields are themselves bastardised, transformed into illegitimate pieces of patrimony no longer connected to the larger aristocratic landscape. Adulterous sexuality challenges the sanctity of aristocratic blood and threatens to dismantle the system of primogeniture. As Michael Neill points out, adultery in *The Revenger's Tragedy* is literally adulterating, associated with unnatural pollution.[62] The aristocratic social order is thus sacrificed to sexual and economic decadence, its decline epitomised by the literal deracination of aristocratic land.

The court, to which aristocrats retreat after they have sold their land, combines conspicuous consumption with disingenuous representation and sexual licence, qualities epitomised by the court revels. Vindice characteristically intermingles the language of sexual licence with that of excessive consumption in his description of the scene:

> Oh think upon the pleasure of the palace,
> Secured ease and state; the stirring meats
> Ready to move out of the dishes,
> That e'en now quicken when they're eaten,
> Banquets abroad by torchlight, musics, sports,
> Bare-headed vassals that had ne'er the fortune
> To keep on their own hats, but let horns wear'em;
> Nine coaches waiting – hurry, hurry, hurry – (II, i, 195–202)

The dishes quicken, as though both pregnant and impregnating, while they are consumed amidst the amusements of the court. As spectacles of conspicuous consumption, the revels foster a surfeit of lust that engenders adultery and rape. The dishes themselves inspire cuckolding; commenting on his own status as the king's bastard son, Spurio remarks, 'some stirring dish / Was my first father ... I was begot in impudent wine and lust' (I, ii, 179–80, 190). This sexual licence not only leads to corruption and violence, as in the rape of Antonio's wife, but it disrupts the already threatened class structure. Spurio, like other theatrical bastards, commits adultery mainly for the sake of disrupting the social order. 'Adultery is my nature' (I, ii, 177), he proclaims, 'a bastard by nature should make cuckolds / Because he is the son of a cuckold maker' (I, ii, 201–2). The bastard is presented as a threat because, unlike his legitimate brothers, he has little stake in the social hierarchy – he embodies the culture's loss of chastity.

Revenger's makes explicit the relationship between adulterous reproduction and usury. Spurio's description of himself as a bastard adulterer suggests that, like usurious transactions, he will reproduce himself almost spontaneously, creating both bastards and cuckolds.[63] Cuckolds, like bastards, are associated with suspect coinage: according to Vindice, 'cuckolds are a-coining, apace, apace, apace, apace' (II, ii, 142). Lussurioso's effort to seduce Castiza is rendered in similar terms, with Vindice averring that the Duke's son hopes to 'turn[]' her 'into use' (II, ii, 97). Invoking an early modern commonplace, Lussurioso hopes that Castiza's 'honour, which she calls her chastity', will be 'br[ought] . . . into expense, for honesty / Is like a stock of money laid to sleep / Which ne'er so little broke, does never keep' (I, iii, 116–19). Lussurioso suggests that virginity, like hoarded money, is of little use because it cannot reproduce. Castiza underscores the ethical implications of his proposition when she refuses to stoop to 'common usury' (IV, iv, 105). By exploiting the discursive link between usury and prostitution, *Revenger's* affirms Thomas Wilson's assertion that 'usurers and bawds may well go together, for they gayne by filthy meanse all that thye geat'.[64]

The actor, like the prostitute, was also associated with usury in the early modern imagination, as a figure who engages in unnatural reproduction and creates an artificial exterior to conceal an empty or corrupt interior. As Jean-Christophe Agnew explains, 'the figure of the usurer incarnated the characterlessness and "infinite purposiveness" of the money he lent out at interest', becoming

> a fungible man, a 'universal equivalent' whose self was effectively interchangeable with any or all of the selves to be found in the seventeenth-century repertoire of 'characters'. The usurer was, like the actor, a liminary: a marginal man perennially poised in midpassage, a figure situated 'betwixt and between' the conventional boundaries of social identity in early modern England.[65]

Vindice's experience reflects the usurious qualities of acting, as his identity is destabilised by his penchant for disguise and dissembling, practices he describes in economic terms. He portrays his alter ego Piato as a 'base-coined pandar' (I, i, 80), someone practised in the twin arts of unnatural reproduction and false representation. When he commands his brother to adopt a disguise with the phrase 'we must coin' (I, i, 102), Vindice overtly links their disguises, or 'counterfeiting', with improper coinage, echoing William Prynne's accusation that actors purchase money 'by their tongues and impudency; they being wise to dissemble, apt to counterfeit'.[66] Like counterfeit coins whose inscriptions do not correspond to their value in specie, the actor's costume occludes the value of the person underneath. As Vindice lingers in his disguise, he comes to embody the representational instability coded in his usury metaphors, and he begins to envision himself in gendered terms as one of the 'wiser' and 'less ashamed' women of the court (I, iii, 15).

Chastity serves in *Revenger's* as an embattled symbol of sexual and representational purity. In its absence, the social world grows degenerate, a condition Vindice encapsulates in his comment, 'All thrives but Chastity, she lies a-cold' (II, i, 223), which ironically connects chastity's scarcity with its inert reproductive capacity. The dual connotations of Vindice's quip capture chastity's mixed status in the play, as it is idealised but also simultaneously depicted as a sterile virtue that cannot be restored in the current social climate. Throughout the play, chastity is associated with the prosperous reign of Elizabeth I, who is invoked in the name of Vindice's deceased lover, Gloriana, whose admirable chastity led to her death.[67] Vindice remembers Gloriana as devoid of the artifice characterising women at court: ''twas a face / So far beyond the artificial shine / Of any woman's bought complexion' (I, i, 20–2). In opposition to the women of the court, Gloriana is neither 'bought' nor in need of cosmetics to augment her beauty, and she therefore does not contribute to her society's economic and moral decline. Furthermore, Vindice presents Gloriana's chastity as working to preserve the social order.

He boasts that she could provoke a usurer's son to 'Melt all his patrimony in a kiss... yet his suit been cold' (I, i, 27; 29). Though her beauty elicits erotic responses from courtiers, her resistance to their pursuits preserves their economic status, albeit against their wishes. In the corrupt and usurious culture of the court, however, such chastity is besieged, and Gloriana is ultimately poisoned for refusing the Duke's advances.

Chastity's embattled state is emphasised visually throughout the play by the presence of Gloriana's skull, which Vindice carries with him as a spur to revenge. Vindice presents the skull's coldness as surpassing the chastity of any woman; its association with death animates its chaste power, allowing it to function as a *memento mori* that forces people to consider their sins. Vindice states,

> Here's an eye
> Able to tempt a great man – to serve God;
> A pretty hanging lip, that has forgot now to dissemble.
> Methinks this mouth should make a swearer tremble,
> A drunkard clasp his teeth, and not undo 'em.
> To suffer damnation to run through 'em.
> Here's a cheek keeps her colour, let the wind go whistle.
> Spout rain, we fear thee not, be hot or cold
> All's one with us. (III, v, 54–62)

The ever-present death's head suggests that chastity is a virtue more likely to be found in dead women than in live ones. Vindice imagines the radical chastity of death as a counterpoint to the artifice of the women of court. Whereas they fear that rain might wash off their cosmetics, Vindice's beloved is completely unadorned. Furthermore, she is incapable of dissembling. If shown the skull, moreover, courtly women would see their own depravity reflected; as Vindice avers, 'Here might a scornful and ambitious woman / Look through and through herself; see, ladies, with false forms / You deceive men but cannot deceive worms' (III, v, 95–7).

False representation, like improper sexuality, is a marker of decay and dissolution, but death, Vindice suggests, will strip this away, ushering in a purified state of final chastity. In short, Gloriana's chastity becomes an object of necrophilic desire.[68] The damaging effect of this necrophilic worship is evident in the death of Antonio's wife, who kills herself after she is raped by the Duke's youngest son. The men universally applaud her decision, with Antonio stating that she 'lived / As cold in lust as she is now in death' (I, iv, 35–6). Although chastity cannot function in conventionally reproductive ways, it serves as a nostalgic ideal that inspires men to potentially purgative revenge.

Only Castiza's chastity is preserved in play, but she is presented as anomalous and is similarly regarded with nostalgia. Castiza affirms her brother's conviction that social corruption might be prevented if women could maintain their chastity, attesting,

> If maidens would [be virtuous], men's words could have no power;
> A virgin honour is a crystal tower
> Which being weak is guarded with good spirits:
> Until she basely yields no ill inherits.   (IV, iv, 152–5)

Castiza's virtue is readily apparent, the 'crystal tower' of her virgin honour indicating a transparency of representation that contrasts with the painted artifice of the court. It is to this chastity that her mother Gratiana refers when she proclaims that Castiza should be 'a glass for maids, and I for mothers' (IV, iv, 158). Although Castiza remains alive and untainted, she remains vulnerable in a corrupt society driven by pecuniary motives. As she laments, 'Were not sin rich there would be fewer sinners: / Why had not virtue a revenue?' (II, i, 6–7). Lacking revenue, chastity proves incapable of effecting transformation in *Revenger's*, as it does in *Pericles* and *Measure*. Castiza never becomes a site of 'honest' reproduction; unlike

Marina and Isabella, she refuses to participate in any exchange, sexual, commercial or theatrical. Castiza therefore reflects the fading monastic ideal of virginity, and in so doing resists the traffic in women. However, this virgin ideal is too embattled in early capitalist society to effect tenable social reform.

Despite Vindice's nostalgic desire for purity, *The Revenger's Tragedy* problematises cultural efforts to assert chastity as a source of redemptive purity, exposing such efforts as both perverse and fantastical. Vindice's fetishisation of the skull implicitly critiques the cultural valorisation of dead women. As Christine M. Gottlieb contends, '*The Revenger's Tragedy* deconstructs the category of the dead chaste woman and shows the absurdity of applying our notions of sexual propriety to dead objects.'[69] In its critique, the play registers disgust at the Catholic veneration of relics. If absolute sexual purity can be embodied only by a piece of bone, then standards of sexual behaviour for women are even more unrealistic. The fetishised death's head, moreover, undermines the play's efforts to assert chastity as a pre-usurious 'Real' beyond the realm of representation. As Karin Coddon contends, Gloriana's skull blurs the line between subject and object, 'playing alternately at being pure referent and pure signifier'.[70] The skull is presented as a relic, materially referencing the body and its saintly death, yet it is also a stage property: As Vindice explains, he 'ha[s] not fashioned this only for show / And useless property, no – it shall bear a part / E'en in it own revenge' (III, v, 99–101). An efficacious stage property, the skull brings about the Duke's death, with Vindice dressing her as a prostitute and putting poison on her lips for the Duke to kiss.

Both prostitution and theatricality mark the murder of the Duke, and the chastity ascribed to Gloriana's skull is compromised by its participation in the act. Not only is the skull accoutred as a prostitute, but, as with the Duke's initial poisoning of Gloriana, the poisoning of the Duke signals

Chastity and the Ethics of Commercial Theatre [71

corrupting sexual exchange, as Gloriana 'shall be revenged / In the like strain and kiss his lips to death' (III, v, 103–4). By deploying the skull in his murder plot, moreover, Vindice effectively puts it to use. Earlier in the play Vindice remarks to the skull that, because the court is asleep, 'Thou mayst lie chaste now!' (III, v, 89), tying its chastity to its inert state and suggesting that this quality will recede with activity. Like the multiplying economic signs of usury, Gloriana's skull becomes active and acquires multiple meanings, coming to signify not only Gloriana's chaste body but also myriad other referents, including Queen Elizabeth, the Duke's crimes, Vindice's vengeance, and the range of social and economic forces Vindice blames for Gloriana's death. This multiple signification indicates not only that chastity fails to constitute a pre-usurious 'Real' but also that chastity operates as a theatrical symbol: not the fixed unity of referent and object, as Shakespeare often implies, but a sign that refers to a web of social, economic and metaphysical concepts. *Revenger's* evocation and simultaneous disavowal of idealised chastity accounts for its nostalgic tone, but ultimately it rejects cultural narratives linking chastity with cultural, economic and mimetic purity.

The play's refusal to reclaim a prior chaste state elucidates the intense metatheatricality of the final scene in which meditations on chastity are abandoned in favour of the free play of usurious signs. In the absence of redemptive chastity that could authenticate mimesis, *Revenger's* revels in the disruptive joy of usurious representation – overt metatheatricality and spectacle that gleefully rejects verisimilitude. Metatheatre's multiplication of theatrical signs parallels usury's multiplication of monetary signs, immaterial fantasies, which Gerard de Malynes accuses usurers of perpetuating: they 'have all their wealth in paper and inke, or parchment, which they accompt as precious as the golden fleece, multiplying the same in their imagination untill they die'.[71] As with money, the signs of the theatre become ends in themselves, provoking accusations of idolatry. Money, according to David Hawkes, seemed to multiply of its own accord, contributing to the 'gradual displacement of things by signs, of reality by representation'.[72] Following Jonathan Dollimore, critics have focused on *Revenger's* metatheatricality, observing that it presents spectacle and simulacra rather than representing the social or natural world directly.[73] This process is captured in the play's association of theatrical signs with usury and in its suggestion that, like usury, spectacle functions simultaneously as a creative force and as a depraved and unreliable means of reproducing signs.

Nowhere is this tendency toward metatheatre more evident than in the murderous masque with which the play concludes. In this final scene, Middleton exploits possibilities present in the revenge tragedy's generic appropriation of the court masque, an aristocratic genre that is in many ways antithetical to the mimetic representation of the public theatre. In contrast to theatrical drama, the court masque relies on allegorical representation, grounded by the presence of the monarch for whom it is performed. As Agnew contends,

> The parts that courtiers enacted were, like those of the moralities, allegorical; they were thus entirely at odds with the concept of role playing simultaneously emerging on the public stage. Roles were ordained in the masque; they were 'investments' only in the older, honorific sense, not in the newer, *credit*able sense. Whatever else they were, they were not the negotiable, promissory agreements about identity that so deeply yet obliquely implicated the playhouse audiences in their performance.[74]

If the public theatre captures the representational strategies of early capitalism, the masques reflect an aristocratic hierarchy, with the monarch and God as homological equivalents at its pinnacle. Acting was reserved for the chaotic antimasque upon which the masque imposed order.

Following in the tradition of Thomas Kyd's *The Spanish Tragedy*, the revenge tragedy often disrupts the court masque with mayhem and murder. In so doing, the theatre assaults the masque's allegorical integrity as well as the social and cosmological systems it purports to reflect. *Revenger's* magnifies this generic convention, rejecting the premise that court masques ever feature stable representation and presenting the audience with a spectacular scene filled with competing forms of signification.

Resolutely metatheatrical, *Revenger's* presents multiple groups of actor-murders competing for violent theatrical supremacy. The masque is compromised even before Vindice interrupts it, as the Duke's sons Supervacuo and Ambitioso plan to use it to kill their older brother Lussurioso. For them, rather than representing proper aristocratic entertainment, masques are opportunities for deception: 'A masque is treason's licence: that build upon – / 'Tis murder's best face, when a visard's on!' (V, i, 178–9). Vindice, the consummate manipulator of courtly modes of representation, sees a similar opportunity for violence in the masque, but he focuses on the theatrical potential to exact poetic justice, and salivates at the prospect of killing the nobles as they enjoy the sordid revels, 'when they think their pleasure sweet and good' (V, ii, 21). The court masque, in Vindice's hands, adopts the techniques of the commercial theatre to seduce the courtiers before killing them, a debt emphasised in Vindice's call to the wings, 'Mark; thunder! / Dost know thy cue, thou big-voiced crier? / Duke's groans are thunder's watchwords' (V, iii, 43–4). By mobilising theatricality, Vindice's masque disrupts the representational power of words and theatrical symbols. The violence of the final scene, with its multiple stabbings, verges on camp, and the identities of the murderers are muddled. When Lussurioso says, 'Those in the masque did murder us' (V, iii, 70), it is unclear to whom he refers. Representation itself loses grounding at the end of the play: signifiers multiply but never point toward a clear culprit. Such heightened theatricality indicates that the court is very far away from reclaiming any chaste world of stable economic and linguistic representation.

Revenger's gestures toward ontological clarity when Vindice, enamoured with his performance, brags of his crimes to Antonio and then confesses to the murders, averring that it would be unfair to have 'nobles clipped' (V, iii, 125) for crimes they have not committed. Having exhausted his dramatic options, Vindice rejects the misrepresentation, associated with 'clipped' coins (nobles), that leads to unjust executions, and he once again voices opposition to usurious behaviour. Despite this brief realignment with clearly identifiable truth, it seems unlikely that Vindice's mass murder of the Duke's family has cleansed the court of its endemic problems. Similarly, the play obviates the potential – developed in *Measure* and *Pericles* – that female chastity might serve as a source of social and mimetic purification. Capitalist transformations – in the economic, social, and sexual realms – prove ineluctable, and the chastity of women such as Castiza is much too embattled to mitigate their effects. By the end of the play, moreover, chastity's symbolic resonance has been largely severed from the experiences of living women, as it is embodied in Gloriana's skull – a relic of an idealised past but also a prop, a sign of the theatre. An overinvestment in anachronistic ideals of chastity contributes, so Vindice's misogynist rhetoric and necrophilic attachments indicate, to the violent scapegoating of women for the ills of their society without addressing larger socioeconomic forces at work. It is perhaps more ethical, *Revenger's* suggests, to abandon the representational security epitomised by chastity and, instead, to revel in the play – and even the depravity – of usurious theatrical signs.

By embodying the power of chastity within the death's head, *Revenger's* illuminates chastity's symbolic power in early modern drama more generally. Peter Stallybrass maintains that, 'in Vindice's overvaluation of and disgust at woman's body, we should find the symbolic burden that women are forced to bear (as well as the semiotic power with which they are invested) when they are conceptualized as mapping both an ideal enclosure and its impossibility'.[75] This is the burden that women bear not only in *Revenger's* but also in *Measure* and *Pericles* where chaste women function to redeem the theatre, figured as a brothel, from accusations of artifice, corruption and commoditisation. In addition to demonstrating the fraught place of women, as symbols of both stability and corruption, *Revenger's*, *Measure* and *Pericles* demonstrate how the questions of exchange inherent in discourses of chastity align with and inform the theatre's reflexive interrogation of its own commercial and mimetic exchanges.

Principled virginity, in each play, indicates resistance to exchange, while the virgin's submission to marriage conversely reflects a willingness to engage in exchange. This acquiescence thus endows exchanges of various types with the virgin's powerful purity and with the state-sanctioned respectability associated with marriage. The theatre's defence against the antitheatrical tracts, in this model, thus depends upon the traffic in women and, more precisely, upon Protestant understandings of virginity as a transitional rather than absolute state. Whereas *Pericles* accepts this premise somewhat unproblematically, modelling the relationship of players and audiences on that of husband and wife, *Measure* reveals the coercion inherent in this solution, noting how closely marriage can resemble prostitution. *Revenger's* takes this critique a step further, suggesting that an overreliance on chastity as both symbol and agent of social, economic and representational stability contributes to a culture of misogyny in which the only truly chaste woman is a dead woman.

Notes

1. Joseph Lenz analyses this association of the theatre with prostitution in 'Base Trade: *Theatre as Prostitution*', *English Literary History* 60.4 (1993): 833–55. For the marginal place of the theatre in the liberties, see Steven Mullaney, *The Place of the Stage: License, Play, and Power in Renaissance England* (Chicago: University of Chicago Press, 1988). For the theatre's role in facilitating prostitution, see Jennalie Cook, '"Bargaines of Incontinencie": Bawdy Behavior in the Playhouses', *Shakespeare Survey* 10 (1977): 271–90.
2. Stephen Gosson, *The Schoole of Abuse [August ?] 1579 and A Short Apologie of the Schoole of Abuse [November?] 1579*, ed. Edward Arber (London: Southgate, 1868), 32.
3. The Malone Society, *Dramatic Records: The Remebrencia*, vol. 1 (New York: Oxford University Press, 1907), quoted in Lenz, 'Base Trade', 836.
4. John Rainolds, *The Overthrow of Stage-Playes* (New York: Jonson Reprint Co., 1972), 18.
5. Stephen Gosson, *Plays Confuted in Five Actions* (New York: Johnson Reprint Corporation, 1972), E3, E4v; Gosson, *Schoole of Abuse*, 2.
6. Gosson, *Schoole of Abuse*, 20.
7. Donald Lupton, *London and the Country carbonadoed and quartered into several characters* (London: Printed by Nicholas Okes, 1632), Folger Copy 1, 79–80.
8. John Northbrooke, *A Treatise wherein Dicing, Dauncing, Vaine playes, or Enterludes, with idle pastimes, &c., commonly used on the Sabbath day, are reproved by the Authoritie of the word of God and auntient writers* (London, 1577), 104.
9. Lenz, 'Base Trade', 842, 834.
10. For these homologies, see Jean-Joseph Goux, *Symbolic Economies: After Marx and Freud* (Ithaca, NY: Cornell University Press, 1990).
11. Gosson, *Schoole of Abuse*, 35.
12. Huston Diehl, *Staging Reform, Reforming the Stage: Protestantism and Popular Theater in Early Modern England*

(Ithaca, NY: Cornell University Press, 1997), 8. See also Michael O'Connell, *The Idolatrous Eye: Iconoclasm and Theater in Early-Modern England* (New York: Oxford University Press, 2000).

13. Paul Yachnin, '"The Perfection of Ten": Populuxe Art and Artisanal Value in *Troilus and Cressida*', *Shakespeare Quarterly* 56.3 (2005): 306–27, esp. 320.

14. Yachnin, '"The Perfection of Ten"', 326–7.

15. See Jacques Derrida, 'White Mythology: Metaphor in the Text of Philosophy', *New Literary History* 6 (1974): 5–21; Jean-Joseph Goux, *Symbolic Economies: After Marx and Freud*, trans. Jennifer Curtiss Gage (Ithaca, NY: Cornell University Press, 1990) and *The Coiners of Language*, trans. Jennifer Curtiss Gage (Norman: University of Oklahoma Press, 1994); and Marc Shell, *The Economy of Literature* (Baltimore: Johns Hopkins University Press, 1978) and *Money, Language, and Thought: Literary and Philosophical Economies from the Medieval to the Modern Era* (Berkeley: University of California Press, 1982).

16. David Hawkes argues that 'the commodification of money implies the commodification of mediation *per se*' (*Shakespeare and Economic Theory*, The Arden Shakespeare [New York: Bloomsbury, 2015], 15).

17. Representations of prostitution in early modern drama have received a great deal of critical attention. For an excellent analysis of the brothel's significance within the theatre's negotiation of early capitalist commerce, see Jean Howard, '(W)holesaling: Bawdy Houses and Whore Plots in the Drama's Staging of London', in *Theater of a City: The Places of London Comedy, 1598–1642* (Philadelphia: University of Pennsylvania Press, 2007), 114–61.

18. Richard Brathwaite, *The English gentlewoman, drawn out in the full body* (London, 1631), 203–4.

19. For the significance of the plague in *Measure*, see Catherine Cox, '"Lord Have Mercy Upon Us": The King, the Pestilence, and Shakespeare's *Measure for Measure*', *Exemplaria* 20.4 (2008): 430–57.

20. William Shakespeare, *Measure for Measure*, ed. J. W. Lever, The Arden Shakespeare (London: Methuen, 1965; reprint 1997), I, iii, 50, hereafter cited parenthetically.
21. For the significance of the convent as means of resisting commoditisation, see Kimberly Reigle, 'Staging the Convent as Resistance in *The Jew of Malta* and *Measure for Measure*', *Comparative Drama* 46.4 (2012): 497–513.
22. The image of the coin is central to the play's themes of value, counterfeiting and exchange. For discussions of the play's financial imagery, see E. Pearlman, 'Shakespeare, Freud, and the Two Usuries, or, Money's a Meddler', *English Literary Renaissance* 2.2 (1972): 217–36; Nigel Smith, 'The Two Economies of *Measure for Measure*', *English* 36.156 (1987): 197–232; Ildikó Limpár, 'Coining Images of Value in Shakespeare's *Measure for Measure*', in *What Does It Mean?*, ed. Kathleen Dubs (Piliscsaba, Hungary: Pázmány Péter Catholic University Press, 2003), 139–45; Teresa Lanpher Nugent, 'Usury and Counterfeiting in Wilson's *The Three Ladies of London* and *The Three Lords of London*, and in Shakespeare's *Measure for Measure*', in *Money and the Age of Shakespeare*, ed. Linda Woodbridge (New York: Palgrave, 2003), 201–18; Stephen Deng, 'Coining Crimes and Moral Regulation in *Measure for Measure*', in *Coinage and State Formation in Early Modern English Literature* (New York: Palgrave, 2008), 103–34; and David Landreth, 'Monetary Policy: *King John* and *Measure for Measure*', in *The Face of Mammon: The Matter of Money in English Renaissance Literature* (New York: Oxford University Press, 2012), 102–49.
23. Michael Neill, 'Bastardy, Counterfeiting, and Misogyny in *The Revenger's Tragedy*', *Studies in English Literature* 36.2 (1996): 397–416.
24. Several critics suggest that Isabella's virginity is transgressive because she resists marriage. See Marcia Reifer, '"Instruments of Some More Mightier Member": The Construction of Female Power in *Measure for Measure*', *Shakespeare Quarterly* 35.2 (1984): 157–69; Mario DiGangi, 'Pleasure

and Danger: Measuring Female Sexuality in *Measure for Measure*', *English Literary History* 60.3 (1993): 589–609; and Hanna Scolnicov, 'Chastity, Prostitution and Pornography in *Measure for Measure*', *Shakespeare Jahrbuch* 134 (1998): 68–81.
25. For discussion of the law in *Measure*, see Jeremy Tambling, 'Law and Will in *Measure for Measure*', *Essays in Criticism* 59.3 (2009): 189–210.
26. Stephen Deng links the play's counterfeiting imagery to its exploration of justice, arguing that 'the deficiency of the coinage described by the coin imagery indicates an inability to establish a stable measure of value for assigning terms of justice within the play' ('Coining Crimes and Moral Regulation in *Measure for Measure*', 104).
27. For more on the significance of incest in relation to exchange, see Marc Shell, *The End of Kinship: 'Measure for Measure', Incest, and the Ideal of Universal Siblinghood* (Stanford: Stanford University Press, 1988).
28. For theatrical exchange in *Measure*, see Jan Kott, 'Head for Maidenhead, Maidenhead for Head: The Structure of Exchange in *Measure for Measure*', in *En Tourno a Shakespeare; Homenaje a T. J. B. Spencer* (Valencia: Universidad de Valencia, Instituto Shakespeare, 1980), 93–113, and Alexander Leggatt, 'Substitution in *Measure for Measure*', *Shakespeare Quarterly* 39.3 (1988): 342–59.
29. Huston Diehl suggests that this emphasis on the limitations of the theatre and its reliance on substitution reflects Shakespeare's appropriation of 'the representational strategies of English Calvinism, distancing his theatre from a fraudulent theatricality widely associated in Protestant England with the Roman Catholic Church while also challenging the vehement antitheatricality of radical Protestants' ('"Infinite Space": Representation and Reformation in *Measure for Measure*', *Shakespeare Quarterly* 49.4 [1998]: 393–410, esp. 396). For discussions of antitheatricality in *Measure*, see Clifford Leech, 'The Meaning of *Measure for Measure*', *Shakespeare Survey* 3 (1950): 66–73; Mary Ellen Lamb, 'Shakespeare's

"Theatrics": Ambivalence Toward Theater in *Measure for Measure*', *Shakespeare Studies* 20 (1988): 129–46; and Richard Hillman, '*Measure for Measure* and the (Anti-)Theatricality of Gasgoigne's *The Glass of Government*', *Comparative Drama* 42.4 (Winter 2008): 391–408.
30. John C. Higgins, 'Justice, Mercy, and Dialectical Genres in *Measure for Measure* and *Promos and Cassandra*', *English Literary Renaissance* 42.2 (2012): 258–93, esp. 289.
31. Francis Bacon, *The Essays, or Counsels Civil and Moral*, ed. Brian Vickers (New York: Oxford University Press, 1999), 4.
32. My reading therefore conflicts with Michael D. Friedman's argument that Isabella's reputation is destroyed by her false confession ('"Oh, let him marry her!": Matrimony and Recompense in *Measure for Measure*', *Shakespeare Quarterly* 46.4 [1995]: 454–64).
33. For an alternate reading of the conflict between discourses of commodities and gifts in *Measure*, see Barbara Sebek, '"By gift of my chaste body": Female Chastity and Exchange Value in *Measure for Measure* and *A Woman Killed with Kindness*', *Journal of Culture and Criticism* 5.1–2 (2001): 51–85.
34. For a discussion of *Measure*'s treatment of justice and mercy, see Victoria Hayne, 'Performing the Social Practice: The Example of *Measure for Measure*', *Shakespeare Quarterly* 44.1 (1993): 1–29; David Lindley, 'The Stubbornness of Barnardine: Justice and Mercy in *Measure for Measure*', *Shakespeare Yearbook* 7 (1996): 333–51; Deborah Kuller Shuger, *Political Theology in Shakespeare's England: The Sacred and the State in* Measure for Measure (New York: Palgrave, 2001); and John C. Higgins, 'Justice, Mercy, and Dialectical Genres in *Measure for Measure* and *Promos and Cassandra*', *English Literary Renaissance* 42.2 (2012): 258–93.
35. Sebek, '"By gift of my chaste body"', 53.
36. For a reading of the Duke in light of James I's rule, see Jeffrey S. Doty, '*Measure for Measure* and the Problem of Popularity', *English Literary Renaissance* 42.1 (2012): 32–57.
37. Critics have interpreted Isabella's silence in response to the Duke's proposal as signalling either compliance or resistance.

I follow Pascale Aebischer in her view that the silences of both Isabella and Angelo 'point to a view of marriage not as a happy comedic resolution but rather as both a form of state control and a kind of rape' ('Silence, Rape and Politics in *Measure for Measure*: Close Readings in Theater History', *Shakespeare Bulletin* 26.4 [2008]: 1–23, esp. 7). For discussions of biopolitics in *Measure*, see Richard Wilson, 'The Quality of Mercy: Discipline and Punishment in Shakespearean Comedy', *Seventeenth Century* 5.1 (1990): 1–41; Jonathan Dollimore, 'Transgression and Surveillance in *Measure for Measure*', in *Political Shakespeare: Essays in Cultural Materialism* (Ithaca, NY: Cornell University Press, 1994), 72–87; Alberto Cacicedo, '"She is fast my wife": Sex, Marriage, and Ducal Authority in *Measure for Measure*', *Shakespeare Studies* 23 (1995): 187–209; Natasha Korda, 'Isabella's Rule: Singlewomen and the Properties of Poverty in *Measure for Measure*', in *Shakespeare's Domestic Economies: Gender and Property in Early Modern England* (Philadelphia: University of Pennsylvania Press, 2002), 159–91; and Benjamin Bertram, '*Measure for Measure* and the Discourse of Husbandry', *Modern Philology* 110.4 (2013): 459–88.

38. Studying *Pericles* is complicated by its dual authorship and by the state of the extant text. I follow the growing consensus that Wilkins wrote Acts 1 and 2 and that Shakespeare wrote the final three acts. For a summary of the long-running debate surrounding the play's authorship, see Suzanne Gossett's introduction to *Pericles*, The Arden Shakespeare, 3rd series (London: Thomas Learning, 2004), 1–163, esp. 62–76.

39. See John Arthos, '*Pericles, Prince of Tyre*: A Study in the Dramatic Use of Romantic Narrative', *Shakespeare Quarterly* 4.3 (1953): 257–70. For a more recent discussion of antitheatricality in *Pericles* and its relationship to patriarchal control, see Deanne Williams, 'Papa Don't Preach: The Power of Prolixity in *Pericles*', *University of Toronto Quarterly: A Canadian Journal of the Humanities* 71.2 (2002): 595–622. See also my essay,

'Authorial Anxieties and Theatrical Instability in John Bale's Biblical Plays and Shakespeare and Wilkins' *Pericles, Prince of Tyre*', in *Stages of Engagement: Drama and Religion in Post-Reformation England*, ed. James D. Mardock and Kathryn R. McPherson (Pittsburgh: Duquesne University Press, 2014), 154–80.

40. William Shakespeare and George Wilkins, *Pericles*, ed. Suzanne Gossett, The Arden Shakespeare, Third Series (London: Thomas Learning, 2004), I, 0, 36, hereafter cited parenthetically. For more on the significance of incest in the play, see Coppélia Kahn, 'The Providential Tempest and the Shakespearean Family', in *Representing Shakespeare*, ed. Murray Schwarz and Coppélia Kahn (Baltimore: Johns Hopkins University Press, 1980), 217–43, and Susan Frye, 'Incest and Authority in Shakespeare's Pericles', in *Incest and the Literary Imagination*, ed. Elizabeth Barnes (Gainesville: University Press of Florida, 2002), 39–58.

41. Gosson, *Schoole of Abuse*, 20.

42. For discussions of Gower as an antitheatrical force, see Walter F. Eggers, 'Shakespeare's Gower and the Role of Authorial Presenter', *Philological Quarterly* 54 (1975): 434–43, and Steven Mullaney, '"All that Monarchs Do": The Obscured Stages of Authority in *Pericles*', in *The Place of the Stage*, 135–51. For more on Gower's significance as a choric figure, see Richard Hillman, 'Shakespeare's Gower and Gower's Shakespeare: The Larger Debt of *Pericles*', *Shakespeare Quarterly* 36.4 (1985): 427–37, and David F. Hoeniger, 'Gower and Shakespeare in *Pericles*', *Shakespeare Quarterly* 33.4 (1982): 461–79.

43. For more on *Pericles*' emphasis on labour, see David Morrow, 'Local/Global *Pericles*: International Storytelling, Domestic Social Relations, Capitalism', in *A Companion to the Global Renaissance: English Literature and Culture in the Era of Expansion, 1559–1660*, ed. Jyotsna G. Singh (Oxford: Blackwell, 2009), 355–77, and Daniel Vitkus, 'Labor and Travel on the Early Modern Stage: Representing the Travail of Travel in Dekker's *Old Fortunatus* and Shakespeare's *Pericles*',

in *Working Subjects in Early Modern English Drama*, ed. Michelle Dowd and Natasha Korda (Burlington, VT: Ashgate, 2011), 225–42.

44. Julia Reinhard Lupton, 'Shakespeare Dwelling: *Pericles* and the Affordances of Action', in *Shakespeare and the Urgency of Now: Criticism and Theory in the 21st Century*, ed. Cary DiPietro and Hugh Grady (New York: Palgrave, 2013), 60–82, esp. 74.

45. Matthew Kendrick, *At Work in the Early Modern English Theater: Valuing Labor* (Madison, NJ: Fairleigh Dickinson University Press, 2015).

46. Phillip Stubbes, *The Anatomy of Abuses* (London, 1583), quoted in *The Oxford Handbook of Shakespeare*, ed. Arthur Kinney (New York: Oxford University Press, 2012), 463.

47. Richard Finkelstein, '*Pericles*, Paul, and Protestantism', *Comparative Drama* 44.2 (2010): 101–29, esp. 123.

48. Finkelstein, '*Pericles*, Paul, and Protestantism', 119. Marina is also considered in relation to miraculous Catholic virgins. For her relation to the Virgin Mary, see Susan Dunn-Hensley, 'Return of the Sacred Virgin: Memory, Loss, and Restoration in Shakespeare's Later Plays', in *Walsingham in Literature from the Middle Ages to Modernity*, ed. Dominic Janes and Gary Waller (Burlington, VT: Ashgate, 2010), 185–97; Ruben Espinosa, 'Marian Miracles and the Theatrical Wonder of *Antony and Cleopatra*, *Pericles*, and *The Winter's Tale*', in *Masculinity and Marian Efficacy in Shakespeare's England* (Burlington, VT: Ashgate, 2011), 149–71; and Garry Waller, 'Traces: Shakespeare and the Virgin – *All's Well That Ends Well*, *Pericles*, and *The Winter's Tale*', in *The Virgin Mary in Late Medieval and Early Modern English Literature and Popular Culture* (New York: Cambridge University Press, 2011), 157–80. For her similarities with Saint Agnes, see Howard Felperin, 'Shakespeare's Miracle Play', *Shakespeare Quarterly* 18.4 (1967): 363–74, and Lorraine Helms, 'The Saint in the Brothel; or, Eloquence Rewarded', *Shakespeare Quarterly* 41.3 (1990): 319–32.

49. Northbrooke, *A Treatise wherein Dicing*, 86.

50. For more on Diana's significance in *Pericles*, see Caroline Bicks, 'Backsliding at Ephesus: Shakespeare's Diana and the Churching of Women', in *Pericles: Critical Essays*, ed. David Skeele (New York: Garland, 2000), 205–27, and F. Elizabeth Hart, '"Great is Diana" of Shakespeare's Ephesus', *Studies in English Literature, 1500–1900* 43.2 (Spring 2003): 347–74.
51. Gossett, Introduction, 147.
52. By contrast, Gossett argues that 'By taking control of the arrangement [Pericles] reestablishes the essential separation between gift and exchange and between commercial and marital sex' (Introduction, 151).
53. Lars Engle, *Shakespearean Pragmatism: Market of His Time* (Chicago: University of Chicago Press, 1993), 3, 6.
54. Yachnin, '"The Perfection of Ten"', 326–7.
55. Although the authorship of *The Revenger's Tragedy* is disputed, I follow the emerging scholarly consensus in attributing it to Middleton.
56. See Aristotle, *Politics*, in *The Basic Works of Aristotle*, ed. Richard McKeon, trans. Benjamin Jowett (New York: Modern Library, 2001), 1127–316, esp. 1:9. For the Aristotelian critique of usury in the sixteenth and early seventeenth centuries, see David Hawkes, *The Culture of Usury in Renaissance England* (New York: Palgrave, 2010), 47–66. See also J. T. Noonan, *The Scholastic Analysis of Usury* (Cambridge, MA: Harvard University Press, 1957) and Odd Langholm, *Wealth and Money in the Aristotelian Tradition* (Bergen: Universitetforlangen, 1983).
57. Thomas Wilson, *A Discourse Upon Usury* (1572; reprint London, 1925), 313.
58. Marc Shell, *Money, Language, and Thought: Literary and Philosophical Economies from the Medieval to the Modern Era* (Berkeley: University of California Press, 1982), 22.
59. For more on the sexual discourse of usury, see David Hawkes, 'Sodomy, Usury, and the Narrative of Shakespeare's Sonnets', *Renaissance Studies* 14.3 (2000): 344–61. See also Hawkes, *Culture of Usury*, 163.
60. David Hawkes, *Shakespeare and Economic Theory*, The Arden Shakespeare (New York: Bloomsbury, 2015), 102.

61. Thomas Middleton, *The Revenger's Tragedy*, ed. Brian Gibbons, New Mermaids (London: A & C Black Publishers, 2008), II, i, 252, hereafter cited parenthetically.
62. Michael Neill, 'Bastardy, Counterfeiting, and Misogyny in *The Revenger's Tragedy*', *Studies in English Literature, 1500–1900* 36.2 (1996): 397–416, esp. 399.
63. For more on usury in Middleton's work, see David Hawkes, 'Middleton and Usury', in *The Oxford Handbook of Thomas Middleton*, ed. Gary Taylor and Trish Thomas Henley (New York: Oxford University Press, 2012), 281–95.
64. Wilson, *A Discourse Upon Usury*, 147.
65. Jean-Christophe Agnew, *Worlds Apart: The Market and the Theater in Anglo-American Thought, 1550–1750* (New York: Cambridge University Press, 1986), 122.
66. William Prynne, *Histrio-Mastix, The Player's Scourge, or, Actors Tragedie* (London, 1633), 133.
67. For a fuller analysis of the play's invocation of Elizabeth I and its discomfort with female power, see Steven Mullaney, 'Mourning and Misogyny: *Hamlet, The Revenger's Tragedy*, and the Final Progress of Elizabeth I, 1600–1607', *Shakespeare Quarterly* 45.2 (1994): 139–62, and Kathryn R. Finin, 'Re-Membering Gloriana: "Wild Justice" and the Female Body in *The Revenger's Tragedy*', *Renaissance Forum* 6.2 (2003): 1–34.
68. For discussions of necrophilia in the play, see Karin S. Coddon, '"For Show or Useless Property": Necrophilia and *The Revenger's Tragedy*', *English Literary History* 61.1 (1994): 71–88; Michael Neill, 'Death and *The Revenger's Tragedy*', in *Early Modern English Drama: A Critical Companion*, ed. Garrett A. Sullivan, Patrick Cheney and Andrew Hadfield (New York: Oxford University Press, 2006), 164–76; and Ashley Denham Busse, '"Quod me nutrit me destruit": Discovering the Abject on the Early Modern Stage', *Journal of Medieval and Early Modern Studies* 43.1 (Winter 2013): 71–98.
69. Christine M. Gottlieb, 'Middleton's Traffic in Dead Women: Chaste Corpses as Property in *The Revenger's Tragedy* and *The Lady's Tragedy*', *English Literary History* 45.2 (2015): 255–74.

70. Coddon, '"For Show or Useless Property"', 125.
71. Gerard de Malynes, *Saint George for England, Allegorically Described* (London, Richard Field for William Tymme, 1601), C8r, EEBO.
72. David Hawkes, *Idols of the Marketplace: Idolatry and Commodity Fetishism in English Literature: 1580–1680* (New York: Palgrave, 2001), 30.
73. See Jonathan Dollimore, 'Two Concepts of Mimesis: Renaissance Literary Theory and *The Revenger's Tragedy*', in *Drama and Mimesis*, ed. James Redmond (Cambridge: Cambridge University Press, 1980), 25–50, and *Radical Tragedy: Religion, Ideology, and Power in the Drama of Shakespeare and his Contemporaries* (Chicago: University of Chicago Press, 1984), 139–50.
74. Agnew, *Worlds Apart*, 146.
75. Peter Stallybrass, 'Reading the Body: *The Revenger's Tragedy* and the Jacobean Theater of Consumption', *Renaissance Drama* 18 (1987): 121–48, esp. 142.

CHAPTER 2

COMMERCIAL CHASTITY AND ARISTOCRATIC VALUE IN *TROILUS AND CRESSIDA*, *THE WHITE DEVIL* AND *THE CHANGELING*

Whereas *Measure for Measure*, *Pericles* and *The Revenger's Tragedy* present chastity as a sign of economic, social and representational stability, characterised by the identity of essence and representation, William Shakespeare's *Troilus and Cressida* (1602), John Webster's *The White Devil* (1612), and Thomas Middleton and William Rowley's *The Changeling* (1621) all invoke commercial discourses to interrogate the concept of intrinsic chastity and in each case reveal it to be a social construct. Although written in different decades of the early seventeenth century, the three plays – tragedies or, in the case of *Troilus*, a semi-tragedy – dramatise the social and epistemological crises that arise from the recognition that market principles may be applied broadly, extending to evaluations of people. Each play presents a society in which market forces have disrupted traditional understandings of intrinsic value and, by extension, have destabilised the aristocratic supremacy that depends on this foundation. Female chastity proves particularly resonant in this context, as a commoditised virtue that also functions as the lynchpin of social and metaphysical hierarchies. Although this dynamic manifests differently in each play, *Troilus*, *The White Devil* and *The Changeling* all emphasise chastity's commodity potential in order to interrogate the constructed nature of value more generally and of aristocratic male selfhood in particular.

Chastity is often presented as a commodity in the conduct literature of the period. Richard Brathwaite in *The English Gentlewoman*, for example, warns women that 'The way to winne an husband is not to wooe him, but to be woo'd by him. Let him come to you, not you to him. Profferd ware is not worth the buying. Your states are too pure, to bee set at sale; too happy, to be weary of them.'[1] Inclined to think in Aristotelian terms, early moderns worried that the intrinsic value of products could be obscured by exchange or by the artful presentation of merchants. Brathwaite points to this concern as it pertains to women, evincing anxiety about women's commoditisation in his depiction of them as 'profferd ware' and in his comment that chaste women are 'too pure' and 'too happy' to 'bee set at sale'. Nonetheless, by situating women's desirability within dynamics of supply and demand, Brathwaite reflects women's commodity potential and suggests that women may, to some extent, manipulate their own value.

A great deal of early modern conduct and medical literature devotes itself to ascertaining whether women are 'authentic' or 'corrupt' commodities. In *The Excellency of Good Women* (1613), subtitled *Infallible Markes Whereby to Know Them*, Barnabe Rich instructs readers in how to interpret women's physical and behavioural signs, explaining that a chaste woman 'openeth her mouth with wisdom, the law of grace is in her tongue', while a harlot can be ascertained by her loose lips, painted features, gaudy clothes and plentiful acquaintances.[2] Where such performative indicators fail, medical examinations endeavoured to provide definitive proof of virginity and were supplemented by virginity potions and displays of wedding sheets.[3] Even the most straightforward of these tests, however, relied on the interpretation of unstable semiotic signs and provided no reliable means of assessing married chastity.[4]

This obsessive focus on external appearance gave rise to the anxiety that the intrinsic value of commodities – including women and their chastity – might be impossible to ascertain, or, more radically, that value may arise solely through artifice, performance or exchange. Because of its commoditised status, chastity becomes a focal point for epistemological anxieties regarding the relationship between personal inwardness and external representation. Such anxieties were prevalent in a culture that, according to Katharine Eisaman Maus, 'nurtures habits of mind that encourage conceiving of human inwardness, like other truths, as at once privileged and elusive, an absent presence "interpreted" to observers by ambiguous inklings and tokens'.[5] Chastity – virginity and, even more inscrutably, married chastity – functions as an 'absent presence' *par excellence*. Although moralists admit that appearances can deceive, they insist that a woman's inner truth can be ascertained through perspicacious analysis of the visual field, a conclusion that exacerbates the fear that chastity may be feigned. As Brathwaite warns, some women

> have learned artfully to gull the world with appearances; and deceive the time, wherein they are Maskers, with vizards and semblances. They can enforce a smile, to perswade you of their affability; counterfeit a blush to paint out their modesty; walke alone, to express their love to privacy; keep their houses, to publish them provident purveyors for their family; receive strangers, to demonstrate their love to hospitality.[6]

Although Brathwaite maintains the male prerogative to penetrate a woman's veneer, her performance threatens to overpower any a priori depravity that it is intended to cover. As Thomas Tuke suggests in *A Treatise Against Painting*, seeming chaste might be the most important component of chastity: 'It is not enough to be good, but she that is good, must seeme good; she that is chast, must seem chast.'[7]

The performative nature of female virtue was highlighted on the public stage where the gendered essence of male actors, such as it was, conflicted with the mimetic representation of the female characters they played. In part for this reason, antitheatricalists scrutinised the player's body, clothing and gestures in a manner that mirrored the conduct writer's scrutiny of women. As Peter Stallybrass contends, 'polemicists insistently dwell upon the theater as a spectacle of the body and of clothes, a spectacle whose corrupting effects depend less upon any textual practices (e.g. whether a play is virtuous or vicious) than upon the actors' corporeal presence'.[8] As the public theatre challenged Protestant sexual morality, it also destabilised traditional assessments of personal value, demonstrating the extent to which virtue could be performed and pointing to the ultimate unreliability of external signs.

Troilus and Cressida, *The White Devil* and *The Changeling* all intensify the transvestite theatre's anti-essentialism by assessing female chastity in relation to explicitly commercial discourses. In this context, the plays interrogate contradictions inherent to viewing chastity as at once a commodity and an absolute, essential virtue. Using chastity – the always already commoditised virtue – as a test case, these plays explore the consequences of assessing people in commoditised terms and ultimately problematise the concept of intrinsic value more generally. As a result, conclusions reached about chastity – the intrinsic value of which is interrogated in *Troilus*, fully demystified in *The White Devil*, and tenuously recuperated in *The Changeling* – influence the plays' presentation of aristocratic men, suggesting that their personal worth may rest not in intrinsic class-based virtue but rather in the more relativistic dynamics of the marketplace.

Chastity and Ontological Stability in Troilus and Cressida's *Market Society*

Economic critics have demonstrated that *Troilus and Cressida* engages with contemporary mercantilist debates as well as with more abstract philosophical questions of value.[9] *Troilus and Cressida* applies mercantile discourse, which focuses on tensions between intrinsic and extrinsic determinations of value, to the characters themselves, their identities having been destabilised by the crumbling of aristocratic hierarchies.[10] The play's treatment of value, in other words, extends to questions of personal value, particularly the value of aristocratic men. These debates about personal value, I argue, are carried out largely in reference to the chastity of Helen and Cressida, whose bodies serve as pawns in the ideological conflicts dramatised in the play.

In *Troilus*, debates about value centre initially on Helen, whose questionable worth serves as the pretext for the war. Hector maintains a traditionalist belief in Helen's intrinsic value, but he doubts that this value is as great as has been reputed, claiming that 'Every tithe soul, 'mongst many thousand dismes, / Has been as dear as Helen'.[11] To Hector, Helen 'is not worth what she doth cost / The holding' (II, ii, 51–2), because her worth is less than that of each of the soldiers who has died in her name. By contrast, Troilus defends the war not by praising Helen's intrinsic value but by suggesting that all value is extrinsically determined. 'What's aught but as 'tis valued?' (II, ii, 52), he asks, suggesting that value is constituted by those who rate it, and he argues that it is politically expedient to honour such constructed value as true. In response to Hector's objection that 'value dwells not in particular will' (II, ii, 53), Troilus explicates the logic of value creation that propels the war, stating, 'Helen must needs be fair / When with your blood you daily paint her thus' (I, i, 86–7). From this perspective, Helen's reputation as the pinnacle of beauty becomes a product of the war itself, with the blood of soldiers cosmetically enhancing her value and, in turn, justifying the war effort. In order to maintain the pretext that Helen's beauty caused the war, Helen's intrinsic worth must be continually proven and re-established by both the Trojans and the Greeks.

Troilus' assessment of Helen's value is shaped largely by market logics, which amplify the dehumanising objectification promoted by the war. Viewing Helen as a commodity, he contends that it would be inappropriate consumer behaviour to freely relinquish a possession the Trojans once sought to acquire, reminding them,

> We turn not back the silks upon the merchant
> When we have spoiled them; nor the remainder viands
> We do not throw in unrespective sieve
> Because we are now full.   (II, ii, 69–72)

Troilus depicts Helen as a purchase that cannot be returned because her value has been debased with use. Like meat that has been eaten and clothes that have been worn, Helen's chastity has been sullied and depleted, making her unsuitable for other buyers. Whereas Paris hopes that winning the war may truly elevate Helen's value, vowing that he 'would have the soil of her fair rape / Wiped off in honourable keeping her' (II, ii, 148–9), Troilus' comments foreshadow his later treatment of Cressida in their indication that something intrinsic has been lost in Helen's 'fair rape'. From this perspective, chastity, unlike beauty, proves resistant to Troilus' relativism, turning the Trojans' valorisation of Helen into propaganda that obscures Thersites's baser interpretation that 'All the argument is a whore and a cuckold' (II, iii, 69–70).

For Troilus, then, the treachery of Hector's anti-war position is not that he is denying Helen's virtue but that he is reneging on the Trojans' initial assessment of her. Turning Marlowe's 'face that launched a thousand ships' into a 'pearl whose price' has done the same, Troilus reminds the Trojans that they instigated the conflict by seeking to possess a highly rated object:

> Is she worth keeping? Why she is a pearl
> Whose price has launched above a thousand ships
> And turned crowned kings to merchants.
> If you'll avouch 'twas wisdom Paris went –
> As you must needs, for you all cried, 'Go, go!';
> If you'll confess he brought home noble prize –
> As you must needs, for you all clapped your hands
> And cried, 'Inestimable!' – why do you now

The issue of your proper wisdoms rate,
And do a deed that never fortune did,
Beggar the estimation which you prized
Richer than sea and land? O theft most base,
That we have stol'n what we do fear to keep!
                                        (II, ii, 81–93)

The item once judged 'richer than sea and land' is now 'beggared' by the Trojans who wish to end the war. Troilus further maintains that the Trojans initiated the market-based value system that Hector opposes. By figuring Helen as 'a pearl whose price' has 'turned crowned kings to merchants', Troilus suggests that the kings not only pursued Helen but participated in creating her value with their public show of support. It would be dishonest business, according to Troilus, for them to disavow the value that they themselves created. Moreover, it would undermine the rationale for their war, turning a lofty quest for 'inestimable' treasure into a 'theft most base'. On these grounds, Hector concedes that it would be dishonourable to return Helen, even if she does rightfully belong to Menelaus. Fighting for Helen, Troilus successfully proves, entails defending the Trojans' powers of discernment and their ability to create value.

The Greek heroes are beset by similar anxieties about the commercial dynamics shaping personal value, but they turn their gaze inward to question their own martial identities. Achilles, in particular, is in danger of losing his reputation, as he refuses to fight. Hoping to prick Achilles's pride, Ulysses suggests that Ajax, the Greek's second-greatest warrior, should face Hector, who has issued a challenge to meet a Greek warrior in one-on-one battle. Ulysses provides a commercial rationale for his choice, explaining,

Let us, like merchants, show our foulest wares,
And think perchance they'll sell; if not,
The lustre of the better yet to show
Shall show the better.   (I, iii, 360–3)

Not only will the selection of Ajax humble Achilles who 'overhold[s] his price so much' (II, iii, 131), but it will make Achilles appear even more redoubtable when he does appear on the battlefield.

Ulysses' mercantilist advice prefigures his subsequent admonition to Achilles that reputations arise not from intrinsic worth but through the 'reflection' of other people's opinions; to him, men

> Cannot make boast to have that which he hath,
> Nor feels not what he owes, but by reflection;
> As when his virtues, shining upon others,
> Heat them, and they retort that heat again
> To the first givers.   (III, iii, 99–103)

Echoing a sentiment common in the conduct literature, Ulysses contends that men's value is not proper to themselves, as it is manifested only when others see it and reflect it back to them. As Brathwaite writes in *The English Gentlewoman*, 'estimation' is 'An unvaluable gemme, which every *wise Merchant*, who tenders his honour, preferres before life. The *losse* of this makes him an irreparable Bankrupt. All persons ought to rate it high, because it is the value of themselves.'[12] As with assessments of women's chastity, public esteem becomes constitutive of men's personal value. In this, Ulysses adopts an essentially Hobbesian perspective that accounts for personal worth in market terms. Hobbes maintained that 'The Value or WORTH of a man, is as of all other things, his Price; that is to say, so much as would be given for the use of his Power; and therefore is not absolute; but a thing dependent on the need and judgement of another.'[13] From this perspective, honour becomes a manifestation of negotiated value: 'To Value a man at a high rate, is to *Honour* him; at a low rate, is to *Dishonour* him. But high and low, in this case, is to be understood, by comparison to the rate that each man setteth on himselfe.'[14] While Hobbes admits the influence of natural faculties, he suggests that a man's reputation arises through the negotiation of his self-assessment with the assessments of those around him. As a result, the Greek heroes in *Troilus and Cressida* must not rest on their laurels but must instead continue to act publically so that their virtues, which are 'subjects all / To envious and calumniating time' (III, iii, 174–5), can be recognised and thus sustained. Ulysses' theory of reflected value – like Brathwaite's discussion of esteem, Hobbes's understanding of honour, and Troilus' assessment of Helen – employs a mercantile logic that emphasises the continual reassessment of value within shifting contexts. Like Troilus, moreover, Ulysses manipulates commercial discourses of value to serve his own military interests: just as Troilus encourages men to fight for Helen, an entity whose value they created, Ulysses encourages his men to defend their own value as heroes and thus to perform valiantly in war.

In his famous speech on degree, Ulysses shifts his position and defends the sanctity of intrinsic value as central to maintaining aristocratic, hierarchical order. Concerned that the Greeks are not respecting authority or fighting to their potential, Ulysses adumbrates the social and cosmological effects that ensue when 'the specialty of rule hath been neglected' (I, iii, 78). When intrinsic value is dislocated, as the Trojans' relativism would have it, natural and social hierarchies are overturned, causing untold turmoil. Such relativism obliterates justice, leaving only power, will and appetite, 'an universal wolf' (I, iii, 121), to reign. In this official statement, which conflicts with his assessments of Achilles's value, Ulysses reveals the power of ideologies of intrinsic value, demonstrating how they can be wielded opportunistically for political gain.[15] Ulysses' subsequent manipulation of Cressida's value – imposing on her an intrinsic lack of chastity – furthers his efforts in this arena, positing female chastity as a site of readily identifiable intrinsic value which, in turn, grounds both intrinsic male virtue and the social hierarchies that support it.

Similar to his depiction of Helen as a pearl whose price can be manipulated, Troilus presents Cressida as a pearl whom he, the merchant adventurer, can possess:

> Her bed is India; there she lies, a pearl.
> Between our Ilium and where she resides
> Let it be called the wild and wand'ring flood,
> Ourself the merchant, and this sailing Pandar
> Our doubtful hope, our convoy and our bark. (I, i, 96–100)

Overtly sexualising the pearl in the bed, Troilus echoes Tarquin's self-aggrandising sentiments in *The Rape of Lucrece*: 'Desire my pilot is, beauty my prize. / Then who fears sinking where such treasure lies?'[16] Cressida understands the implications of this commercial imagery, highlighted as well in Pandarus' attempts to raise her value. Her statement that 'Men price the thing ungained more than it is' (I, ii, 280) reflects her recognition that women acquire power as desired objects that they lose once they are possessed.

When Cressida is taken to the Greek camp in exchange for the Trojan elder Antenor, Shakespeare dramatises the process by which men determine female value and, subsequently, characterise this value as intrinsic to the woman herself. As Hugh Grady argues, *Troilus* demystifies foundational ideologies, only to reveal the means by which they are reified in early modern culture.[17] Ideologies of female value are central to this process. Just as the Trojans created Helen's value by fighting on her behalf, the Greeks collectively attribute value to Cressida; in this case her beauty and chastity are devalued by her liaison with Troilus and by her status as a foreigner.[18] Assessing Cressida's charms, the Greek commander Diomedes notes only that 'The luster in [her] eye, heaven in [her] cheek, / Pleads [her] fair usage' (IV, v, 117–18), inflecting the word 'usage' with sexual connotations. Not only do the Greeks determine Cressida's sexual value but they also impose on her an intrinsic nature, marked by wanton licentiousness. After Cressida submits to a round of kissing by the Greeks, Ulysses interprets her bodily movements as unchaste, further degrading her value and claiming access into an inner self that she has not in fact revealed:

> There's language in her eye, her cheek, her lip,
> Nay, her foot speaks; her wanton spirits look out
> At every joint and motive of her body.
> O, these encounterers, so glib of tongue,
> That give accosting welcome ere it comes,
> And wide unclasp the tables of their thoughts
> To every ticklish reader! Set them down
> For sluttish spoils of opportunity
> And daughters of the game. (IV, v, 56–64)

As feminist critics have noted, it is by no means clear that Cressida has any choice but to kiss the Greeks, who are her captors.[19] Nonetheless, Ulysses interprets her behaviour as voluntary and attributes to her an intrinsic core of value. In so doing, he surpasses Troilus' position that women 'are as they are valued' and actively attributes his perceptions to Cressida's core being. Her body parts bespeak her licentiousness, and the image of her actions 'unclasp[ing] the tables of their thoughts', suggests that her comportment reflects a deep inner essence, which Cressida shares liberally with 'every ticklish reader'. The Greeks' collective assessment of Cressida is thus configured as innate, a conclusion that Ulysses subsequently imparts to Troilus as he figures Cressida's betrayal in terms of her intrinsic depravity.

As they surreptitiously watch Cressida in Diomedes' tent, Ulysses attempts to convert Troilus to his understanding of her value as intrinsic and, in so doing, to assert that his assessments of value outweigh Troilus'. Even before Troilus observes her in the tent, Ulysses casually insults Cressida's chastity, saying 'She will sing any man at first sight' (V, ii, 10), preparing Troilus to interpret the encounter in a negative light. Troilus is ultimately swayed to Ulysses' view when he sees her with Diomedes, crying 'O withered truth' (V, ii, 48) as his former vision of Cressida slips away. As his perception of Cressida is destroyed, so too is his belief in his own power to create value. Although Troilus initially acknowledges the complexity of Cressida's situation in his statement 'this is and is not Cressid' (V, ii, 153), he ultimately concurs with Ulysses' assessment of her character and concedes that she possesses a corrupt nature independent of his estimation.[20] Her chastity unravelled, Cressida's body becomes associated with the 'fragments, scraps, the bits and greasy relics / Of her o'ereaten faith' (V, ii, 166–7). As they witness Cressida giving Troilus' sleeve to Diomedes, Ulysses concludes, 'All's done, my lord', and Troilus, now swayed, finishes the line with 'It is' (V, ii, 121). By asserting the intrinsic nature of value, the master strategist Ulysses has ensured that his own vision of truth – his particular estimation of Cressida as a whore – has prevailed. It is this ability to make truth, *Troilus* suggests, that creates power, and Ulysses uses this power to his own political advantage. In this way, Ulysses uses Cressida's body as a pawn in his campaign against the Trojans' relativism, an ideological battle he perceives as necessary to winning the military war even if he does not believe it to be ontologically true. Moreover, this reassertion of intrinsic value – most readily located in unchaste women – affirms the metaphysical hierarchies Ulysses identifies as central to the aristocratic order.

Troilus himself further illuminates the ideological function of intrinsic chastity in his definitive condemnation, 'O Cressid! O false Cressid! False, false, false! / Let all untruths stand by thy stained name, / And they'll seem glorious' (V, ii, 185–7). In his formulation, all claims to truth will be judged against the inherent negative value of Cressida's unchastity. This category of 'untruths' includes the precarious identities of the warriors, who will now be evaluated not on their own merits but through an advantageous comparison to Cressida's valueless identity. Having recuperated intrinsic value, at least where female chastity is concerned, it becomes possible to imagine that men similarly possess a kernel of intrinsic worth independent of public estimation. This point is made explicit in Pandarus' prophesy: if all 'false women be Cressids', it follows that, 'all constant men be Troiluses' (III, ii, 198, 197). Memorialising Cressida's intrinsic corruption solidifies Troilus' more reputable legacy, eliding his questionable behaviour. Likewise, the spectre of female corruption underlies the political and metaphysical schema purveyed by Ulysses. As with Ulysses' plan to present Ajax to the Trojans so that Achilles 'Shall show the better' (I, iii, 363) once he is revealed, Ulysses' politically expedient 'untruths' will seem 'glorious' only when juxtaposed with the obvious falsehood embodied by Cressida. This association of Cressida with absolute corruption, then, not only reaffirms that women's sexual status is discernable and constitutive of their personal worth, but also bolsters tenuous ideologies of intrinsic value and the aristocratic hierarchy that depends on them. In its ironic mode, however, *Troilus and Cressida* stops short of embracing this conservative conclusion, as it has too fully demystified the process through which it was fabricated.

The White Devil's *Rejection of Intrinsic Chastity*

As in *Troilus and Cressida*, female chastity functions in *The White Devil* as a locus for concerns about personal value in a declining aristocratic society. Set in Catholic Italy, *The White Devil* interrogates the artifice and performativity that may obscure, or even constitute, the self. Unlike Cressida, *The White Devil*'s female protagonist Vittoria resists the attempts of male authorities to either penetrate her being or to impose upon her an inner core of value. Furthermore, whereas Cressida remains trapped within a patriarchal system, Vittoria appropriates mercantile discourse to reject the concept of intrinsic chastity altogether, exposing it as a patriarchal construct used to buttress aristocratic male supremacy. Vittoria's rejection of intrinsic chastity in favour of performative subjectivity, I suggest, ultimately points toward new modes of selfhood attractive to aristocratic men whose identities have been decentred by the contingencies of early capitalist society.

As with Cressida and Helen, Vittoria's chastity is invested with economic resonances from the beginning of the play. In an effort to draw Vittoria into an adulterous relationship, Duke Brachiano engages her in repartee about her 'jewel', referring not only to the jewel on her dress but also to her chastity and genitalia. In his sexually charged banter, Brachiano eschews the elevated language of women's 'inestimable' treasure, immediately assuming that Vittoria's jewel can be priced and therefore purchased in his question, 'What value is this jewel?'[21] Like Troilus, Brachiano initially thinks in terms of conquest, stating 'In sooth I'll have it' (I, ii, 206), but then turns to the less forceful language of trade in his offer, 'nay I will but change / My jewel for your jewel' (I, ii, 206–7). The intermingling of sexual and commercial discourse in the exchange is underscored by the commentary from Vittoria's brother – and bawd – Flamineo, who remarks, 'Excellent, / His jewel for her jewel; well put in Duke' (I, ii, 207–8). The phrase 'well put in' carries the sexual connotation of penetration and also means 'to make a claim or a bid' on something.[22] Although this exchange of jewels seems egalitarian, Flamineo's praise indicates that Brachiano will benefit unduly from the trade: Vittoria will relinquish her chastity and her reputation while the Duke will face few consequences.

Brachiano's very literal identification of Vittoria's genitalia with the jewel prefigures the complex matrix of economic and sexual discourses invoked in the courtroom, where Vittoria is tried for adultery and for the murders of her husband and Brachiano's wife, Isabella. Much like Vindice in *The Revenger's Tragedy*, the presiding magistrate, Cardinal Monticelso, associates women with generalised economic crisis, imaged in terms of alchemy, counterfeiting, corrupt wares, extortion, exorbitant taxation and the expropriation of land. In his expansive diatribe 'expound[ing]' the 'perfect character' (III, ii, 79–80) of a whore, he compares the whore to an overvalued coin or commodity, her superficial appearance luring unsuspecting customers, and he concludes his speech with the statement that she is 'like the guilty counterfeited coin / Which whosoe'er first stamps it brings in trouble / All that receive it' (III, ii, 100–2).[23]

With his emphasis on counterfeiting and 'coz'ning alchemy' (III, ii, 82), Monticelso charges women with disrupting metaphysical hierarchies, as these unauthorised forms of production upset the status of gold as a transcendental signifier and decentre the monarch's power to create and evaluate worth. By extension, Monticelso holds unchaste women responsible for disintegrating social hierarchies, particularly the decline of the aristocracy. Monticelso's whores overtax the men who 'buy' them, demanding 'Exactions upon meat, drink, garments, sleep; / Ay even on man's perdition, his sin' (III, ii, 80–91). Like legal quibbles 'Which forfeit all a wretched man's estate' (III, ii, 91), this sinful financial drain contributes to the loss of aristocratic land. Furthermore, Monticelso's image that 'rich whores / Are only treasuries by extortion filled, / And emptied by curs'd riot' (III, ii, 94–6) captures the sense of political unrest that he associates with uncontrolled female sexuality. The women have acquired their luster by extorting riches from their lovers, in turn intensifying their inner degradation. The women are then emptied, it seems, by the 'riot' of the lover's lust, but Monticelso's dense syntax also conjures fears of political riots that may empty aristocratic coffers. Ultimately, in Monticleso's framework, the whore threatens the aristocracy by literally draining pocketbooks and by destabilising value, including the intrinsic value that buttresses aristocratic power.

Throughout the trial, Monticelso endeavours to expose what he presumes to be Vittoria's corrupt inner core, paradoxically seeking to fix the unstable value associated with unchaste women by uncovering an identifiable core of 'black lust' (III, i, 7). This attempt to locate Vittoria's value by means of the very unstable category of the whore reflects a tension that Dympna Callaghan identifies in efforts to enforce gender binaries. As she notes: 'The problem with the category of woman is in keeping it in its place and out of the ideal order. The process is, however, always and necessarily incomplete. In tragedy there is a constant reiteration of misogynistic discourse which "fixes" women in conceptual terms and yet, paradoxically, fixes them as unstable.'[24] Although whores are defined precisely by their inherent instability, the tribunal seeks to mitigate this instability by exposing it, naming it, and defining it as absolute evil and as the binary opposite of pure chastity. As in tracts such as Rich's *The Excellency of Good Women* and Brathwaite's *The English Gentlewoman*, Monticelso assumes that the masculine gaze of the court will effortlessly penetrate Vittoria's veneer, exposing the 'soot and ashes' (III, ii, 67) of her sexual sin.

In opposition to Monticelso's gaze, Vittoria refuses to relinquish any inner reality and instead exposes the patriarchal mechanisms through which the court attempts to define her being and assign her guilt. As Kathryn R. Finin-Farber has demonstrated, Vittoria acknowledges that the court is inhospitable to women when she asks an ineloquent lawyer to speak in the vernacular rather than in Latin, as she is worried that 'this auditory / Which come to hear [her] cause, the half of more / May be ignorant in't' (III, ii, 15–17).[25] By challenging the court's superfluous use of Latin, Vittoria undercuts the stability of legal discourse and exposes the trial as a spectacle of patriarchal power. Moreover, Vittoria appropriates the court's spectacle – in which guilt or innocence rests on the interpretation of signs – to her own ends, using it to appeal to potentially sympathetic audience members and to construct an overtly performative sense of self.[26]

At each turn, Vittoria thwarts Monticelso's efforts to identify inner corruption in her external appearance. In his accusations, Monticelso relies on commonplace associations between a woman's complexion and her moral character, threatening to 'paint out / [Her] follies in more natural red and white / Than that upon [her] cheek' (III, ii, 51–3). Here he employs misogynist discourses surrounding the blush, which Rich calls 'the common treasure of feminine virtue', in contrast to the use of cosmetics, which functions as a sign that a woman 'will make little conscience to adulterate the inward beauty of the mind'.[27] Vittoria, however, rejects the idea of a correlation between her external and internal features, retorting, 'You raise a blood as noble in this cheek / As ere was your mother's' (III, ii, 53–5). Here she accuses the magistrate of literally 'painting out' her follies, drawing them where they did not previously exist. This exchange exemplifies Vittoria's dominant tactic. Although she rejects the claim that her blush is cosmetic, she does not resort to protestations of innocence; instead, she turns Monticelso's evidence back on him, suggesting that the blush arises neither from her guilt nor from her innocence but from the words and actions of the court. By extension, Vittoria suggests that men create the very whores they wish to scapegoat, not only by seducing them but by shaping them discursively in the image of their fantasies and fears. In so doing, she overtly critiques the process that Shakespeare dramatises in *Troilus and Cressida* by which men impose intrinsic value on women to further their own psychological and political interests.

Unable to prove Vittoria's guilt based solely by her external appearance, which she presents as a compilation of meaningless and unstable signs, Monticelso shifts his focus toward the portended exposure of her inner, rotten, core. To do so, he draws the outlines of a character that she herself refuses to reveal:

> You see my lords what goodly fruit she seems,
> Yet like those apples travellers report
> To grow where Sodom and Gomorrah stood:
> I will but touch her and you straight shall see
> She'll fall to soot and ashes. (III, ii, 63–7)

Monticelso not only presumes that Vittoria's depravity is intrinsic but also creates for her a sense of interiority, much like that which Ulysses imposes on Cressida. Like the apples of Sodom and Gomorrah, Vittoria is assumed to possess an essence that can be uncovered, once 'touched' by the tribunal. Even in Monticelso's image, however, this core cannot be held up for examination by the court, as it disintegrates into ephemeral 'soot and ashes' the moment it is uncovered. Monticelso's imagery inadvertently corroborates Vittoria's contention that the interiority he references is a product of the court's machinations; at the very moment it is 'exposed', it ceases to exist. Vittoria underscores the reflexive quality of Monticelso's accusations in her retort that, if she did 'fall to soot and ashes', the court's 'envenomed pothecary should do't' (III, ii, 68), characteristically insisting that the juridical men, rather than her own guilt, would cause her disintegration.

Vittoria's most forceful rejection of the court's impositions comes when Monticelso returns to the play's economic motifs and casts her as a 'counterfeit jewel' of the kind that 'Make true ones oft suspected' (III, ii, 141–2). In response, Vittoria rejects this binary distinction between 'true' and 'counterfeit' jewels and insists that she fits neither category.

Moreover, she calls attention to the court's intrusive and ultimately futile attempts to first create and then expose her inner reality, stating:

> You are deceived,
> For know that all your strict combined heads,
> Which strike against this mine of diamonds,
> Shall prove but glassen hammers, they shall break;
> [. . .] for your names
> Of Whore and Murd'ress, they proceed from you,
> As if a man should spit against the wind,
> The filth returns in's face.   (III, ii, 142–51)

The men whom Monticelso envisioned as 'touch[ing]' (III, ii, 66) Vittoria are now figured as hammering against diamonds and spitting in the wind, gestures that only expose their own impotence. Vittoria thus appropriates the jewel imagery that has been used throughout the play, using it to fashion her own stoic exterior. In contrast to the men's image of a secret jewel that can be uncovered, scrutinised, and judged either precious or counterfeit, Vittoria depicts her inner core as an entire diamond mine, irreducible either to the names of 'Whore and Murd'ress' or to the chastity that is their alternative. Instead of opening itself to exposure, this self is defined by its solidity and inaccessibility, by its resistance to the impositions of the court.[28] Vittoria's reconstituted self, then, arises largely from her rejection of the imposed ideal of intrinsic chastity and its obverse category of essential sexual corruption. Her indictment of the trial as a rape underscores the sexual violence inherent in the magistrates' attempt to penetrate her fortress of jewels with their phallic 'combined heads' (III, ii, 143). This attempted rape remains unsuccessful, however, in Vittoria's formulation, as the court has 'ravished Justice' (III, ii, 274) but not Vittoria herself.

Rather than being diminished by her interrogation, Vittoria exits the trial possessing a heightened sense of personal integrity, formed in resistance to the Court's penetrating gaze. This impenetrable female self no longer absorbs the displaced anxieties of men; instead, it reflects and refracts their negative qualities and, in addition, shines its own light. As a result, Vittoria pledges to transform the 'house of convertites' to which she is committed into a place of clarity, claiming that, 'Through darkness diamonds spread their richest light' (III, ii, 294). Upending traditional associations between chastity and conversion, Vittoria uses the house of convertites not as a site of religious repentance but as an opportunity to display the power of her newly strengthened self. There, she resists psychic penetration from her lover Brachiano, who refuses to accept that even he cannot uncover and thus possess her inner essence. Amending her depiction of her subjectivity as a mine of diamonds, he exclaims,

> How long have I beheld the devil in crystal?
> Thou hast led me, like an heathen sacrifice,
> With music and with fatal yokes of flowers
> To my eternal ruin. Woman to man
> Is either a god or a wolf. (IV, ii, 84–8)

Although he acknowledges her crystalline exterior, Brachiano insists on identifying an essential devilishness within it, so as to uphold his binary conclusion that 'Woman to man / Is either a god or a wolf'. This binary is disrupted, however, as Sheryle Stevenson contends, by the simultaneously transparent and reflective nature of the crystal, which reinforces the psychoanalytic dictum that 'woman' is 'the mirror and projection of man'.[29] Redirecting Brachiano's accusations, as she did those of the magistrates, Vittoria indicates that, as her lover, he is complicit in the faults he finds in her. She asks, 'What have I gained by thee but infamy?' (IV, ii, 103) and blames him for sending her to the house of penitent women. Although she assigns Brachiano responsibility for her transgressions, making him 'full executor / To all [her] sins' (IV, ii, 120–1), she refuses to cede him possession of her person. In response to his plea, 'Is not this lip mine?' (IV, ii, 129), she retorts, 'Yes: thus to bite it off, rather than give it thee' (IV, ii, 130). Although her affirmative answer acknowledges Brachiano's role in creating her current self, she quickly reclaims the right to use, manipulate, and even do violence to her body parts. Though men have participated in Vitttoria's transformation, her newfound identity has escaped their control as well as their understanding.

As she exposes the patriarchal dynamics of subject formation, Vittoria also calls attention to the unstable identities of men. In particular, Vittoria's stoicism is juxtaposed with the fragmented identity of her brother Flamineo, a dissolute aristocrat who has lost his land and whose sense of self grows increasingly tenuous after he is dismissed from Brachiano's service. Whereas Vittoria directly rejects the court's accusations, Flamineo feigns madness in an attempt to hide his complicity in the crimes of adultery and murder, a decision that belies a more genuine disintegration evident in his lament, 'I am falling to pieces already – I care not, though, like Anacharsis, I were pounded to death in a mortar' (V, iv, 22–4). In contrast to Vittoria's stoicism, Flamineo admits to being a whore of the court, forced by his insecure financial status to grub for gold, 'that cursed mineral' (III, iii, 20–1) which 'will corrupt and putrefy' (III, iii, 24) anything it touches. Reversing Monticelso's assertion that unchaste women cause economic corruption, Flamineo demonstrates that financial precarity produces an environment characterised by widespread prostitution, as he himself is depicted as a whore as well as a bawd.

Having exhausted all financial means of reconstructing his identity, Flamineo turns to Vittoria's model of chaste subjectivity as he faces death, asserting, 'My life hath done service to other men; / My death shall serve mine own turn' (V, vi, 49–50). At this moment, his pledge not to 'live at any man's entreaty / Nor die at any's bidding' (V, vi, 47–8) echoes his sister's earlier retort to Monticelso, 'I scorn to hold my life / At yours or any man's entreaty' (III, ii, 47–8). In addition to following Vittoria in extracting himself from patriarchal bonds, Flamino takes inspiration from her death, admiring her unflinching refusal to either faint or blush as she submits to her enemies. Vittoria maintains bodily and mental integrity throughout the ordeal, responding to the suggestion that she will dissolve from fear with the statement 'I am too true a woman: / Conceit can never kill me' (V, vi, 219–20). By rejecting notions of intrinsic personal value, Vittoria reconfigures what it means to be 'too true a woman'. Her performance of identity, even in death, is shaped by negation: by what is concealed rather than by what is revealed. Using the strategy she developed in her arraignment, Vittoria restricts access to signs that may be used to discern her inner state and thus exerts control over her self-representation. Flamineo attempts to follow her example in his own death, remarking:

> Th'art a noble sister –
> I love thee now. If woman do breed man
> She ought to teach him manhood: fare thee well.
> Know many glorious women that are famed
> For masculine virtue have been vicious
> Only a happier silence did betide them.
> She hath no faults, who hath the art to hide them.
>
> (V, vi, 237–43)

Recognising the performative nature of identity, Flamineo inverts gender expectations, suggesting that men should take Vittoria's example. Here it is women who 'teach . . . manhood', as Flamineo equates masculinity with impenetrable self-presentation. The residual misogyny in Flamineo's maxim, 'She hath no faults, who hath the art to hide them', however, occludes the process by which Vittoria's stoic veneer came into being. As the arraignment scene elucidates, Vittoria develops her persona not to cover faults – for she neither claims innocence nor acknowledges sin – but to supersede them: to reject the patriarchal imposition of intrinsic value onto her core being and to insist that the self she does possess was created through her own agency. In so doing, she articulates a new model of subjectivity, which, though formed in opposition to external threats, transcends the aristocratic model of servitude to which Flamineo is beholden.

Flamineo's emulation of Vittoria points toward the centrality of chastity in theatrical articulations of early capitalist selfhood. In resistance to patriarchal assertions of women's intrinsic value, such as those displayed by Ulysses and Monticelso, Vittoria develops a self-contained, stoic selfhood. The self that she creates – based not in gendered or class-based value but in performativity – ultimately serves as a model for men whose identities have been fragmented in early capitalist society. Vittoria's denunciation of intrinsic value has profound ideological consequences, as it not only disrupts established gender codes but also unsettles the metaphysical basis of aristocratic supremacy. Rulers such as the banished Count Lodovico or the murderous Brachiano are frequently criticised in the play, not only for their personal flaws but also for more political failures, such as their willingness to allow men to die in futile wars and for not adequately remunerating their soldiers. Flamineo gestures toward the rulers' callous disregard for the lives of commoners when he calls Brachiano the 'kind of statesman that would sooner have reckoned how many cannon bullets he had discharged against a town, to count his expense that way, than how many of his valiant and deserving subjects he lost before it' (V, iii, 61–4). Neither Brachiano's personal morality nor his political leadership indicates that he is worthy of his social position. Vittoria's deconstruction of intrinsic personal value provides a philosophical foundation for these critiques, showing that such nobles are not inherently worthy of their positions. Only from this perspective can we fully understand the fear that the dissolution of chastity may portend social and economic collapse.

Chastity, Labour and the Recuperation of Aristocratic Integrity in The Changeling

Like the other plays discussed in this chapter, Middleton and Rowley's *The Changeling*, whose very title connotes exchange, reflects concerns about commercial assessments of men through the lens of female chastity. The commoditisation of Beatrice-Joanna's virginity informs the play's subsequent objectification of male bodies and obliquely illuminates the alienating effects of capitalist labour relations. *The Changeling*, as Bradley Ryner demonstrates, 'powerfully articulates anxieties about the instability of value arising from England's precarious place in the international market economy'.[30] In this context, the play explores the prospect that men might be judged in the commercial terms generally reserved for women and raises the more threatening possibility that women themselves might treat men as exchangeable commodities in a sexual marketplace. *The Changeling*, however, ultimately works to transcend this established paradigm evaluating men in terms of female chastity and instead scapegoats women for the disconcerting effects of the market economy.

The Changeling is preoccupied with the challenges of assessing personal value, and it repeatedly expresses these preoccupations in commercial terms. Jasperino commoditises Beatrice-Joanna's maid Diaphanta, for example, when he depicts her as a merchant ship waiting to be conquered; 'I meant to be a venturer in this voyage', he pledges, 'Yonder's another vessel, I'll board her – if she be lawful prize, down goes her top-sail'.[31] With his treasure imagery, Jasperino depicts Diaphanta as a conquest who will enrich her possessor so long as she is 'lawful' – a judgement call that men in *The Changeling* find especially difficult to make. Male characters are similarly assessed within patriarchal networks of desire, although in less grossly materialistic terms. Beatrice-Joanna's father, Vermandero, lusts after Alonzo as a son-in-law, asserting,

> the gentleman's complete,
> A courtier and a gallant, enriched
> With many fair and noble ornaments:
> I would not change him for a son-in law
> For any he in Spain.   (I, i, 205–9)

While Vermandero's reference to Peacham's *The Complete Gentlemen* points toward Alonzo's aristocratic integrity and self-containment, it also reflects his objectifying gaze. Vermandero's possessiveness becomes evident in his vow, 'He shall be bound to me, / As fast as this tie can hold him, I'll want / My will else' (I, i, 211–13), thus placing Alonzo in a subordinate position usually associated with women. The self-contained integrity of men in *The Changeling* is further compromised by their desire for women, with the once stoic Alsemero admitting 'I am not myself' (II, i, 152) as a result of his love for Beatrice-Joanna. The subplot underscores this sense of instability, both through the madmen 'That act their fantasies in any shapes / Suiting their present thoughts' (III, iii, 186–7) and through the aristocrats who present themselves as mad with love for the captive Isabella.

For her part, Beatrice-Joanna embraces the commodity potential of both her person and her chastity, using it to her advantage. In contrast with Vittoria's rejection of interiority in *The White Devil*, Beatrice-Joanna accepts that her exterior appearance need not reflect her inner reality, creating a double persona reflected in her compound name. Ruminating on her hatred for her servant Deflores, for example, she asks, 'Must I needs show it? Cannot I keep that secret, / And serve my turn upon him?' (II, ii, 68–9). She skillfully manages her self-presentation both to raise her value on the marriage market and to serve her own personal desires. To this end, she asks to retain her maidenhead, 'the dear companion of [her] soul' (I, i, 186), for a few days longer, thus postponing her unwanted marriage to Alonzo and presenting herself as chaste and therefore valuable. Despite her spiritual language, however, Beatrice-Joanna acknowledges her virginity's status as 'a toy' (I, i, 190), as her father refers to it, not just a trifle but also a commodity exchanged in a sexual transaction. Her frank acknowledgement of virginity's commodity status informs her plan to pay Diaphanta one thousand ducats to serve as a substitute on her wedding night. As Beatrice-Joanna remarks, ''tis a nice piece / Gold cannot purchase' (IV, i, 56–7), suggesting that even the most virginal woman can be bought.

Intimately acquainted with commercial dynamics of desire, Beatrice-Joanna assesses her suitors in similar terms, and she voices anxieties traditionally expressed by men about the difficulty of evaluating potential mates. Questioning the sudden love that arises between herself and Alsemero, she observes,

> Our eyes are sentinels unto our judgements,
> And should give certain judgement what they see;
> But they are rash sometimes, and tell us wonders
> Of common things, which when our judgements find,
> They can then check the eyes, and call them blind.
>
> (I, i, 68–72)

Love at first sight is limited, she suggests, because the eyes may overvalue the object of desire, 'tell[ing] us wonders of common things'.[32] Judgement therefore must affirm this initial assessment to determine whether the beloved's outward appearance truly indicates inner substance. Because Beatrice-Joanna's 'eyes were mistaken' (I, i, 80) in her initial selection of Alonzo as a fiancé, she succumbed to the unruly nature of sexual desire that cathects onto unworthy objects. Though she believes firmly that she sees 'now with the eyes of judgement' (II, i, 13), her assessment of Alsemero seems similarly driven by desire, as he appears equal in substance to Alonzo. Less worldly than Beatrice-Joanna, Alsemero lacks her circumspection and fatally avers that his vision and his judgement 'are both agreed' (I, i, 75) in his choice of her as a wife.

Whereas Alsemero lacks the ability to penetrate female artifice, Beatrice-Joanna appropriates for herself the prerogative to assess male value. She uses the treasure imagery associated with female chastity in her comment that 'A true deserver like a diamond sparkles' (II, i, 13). Though indicating that intrinsic virtue shines through a man's exterior, her diamond imagery also suggests that men, like jewels, can be exchanged, and she hopes that, if she can remove Alonzo, Alsemero 'Shall soon shine glorious in my father's liking / Through the refulgent virtue of my love' (III, iii, 16–17). Like commodities – or women – men's value is relative to the value of those around them. Here, *The Changeling* reflects what Ryner calls 'an uneasiness about proper valuation and perhaps even a terror about the vicissitudes of exchange', a psychological condition reflecting 'a larger anxiety about valuation made pressing by the period's economic conditions'.[33] This anxiety is compounded by Beatrice-Joanna's appropriation of the male gaze, the transgressive nature of which is revealed in her decision to murder Alonzo so that she may marry Alsemero. Rejecting the suggestion that the men duel for her favour, she seeks a more masculine agency, complaining to Deflores that, if she were a man, she would 'have power / Then to oppose [her] loathings – nay, remove 'em / Forever from [her] sight' (II, ii, 111–13). Hoping to enter Beatrice-Joanna's good graces, Deflores presents himself as a supplement to her person, promising, 'Without change to your sex, you have your wishes. / Claim so much man in me' (II, ii, 114–15). Having appropriated the masculine privilege of evaluating potential mates, Beatrice-Joanna subsequently seeks the ability to select one herself. Within a patriarchal society this opportunity is closed to her, however, leaving her with few means of achieving her will other than to commit murder using Deflores as a masculine prosthetic.

The perversity of Beatrice-Joanna's desire to exchange men is encapsulated in the image of Alonzo's finger, severed by Deflores, still bearing Beatrice-Joanna's diamond ring. In its normative context as 'the first token my father made me send him' (III, iii, 33), the ring signals Beatrice-Joanna's constricted position within patriarchal exchange, as it figuratively links the jewel of chastity to the vaginal ring. Alibius underscores this sexual meaning of rings when he describes his anxieties about being cuckolded, saying, 'I would wear my ring on my own finger; / Whilst it is borrowed it is none of mine, / But his that useth it' (I, ii, 27–9). The presence of the ring on the dismembered finger evokes sexual penetration, and Deflores's observation that the ring 'stuck' to the finger 'As if the flesh and it were both one substance' (III, iii, 37–8) attests to Alonzo's lasting unwillingness to relinquish patriarchal ownership of Beatrice-Joanna's body. In its reconfigured association with death and dismemberment, however, the ring comes to signify Alonzo's objectification by both Beatrice and her father, and it highlights not only Beatrice's transgressive gender reversal but also the more general perversity of objectifying people, women as well as men, through the jewel discourse associated with commoditised chastity. The castrated finger, stuck in the vaginal ring and adorned with a diamond, thus literalises the objectifying power of chastity discourse and evinces the play's horror at the idea that men might be evaluated in the same terms as women.

Beatrice-Joanna and Deflores's struggle over the ring's significance reflects their competing understandings of virginity, service and personal value in the early modern economy. Beatrice-Joanna emphasises the ring's status as an alienable commodity, noting its monetary value of three hundred ducats and encouraging Deflores to 'make use on' it (III, iii, 42).

Deflores, by contrast, persists in associating the ring that '[t]hrew sparkles in [his] eye' (III, i, 31) with Beatrice-Joanna's virginity, which he hopes to possess. Regarding the ring in terms of the affective, social bonds of both marriage and aristocratic service, Deflores resists Beatrice-Joanna's attempts to present the ring, or other riches, as payment for services rendered. Recoiling at the spectre of wage labour, he asks,

> Do you place me in the rank of verminous fellows
> To destroy things for wages? Offer gold?
> The life blood of man! Is any thing
> Valued too precious for my recompense?   (III, iii, 64–7)

Deflores evinces disgust at Beatrice-Joanna's commoditisation of human life and, more to the point, of his service. In a period in which, as Michelle Dowd observes, 'increasing numbers of servants were negotiating yearly contracts with their masters rather than assuming long-term positions', Deflores represents not merely the threat of an upstart servant but also the fate of a dissolute gentleman whom 'hard fate has thrust . . . out to servitude' (II, i, 48).[34] Compounding the implications of the ring on Alonzo's disembodied finger, Beatrice-Joanna's actions suggest that men's work and lives can be commoditised in the early modern economy, a point Alsemero later underscores when he asks Deflores, 'What price goes murder' (V, iii, 102). A similar commoditisation is present in the subplot, where Alibius makes 'a fine trade' (III, ii, 265) by farming out the residents of his asylum as entertainment, turning 'Madmen and fools' into 'a staple commodity' (III, ii, 266).

It is this objectification of labour that Deflores resists, and he instead seeks to bind himself to his employer. He insists that the social distance between himself and Beatrice-Joanna has been collapsed by their shared sin, rendering them 'engaged so jointly' (III, iii, 88). To tighten this bond further, he demands that his service must be 'paid for' (III, iii, 106) not with money but with Beatrice-Joanna's virginity, which he regards as the seal of an affective bond resembling marriage.[35] Moreover, he recognises Beatrice-Joanna's virginity as a non-renewable, and therefore intensely desirable, object of homosocial competition, admitting to her, 'were I not resolved in my belief / That thy virginity were perfect in thee / I should but take my recompense with grudging' (III, iii, 116–18). Perversely invoking dictums rendering virginity 'invaluable', Deflores maintains that 'The wealth of all Valencia shall not buy / My pleasure from me' (III, iii, 159–60). His excessive, extra-economic desire is both sexual and social, reflecting his efforts to level class distinctions and to establish sexual primacy not only over Beatrice-Joanna but also over Alonzo and Alsemero. Once Deflores has attained 'her honour's prize' (V, ii, 167), he gloats that there is nothing left for anyone else: 'it was so sweet to me / That I have drunk up all, left none behind / For any man to pledge to' (V, ii, 167–71). Regarding virginity as a quasi-commodity within homosocial economies, Deflores refuses to divorce its value from Beatrice-Joanna's body, as she herself wishes to do by reifying it in the ring. Similarly, he refuses to alienate his own murderous labour by accepting cash payment, using his action to coerce Beatrice-Joanna into sexual submission so as to sadistically tighten his bonds of service.

Despite his investment in patriarchal understandings of virginity, Deflores's class resentments lead him to deflate conventional ideologies associating morality with sexual purity. When Beatrice-Joanna accuses him of making Alonzo's death 'the murderer of my honour' (III, iii, 122), he chastises her for equating honour with virginity, saying 'Push! You forget yourself: / A woman dipped in blood, and talk of modesty?' (III, iii, 125–6). As Alsemero later affirms when he calls their bed 'a charnel, the sheets shrouds / For murdered carcasses' (V, iii, 84–5), a woman cannot commit murder and remain chaste. Despite his obsession with Beatrice-Joanna's physical body, Deflores emphasises the performative aspects of personal value, contending that her honour rests not in her unbroken hymen but in her actions. Having commissioned Alonzo's murder, she becomes 'the deed's creature', having 'by that name ... lost [her] first condition' (III, iii, 137–8). As such, Deflores insists, she becomes 'one with' (III, iii, 140) him, to whom she must 'forget [her] parentage' (III, iii, 136). Reborn through murder, Beatrice-Joanna owes her new self to Deflores. As Jonathan Dollimore argues, this scene reveals the concepts of '"blood" and "birth" to be myths in the service of historical and social forms of power'; as in *The White Devil*, the dismantling of chastity's intrinsic value disrupts ideologies of aristocratic supremacy more broadly.[36]

In a more literal sense, Beatrice-Joanna emphasises the performative aspects of chastity when she feigns her response to the virginity test. While she accepts virginity as a physical fact, causing Diaphanta to fear that she will search her 'Like the forewoman of a female jury' (IV, i, 99), her machinations reveal that perceptions of chastity can be shaped through artifice.[37] Fittingly for a stage play, the virginity potion reveals itself through action, as it purports to make a virgin 'incontinently gape, then fall into a sudden sneezing, last into a violent laughing – else dull heaving and lumpish' (IV, i, 48–50), signs associated with female orgasm.[38] Beatrice-Joanna thwarts this attempt at penetration, however, disclosing in an aside, 'I'm put now to my cunning: th'effects I know, / If I can now but feign 'em handsomely' (IV, ii, 137–8). Her performance successfully convinces Alsemero that she is 'Chaste as the breath of heaven, or morning's womb / That brings the day forth' (IV, ii, 149–50). Alsemero is similarly swayed by Beatrice-Joanna's more general performance of self, believing that 'Modesty's shrine is set in yonder forehead' (IV, ii, 125), and by Diaphanta's bedroom performance on his wedding night.

In contrast to *The White Devil*'s use of performative chastity as the basis of early capitalist subjectivity, *The Changeling* ultimately forecloses this radical potential and instead reaffirms the central premise of the chastity test: that there exists an intrinsic and knowable core of female sexual essence.[39] Echoing Monticelso's discourse from *The White Devil*, the still suspicious Jasperino encourages Alsemero to penetrate Beatrice-Joanna's veneer: 'Touch it home then', he instructs, ''tis not a shallow probe / Can search this ulcer soundly; I fear you'll find it / Full of corruption' (V, iii, 7–9). In response, Alsemero promises to 'demolish and seek out truth' (V, iii, 37) in Beatrice-Joanna, to remove the 'visor / O'er that cunning face' (V, iii, 47–8), and to 'ransack / And tear out [his] suspicion' (V, iii, 39–40). Whereas Vittoria resists such penetration, Beatrice-Joanna admits that ''Tis an easy passage' (V, iii, 40–1) to her heart and, after dissembling for a bit, admits that she has murdered Alonzo and had sex with Deflores.

Despite this seeming closure, however, *The Changeling* evinces residual anxiety about the legibility of women's sexual status. Even after rooting out Beatrice-Joanna's sins, Alsemero laments, 'O cunning devils, / How should blind men know you from fair-faced saints?' (V, iii, 109–10). This insecurity stems from the play's acknowledgment that chastity, like the sexual satisfaction mimicked by the virginity test, is in many aspects performative and constitutes only a portion of a woman's honour. Even if a woman's sexual status is knowable, *The Changeling* demonstrates, this knowledge offers only minimal insight into her character. In contrast to Alibius's tolerant conversion from 'jealous coxcomb' (V, iii, 210) to 'better husband' (V, iii, 213), the main plot resolves anxieties about the inscrutability of female chastity by expelling women from the homosocial order altogether. As she is dying, Beatrice-Joanna figures herself as contaminated blood that has been let from the family line to ensure her father's 'better health' (V, ii, 151), asking him to 'look no more upon't, / But cast it to the ground regardlessly, / Let the common sewer take it from distinction' (V, ii, 150–3). With her honour defiled and depleted, Beatrice-Joanna's personal integrity fragments to the point of indistinction. Here, *The Changeling*'s conservative gender politics override its potentially radical critique of aristocratic supremacy.

In the face of Beatrice-Joanna's dissolved chastity, the aristocratic men attempt to reconstitute the social hierarchy that Beatrice-Joanna and Deflores have disrupted. In the face of the wreckage caused by the upstart servant and the transgressive woman, Alsemero instantiates regenerative homosocial bonds, promising the surviving men,

> Your only smiles have power to cause re-live
> The dead again, or in their rooms to give
> Brother a new brother, father a child –
> If these appear, all griefs are reconciled.   (V, iii, 223–6)

Alsemero thus fulfills Vermandero's desire to have a son, but sidesteps the complications of triangulating this desire through a woman. He similarly substitutes himself for Tomazo's lost biological brother, and the three men forge a family free of female bonds. In this context, the men's stoic aristocratic integrity – earlier threatened by Alsemero's sexual passion for Beatrice-Joanna and by Tomazo's parallel passion for revenge – is restored, buttressed by male relationships. With this fantasy of homosocial stability, *The Changeling* evades the implication made earlier in the play – and in *Troilus* and *The White Devil* – that aristocratic men are subject to the commoditising forces shaping evaluations of female chastity. Instead, *The Changeling* recuperates aristocratic subjectivity by blaming any sense of personal dislocation not on objectifying early capitalist labour relations, but on women's seductive artifice and transgressive sexuality. In this way, the play's conclusion displaces anxieties about declining aristocratic supremacy and the commoditisation of male bodies in early capitalist markets.

The Changeling's idealised conclusion remains haunted, however, by the image of Alonzo's adorned, disembodied finger, which reminds audiences of the commoditising forces to which men can be subjected, not only by women seeking to change husbands but by capitalist divisions of labour. Although the courtiers themselves do not consider these economic developments, they are central to Deflores's trajectory as he desperately seeks to avoid the fate of the wage labourer. This fate, by contrast, is embodied by the dancing madmen, forced – much like theatrical actors – to perform for the entertainment and profit of others, their addled minds at once symptoms and causes of their exploitation. Contravening Alsemero's comforting pronouncements, the experiences of Alonzo, Deflores and the madmen suggest that men may have more in common with commoditised women than they would like to admit.

Whereas *Troilus and Cressida* and *The White Devil* raise essentially mercantile questions of value – asking how understandings of personal subjectivity would shift if ideologies of intrinsic value were replaced by commercial paradigms – *The Changeling* asks what would happen if male bodies and labour were literally commoditised rather than simply assessed in commercial terms. Reflecting concerns that intensified in the 1620s about the proletarianisation of service and of labour more generally, *The Changeling* reveals this shift to be catastrophic, and its conservative ending tenuously recuperates aristocratic identity by displacing economic anxieties onto women. Although *The Changeling* reflects one discursive trajectory in the coarticulation of female chastity and male subjectivity, this inquiry into the commoditisation of male bodies is explored in somewhat more positive terms in the London city comedies treated in the next chapter. There, playwrights such as Middleton and Ben Jonson invoke the commoditised bodies of chaste female characters to articulate workable models of bourgeois subjectivity in an early capitalist marketplace that is at once alienating and seductive.

Notes

1. Richard Brathwaite, *The English gentlewoman, drawne out to the full body: expressing, what habilliments doe best attire her, what ornaments doe best adorne her, what complements doe best accomplish her* (London: Printed by B. Alsop and T. Favvcet, for Michaell Sparke, 1631), 105, Folger Copy.
2. Barnabe Rich, *The Excellency of Good Women. The Honour and Estimation that Belongeth unto Them. The Infallible Markes Whereby to Know Them* (London: 1613), 7, EEBO.
3. For a discussion of virginity tests in the period, see Dale B. J. Randall, 'Some Observations on the Theme of Chastity in *The Changeling*', *English Literary Renaissance* 14.3 (1984): 347–66.
4. For interpretive dilemmas evoked by virginity, see Marie Loughlin, *Hymeneutics: Interpreting Virginity on the Early Modern Stage* (Lewisburg: Bucknell University Press, 1997) and Mara Amster, 'Frances Howard and Middleton and Rowley's *The Changeling*: Trials, Tests, and the Legibility of the Virgin Body', in *The Single Woman in Medieval and Early Modern England: Her Life and Representation*, ed. Laurel Amtower and Dorothea Kehler (Tempe: Arizona Center for Medieval and Renaissance Studies, 2003), 211–32. For a discussion of the performance of chastity in conduct literature, see Ann Rosalind Jones, 'Nets and Bridles: Early Modern Conduct Books and Sixteenth Century Women's Lyrics', in *The Ideology of Conduct: Essays on Literature and the History of Sexuality*, ed. Nancy Armstrong and Leonard Tennenhouse (New York: Methuen, 1987), 39–72.
5. Katharine Eisaman Maus, *Inwardness and Theater in the English Renaissance* (Chicago: University of Chicago Press, 1995), 11.
6. Brathwaite, *The English gentlewoman*, 114.

7. Thomas Tuke, *A Treatise Against Painting* (London: 1616), D1v.
8. Peter Stallybrass, 'Reading the Body: *The Revenger's Tragedy* and the Jacobean Theater of Consumption', *Renaissance Drama* 18 (1987): 121–48, 125.
9. See especially W. R. Elton, 'Shakespeare's Ulysses and the Problem of Value', *Shakespeare Studies* 2 (1966): 95–111; Lars Engle, 'Always Already in the Market: The Politics of Evaluation in *Troilus and Cressida*', in *Shakespearean Pragmatism: Market of his Time* (Chicago: University of Chicago Press, 1993), 147–63; Jonathan Gil Harris, '"The Enterprise is Sick": Pathologies of Value and Transnationality in *Troilus and Cressida*', *Renaissance Drama* 29 (1998): 3–37; and Paul Yachnin, '"The Perfection of Ten": Populuxe Art and Artisanal Value in *Troilus and Cressida*', *Shakespeare Quarterly* 56:3 (2005), 306–27.
10. See Stephen Mead, 'Thou Art Chang'd: Public Value and Personal Identity in *Troilus and* Cressida', *Journal of Medieval and Renaissance Studies* (1992): 237–59, and Mario Domenichelli, '"Voila la belle mort": The Crisis of the Aristocracy in *Troilus and Cressida*', in *Shakespeare, Italy, and Intertextuality*, ed. Michele Marrapodi (New York: Manchester University Press, 2004), 59–70.
11. William Shakespeare, *Troilus and Cressida*, ed. David Bevington, The Arden Shakespeare, Third Series (Walton-on-Thames: Thomas Nelson and Sons Ltd., 1998), II, ii, 19–20, hereafter cited parenthetically.
12. Brathwaite, *The English gentlewoman*, 101.
13. Thomas Hobbes, *Leviathan*, ed. C. B. Macpherson (New York: Penguin Books, 1985), 151–2.
14. Hobbes, *Leviathan*, 152.
15. Jonathan Gil Harris notes that Ulysses' speech exposes the tensions, common in mercantilist discourse, inherent in asserting simultaneously that value is fixed yet is in danger of becoming unfixed, and reflects the desire, also evident in Hobbes, for an external force to stabilise value ('"The Enterprise is Sick"', 20).

16. William Shakespeare, *The Rape of Lucrece*, in *The Poems*, ed. John Roe (New York: Cambridge University Press, 2006), ll. 279–80.
17. Hugh Grady, '"Mad Idolatry": Commoditization and Reification in *Troilus and Cressida*', in *Shakespeare's Universal Wolf: Studies in Early Modern Reification* (Oxford: Clarendon Press, 1996), 58–94.
18. For a fuller discussion of the status of Troilus and Cressida's relationship, see Emily Ross, '"Words, Vows, Gifts, Tears and Love's Full Sacrifice": An Assessment of the Status of Troilus and Cressida's Relationship According to Customary Elizabethan Marriage Procedure', *Shakespeare* 4.4 (2008): 413–37.
19. For feminist criticism of the play, see Gayle Greene, 'Shakespeare's Cressida: "A Kind of Self"', in *The Women's Part: Feminist Criticism of Shakespeare*, ed. Carol Lenz et al. (Urbana: University of Illinois Press, 1980), 133–49; Alan Sinfield, 'Kinds of Loving: Women in the Plays', in *Self and Society in Shakespeare's Troilus and Cressida and Measure for Measure*, ed. J. A. Jowitt and R. K. S. Taylor, Bradford Center Occasional Papers, no. 4 (1982), 27–44; and Sharon M. Harris, 'Feminism and Shakespeare's *Troilus and Cressida: If* I be false...', *Women's Studies* 18 (1990): 65–82.
20. For a discussion of Cressida's complex identity in this moment, see Cora Fox, 'Blazons of Desire and War in Shakespeare's *Troilus and Cressida*', in *Staging the Blazon in Early Modern English Theater*, ed. Deborah Uman and Sara Morisson (Burlington, VT: Ashgate, 2013), 189–99.
21. John Webster, *The White Devil*, ed. Christina Luckyj, New Mermaids (London: Methuen, 2008), I, ii, 204, hereafter cited parenthetically. For an extended discussion of this jewel imagery, see Samuel Schuman, 'The Ring and the Jewel in Webster's Tragedies', *Texas Studies in Literature and Language* 14.2 (1972): 253–68.
22. Luckyj, *The White Devil*, 21n.208.
23. As Dympna Callaghan points out, Monticelso also implicates men in the abuses he lists, as evidenced by his admission that

it is a man who first 'stamps' the whore (*Woman and Gender in Renaissance Tragedy: A Study of King Lear, Othello, The Duchess of Malfi and The White Devil* [Atlantic Highlands, NJ: Humanities Press International, 1989], 124).

24. Callaghan, *Woman and Gender in Renaissance Tragedy*, 109.
25. See Kathryn R. Finin-Farber, 'Framing (the) Woman: *The White Devil* and the Deployment of Law', *Renaissance Drama* 25 (1994): 219–45.
26. For a discussion of Vittoria's use of metatheatre to subversive ends, see Lisa Dickson, '*Theatrum Mundi*: Performativity, Violence, and Metatheater in Webster's *The White Devil*', in *Beholding Violence in Medieval and Early Modern Europe*, ed. Allie Terry-Fritsch and Erin Felicia Labbie (Burlington, VT: Ashgate, 2012), 163–78.
27. Rich, *The Excellency of Good Women*, 23, 22.
28. For a discussion of Vittoria's self-fashioning, see Christina Luckyj, 'Gender, Rhetoric, and Performance in John Webster's *The White Devil*', in *Enacting Gender on the English Renaissance Stage*, ed. Viviana Comensoli and Anne Russell (Urbana: University of Illinois Press, 1999): 218–32.
29. Sheryle A. Stevenson, '"*As* Differing as Two Adamants": Sexual Difference in *The White Devil*', in *Sexuality and Politics in Renaissance Drama*, ed. Carole Levin and Karen Robertson (Lewiston, NY: The Edwin Mellen Press, 1991), 159–74, esp. 160.
30. Bradley Ryner, 'Anxieties of Currency Exchange in Middleton and Rowley's *The Changeling*', in *Money, Morality, and Culture in Late Medieval and Early Modern Europe*, ed. Juliann Vitullo and Diane Wolfthal (Burlington, VT: Ashgate, 2010), 109–25.
31. Thomas Middleton, *The Changeling*, ed. Michael Neill, New Mermaids (New York: Bloomsbury, 2006), I, i, 85–7, hereafter cited parenthetically.
32. For iconophobic anxieties surrounding vision in the play, see Andrew Stott, 'Tiresias and the Basilisk: Vision and Madness in Middleton and Rowley's *The Changeling*', *Revista Alicantina de Estudios Ingleses* 12 (1999): 165–79.

33. Ryner, 'Anxieties of Currency Exchange', 110.
34. Michelle M. Dowd, 'Desiring Subjects: Staging the Female Servant in Early Modern Tragedy', in *Working Subjects in Early Modern English Drama*, ed. Michelle M. Dowd and Natasha Korda (Burlington, VT: Ashgate, 2011), 132–43, esp. 133. For more on service in *The Changeling*, see Mark Thornton Burnett, '*The Changeling* and Masters and Servants', in *Early Modern English Drama: A Critical Companion*', ed. Garrett A. Sullivan, Jr., Patrick Cheney and Andrew Hadfield (New York: Oxford University Press, 2006), 298–308.
35. For more on the dynamics of eroticism and sexual submission in the play, see Christina Malcolmson, '"As Tame as the Ladies": Politics and Gender in *The Changeling*', *English Literary Renaissance* 20.2 (1990): 320–39; Deborah G. Burks, '"I'll Want My Will Else": *The Changeling* and Women's Complicity with their Rapists', *English Literary History* 62 (1995): 759–90; Judith Haber, '"I(t) could not choose but follow": Erotic Logic in *The Changeling*', *Representations* 81.1 (2003): 79–98; and Francis E. Dolan, 'Rereading Rape in *The Changeling*', *The Journal for Early Modern Cultural Studies* 11.1 (2011): 4–29.
36. Jonathan Dollimore, *Radical Tragedy: Religion, Ideology, and Power in the Drama of Shakespeare and His Contemporaries* (Chicago: Chicago University Press, 1984), 147.
37. Several critics draw connections between *The Changeling*'s chastity test and the annulment trial of Frances Howard, who was believed to have substituted a virginal woman for herself during a physical examination. See for example, Haber, '"I(t) could not choose but follow"'; Amster, 'Frances Howard and Middleton and Rowley's *The Changeling*'; and Sara D. Luttfring, 'Bodily Narratives and the Politics of Virginity in *The Changeling* and the Essex Divorce', *Renaissance Drama* 39 (2010): 97–128. See also Duncan Douglas, 'Virginity in *The Changeling*', *English Studies in Canada* 9.1 (1983): 25–35.
38. See Marjorie Garber, 'The Insincerity of Women', in *Desire in the Renaissance: Psychoanalysis and Literature*, ed. Valeria Finucci and Regina Schwarz (Princeton: Princeton University

Press, 1994), 19–38, esp. 25, for comparison of the test's effects to Freud's discussion of female orgasm.

39. For more on the play's obsession with exposing and thus destroying interiority, see Michael Neill, '"Hidden Malady": Death, Discovery, and Indistinction in *The Changeling*', *Renaissance Drama* 22 (1991): 95–121, and Bruce Boehrer, 'Alsemero's Closet: Privacy and Interiority in *The Changeling*', *Journal of English and Germanic Philology* 96.3 (1997): 349–68.

CHAPTER 3

CHASTE SELFHOOD: BEN JONSON'S CRITIQUE OF URBAN CHASTITY TROPES

Ben Jonson's marriage masque *Hymenaei* (1606) features a competition between virginity, represented by Opinion, and married chastity, represented by Truth, in which marriage predictably triumphs. Jonson's seeming admiration for the virgin's autonomy complicates this generic trajectory, however.[1] Although the 'unprofitable virgin' is maligned by Truth for her greedy hoarding, Opinion's depiction of virginity bears a close resemblance to Jonson's famed masculine ideal, what Thomas Greene calls the 'centered self'.[2] Like this masculine subject, *Hymenaei*'s virgin possesses qualities associated with centeredness and circularity, both of which, in Jonson's corpus, 'become symbols not only of harmony and completeness but of stability, repose, fixation, duration'.[3] Virgins, Opinion extolls, 'Have all things perfect, spin their own free fate, / Depend on no proud second, are their own / Center and circle, now and always one' (718–20). The virgin thus serves as an analogue to Jonson's masculine ideal, in which the virtuous man is defined by his impenetrability.[4] In *Hymenaei*, however, in which union signifies not only heterosexual marriage but also the yoking of Scotland to England and King James to his people, the virgin must submit to a higher power, compromising her autonomous integrity for 'Eternal Unity'

(821), cemented 'In th'one's obedience and the other's sway' (730). Traditionally, the marriage contract, as Victoria Kahn demonstrates, functioned as a foundational analogy for the subject's relationship to the state.[5] Here, the virgin's fate parallels that of the masculine subject in a monarchal society, sacrificing autonomy as she submits to potentially advantageous, though patriarchal, authority. This intermingling of erotic and political discourse, Melissa Sanchez points out, produces a subject who desires his own subjection and even abjection.[6] Though ostensibly male, the subject is queered not only through this abjection but through repeated comparisons to the chaste – first virginal and then married – woman, figured in sexual relation to the male sovereign.

This chapter explores the permutations of this paradigm in London city comedy, where, I argue, chastity is invoked to explore the particular subjectivity of *homo economicus*. Throughout city comedy, female chastity functions as an analogue to masculine temperance and is invoked to explore men's subjugation to commercial forces. As Jean Howard demonstrates, prostitution plots often functioned as a means of negotiating the limits of traffic and its effect on the early modern subject.[7] Despite being positioned as antithetical to the prostitute, the chaste woman is also invoked in city comedy to explore commercial subjectivity; specifically, she models forms of selfhood capable of withstanding potentially compromising commercial environments. Plays such as Thomas Middleton's *A Chaste Maid in Cheapside* (1613), the anonymous *Fair Maid of the Exchange* (1607), Middleton and Thomas Dekker's *The Roaring Girl* (1611), and Jonson's *Volpone* (1606), *Epicoene* (1609) and *Bartholomew Fair* (1616) all juxtapose chaste women with desiring, fragmented male characters as a means of critiquing an ineffectual masculinity incapable of withstanding the dangers and temptations of the market. As such, the chaste woman's ability to guard her bodily boundaries and sexual riches points to potentially efficacious forms of capitalist subjectivity, and her entrance into a marriage contract often signals appropriate modes of maintaining integrity while participating in exchange.

Although female characters in city comedy reflect anxieties about actual early modern women, who, as Karen Newman observes, were 'the focus of cultural ambivalence toward social mobility, urbanization, and colonization', they also function as abstractions.[8] Elizabeth Hanson reminds us that, despite their veneer of realism, city comedies operate at least in part on the level of allegory; as such, she advises, 'we must also attend to representational traditions which urge upon us a hermeneutic of abstraction, a movement away from women as historical subjects and toward things which they can be made to signify'.[9] Reading in this vein, Shannon Miller demonstrates that the grotesque female body often stands in for the economy itself, offering 'one site upon which to explore the metaphoric associations generated by a carnivalesque and equally incomprehensible market'.[10] In addition to representing the closed, stable antithesis of the carnivalesque market, the chaste woman operates as an analogy for early modern man, anxious about his own integrity in the early capitalist economy.[11]

Despite disparate behavioural expectations for men and women in the early modern period, language surrounding female chastity in many ways mirrors discourses of temperance, an aspect of aristocratic virtue that was appropriated by bourgeois conduct writers as a key component of commercial success. Although temperance is not deemed wholly constitutive of personal value in the same way that chastity is, aristocratic conduct books such as Richard Brathwaite's *The English Gentleman* (1630) posit it as the basis of all virtue, encouraging men to use moderation 'in their restraint of every *pleasure*; laboring to become commanders of themselves in the *desires* and *affections* of this life'.[12] Similarly Henry Peacham emphasises stoic containment in *The Complete Gentleman*

(1634), describing temperance as 'a bridle' with which 'we curbe and breake our ranke and unruly Passions, keeping as the Caspian Sea, ourselves ever at one height without ebbe or refluxe'.[13] Bourgeois tracts such as William Scott's *An Essay of Drapery: or The Compleate Citizen* (1635) modify this aristocratic ideal to address the demands of living in and profiting from London's market economy. In addition to advising merchants to speak and consume sparingly, Scott counsels them to exercise temperance in both their saving and their earning: the citizen should 'save anything hee can save, without hurt to his conscience, or losse to his credit', and should 'be diligent in the Quest of riches, and credit; but not over-violent and long'.[14] For Scott, temperance cultivates the self-control necessary to succeed financially without compromising virtue, 'as it is the way to Vertue, so the way to profit'.[15]

In both the aristocratic and the bourgeois conduct literature, temperance encompasses sexual chastity, as sexual appetite constitutes one of the many appetites men must control. Brathwaite, for example, comments that temperance enables men to defend themselves against temptresses such as Cleopatra who 'in the last tragicke Scene of her disasters, kneeling at the feet of *Caesar*, laid baits for his eyes; but in vaine; her beauties were beneath that Prince's chastity'.[16] This restraint, he suggests, is integral to the health of the state, ensuring that 'the Realme be not corrupted with riot and wanton delights, whereby diverse States have been cast away'.[17] It is in this sexual aspect that temperance relates most closely to female chastity, which Robert Greene calls in *Penelope's Web* (1601) 'the shield against luxuriousness', and 'an enemy to the disordered will of the soul'.[18] Influenced by stoic philosophy as well as by Elizabeth I's virginal authority which signalled England's impenetrable borders, conduct writers deemed temperance, like chastity, necessary to the maintenance of personal integrity and national stability. City comedies, I argue, draw on this connection between female chastity and male temperance to interrogate the nature of male subjectivity in commercial contexts in which the male self – like the body of the chaste woman – is in perpetual danger of becoming undone, either by the market's commoditising energies or by its own desires.

In what follows, I first discuss the ways in which *A Chaste Maid in Cheapside*, *Fair Maid of the Exchange* and *The Roaring Girl* employ chastity to think through the fate of temperance and integrated selfhood in urban London and invoke marriage as an often imperfect, and even queer, means of fulfilling the desiring subject and militating against the often threatening exchanges of the marketplace. I then turn to the plays of Ben Jonson, the city dramatist who engages most critically with this generic use of chastity to represent male subjectivity. Although Jonson deploys marriage in *Hymenaei* as a metaphor for the relationship of subject to sovereign, he questions the applicability of this paradigm to commercial London. In *Volpone* he juxtaposes Celia's contained chastity to the unravelling bodies and souls of the men around her, but he presents her chaste selfhood, also adopted by Bonario, as impotent in debased commercial environments marked by artifice and greed. *Epicoene* more fully satirises the generic association of chastity and stoic masculinity, rendering both chastity and personal integrity impossible in urban London. By revealing the chaste Epicoene to be a boy, Jonson rejects heterosexual models of subject formation in favour of modes of subjectivity grounded in homosocial bonds, forged in part through men's ability to ascertain the value of female chastity and other comparable commodities. Jonson reconsiders connections between chastity and subjectivity in *Bartholomew Fair*, where he exploits chastity's commodity status to articulate a dynamic model of contingent subjectivity grounded in the subject's compromised relation to the marketplace. In *Bartholomew Fair*, I argue, Jonson applies this model of chaste, commoditised subjectivity to the playwright, grounding his own authority in his ability to comprehend and manipulate the commercial dynamics to which he is nonetheless beholden.

Maintaining Moral and Bodily Integrity in *Chaste Maid in Cheapside*, *The Fair Maid of the Exchange* and *The Roaring Girl*

Chaste Maid in Cheapside, *The Fair Maid of the Exchange* and *The Roaring Girl* all draw on female chastity to examine the effects of market activity on the male subject, suggesting that men have something to learn from the conduct and personal presentation of chaste women. These plays reveal the difficulty of maintaining absolute personal integrity in the London marketplace and, owing in part to their comic genre, invoke marriage as a means of managing the destabilising effects of commerce, presenting it as a normative sexual analogue to potentially problematic traffic. While *Chaste Maid* embraces marriage as the only available means of cultivating temperance in commercial London, queer and/or disabled chaste figures in *Fair Maid* and *Roaring Girl* point to potentially compromising aspects of this generic reliance on marriage.

A *Chaste Maid in Cheapside* provides a paradigmatic example of city comedy's use of chastity and marriage to conceptualise commercial subjectivity. Middleton invokes exceptional female chastity as a means of exposing widespread intemperance, which is intensified in Cheapside, the commercial centre of the city. Ironically set in the Lenten season, the play is populated by characters who cannot control their sexual, gustatory or consumer urges. The women are open, leaky vessels who eat, drink, copulate, cry and urinate excessively, while the men find their patriarchal prerogatives jeopardised both by these unruly women and by their own unbalanced sexuality.[19] Touchwood Senior and his wife, for example, have grown destitute because of their rampant procreation, as their 'desires / Are both too fruitful for [their] barren fortunes'.[20] Mr. Allwit, alternately, has become a wittol, or willing cuckold, ceding control over his family to Sir Walter Whorehound in exchange for financial security.[21] Allwit's experience, like that of Sir Oliver Kix, who pays Touchwood Senior to impregnate his wife, demonstrates that the status of husband and father, once naturalised within the social hierarchy, can now be bought and sold. The commoditisation of patriarchal prerogatives, compounded by the sensual temptations of the city, leads to a sense that masculine identity has become dislocated and dissolute.

Moll, the eponymous chaste maid, resists these cultural influences and largely overcomes her commoditised position as a marriageable woman, ultimately maintaining her virtue and achieving the marriage she desires. Moll's commodity potential is highlighted by her association with the gold that her father Yellowhammer keeps in his shop. Similarly, Sir Walter wishes to profit by marrying her, as he anticipates 'two thousand pound in gold, / And a sweet maidenhead / Worth forty' (IV, ii, 92–4). This overt monetisation links Moll not only with the gold but also with the Welsh prostitute whom Sir Walter hopes to marry off, establishing Cheapside, as Karen Newman argues, as 'a place of never-ending exchange and circulation, symbolized . . . by gold and its various equivalents'.[22] Although Moll disobeys her greedy father, who has 'lock[ed] up this baggage / As carefully as my gold' (III, i, 43–4), her chastity is redefined over the course of the play as fidelity to her future husband Touchwood Junior, who rests assured that, 'though she be locked up, her vow is fixed only to me' (III, iii, 3).

Chaste Maid embraces companionate marriage as a necessary and normative means of mitigating the deleterious effects of the early modern economy. As Touchwood Senior learns, for example, husbands and wives must control their sexual appetites in order to protect their financial interests, proclaiming that 'The feast of marriage is not lust but love, / And care of the estate' (II, i, 50–1). Sanctioned sexual unions contain desire, *Chaste Maid* suggests, and in so doing provide a bedrock of social and financial security. Moll's marriage to Touchwood Junior offers the play's most effective model for negotiating the temptations of the early modern marketplace, grounded as the union is in Moll's exceptional chastity. This chastity is underscored in the fake deaths that both Moll and Touchwood Junior endure as a means of facilitating their union, permitting time for Touchwood Senior to cultivate remorse in Moll's parents and to eulogise 'The true, chaste monument of [Moll's] living name, / Which no time can deface' (V, iv, 12–13). In contrast to plays such as *Much Ado Nothing* or *All's Well That Ends Well*, in which fake deaths recuperate a woman's sullied honour, the redemptive slumber in *Chaste Maid* extends to Touchwood Junior, cleansing him of the intemperance that suffuses his society and which is most evident in his excessively virile brother, Touchwood Senior. The redemptive power of marriage is subsequently affirmed by the Welsh prostitute who, after marrying Moll's brother, exclaims, 'There's a thing called marriage, and that makes me honest' (V, iv, 117). By the end of *Chaste Maid*, marriage has transformed from commercial contract to chaste union. This union cultivates the temperance – a virtue modelled in the chaste maid – needed to live ethically and profitably in early modern London.

The Fair Maid of the Exchange and *The Roaring Girl* similarly employ chastity and marriage as means of containing commercial desire. As its title suggests, *Fair Maid* examines the fate of chastity in commercial environments. Phillis, the fair maid, works as a seamstress and vendor of textiles in the Exchange, where her customers routinely conflate her body with her wares. Throughout the play, the virginal Phillis is juxtaposed both with Cripple, a disabled drawer, and with her many suitors, whose identities have been destabilised by sexual as well as economic desire. Although Phillis surpasses her suitors in maintaining her psychological and bodily integrity despite daily exposure to the Exchange, her ardent virginity does not ultimately prove as resistant either to external threats or to internal desires as does the disabled body of

Cripple, who helps to rescue her from an attempted rape. In contrast to Phillis's not-yet-penetrated wholeness, Cripple is defined by a queer supplementarity, his crutches endowing him with 'more legs than nature gave [him]'.²³ This phallic excess engenders a sense of self-completion and a resultant lack of desire that proves erotically enticing, even to Phillis; as Cripple explains, 'I detest the humor of fond love: / Yet am I hourly solicited' (887–8). Defined against both Phillis and her suitors, Cripple represents a particular kind of capitalist worker/consumer: one in many ways compromised and characterised by lack, but who is fulfilled both by his labour and by the judicious use of commodities.²⁴ Unlike the multitude in whom consumer capitalism breeds desire, Cripple's supplemental fulfilment leaves him stoically detached and free to manage the desires of those around him.

These efforts culminate in the marriage of Phillis to the able-bodied Frank, as Cripple channels the eroticism of the marketplace into the normative sexuality of marriage. *Fair Maid* thus proffers marriage as a means of mitigating the market's destabilising effects, providing supplemental fulfilment analogous to that embodied in Cripple. As a sanctioned form of exchange, marriage allows men and women to maintain personal integrity even while profiting from commercial activity. Nonetheless, by comparing marriage to the disabled body, *Fair Maid* presents it as a somewhat unnatural state, less autonomous than the stoic individualism that Frank flaunts before falling in love.

Middleton and Dekker's *The Roaring Girl* draws more overt attention to the queer dynamic inherent in using chaste female characters to delineate commercial masculine subjectivity. Chaste virtue in *The Roaring Girl* is shared by two characters, both named Mary: the marriageable Mary Fitzallard and the autonomous Moll Cutpurse, whose swashbuckling androgyny is reminiscent of Elizabeth I. A cross-dressed figure deemed 'woman more than man, / Man more than woman',

Moll is presented as completing herself whereas others seek fulfilment from commodities or sexual partners.[25] Like Cripple in *Fair Maid*, she is defined by a self-fulfilling supplementarity that obviates the need for marriage; as she explains, 'I have no humour to marry, I love to lie o'both sides o'the'bed myself' (II, ii, 36–7). For Moll, marriage reflects the commercial ethos of urban London, and she critiques the institution as 'but a chopping and changing, where a maiden loses one head and has a worse i'th'place' (II, ii, 43–5). Again, traffic, both sexual and commercial, dismantles personal integrity. Rather than submitting to patriarchal exchange, Moll vows that her 'spirit shall be mistress of [her body] / As long as [she] have time in't' (III, i, 139–40).

Moll's chaste self-sufficiency is juxtaposed not only with Mary's more normative chastity and with the sexual availability of the city wives, but also with the inadequacy of men who have been emasculated by the early modern economy. These men, like those of *The Fair Maid of the Exchange*, are haunted by the vendor's call 'What is't you lack? (II, i, 1), which as Jonathan Gil Harris notes signals 'widespread insufficiency . . . for which material goods provide the fetishistic stopgap'.[26] This lacking masculinity, evident in effeminate gallants and passive city husbands, is most fully embodied in Laxton, whose name indicates the absence of both land and testicles. When Laxton tries to seduce Moll, believing that 'money is that aqua fortis that eats into many a maidenhead' (II, i, 180–1), Moll subdues him with her sword, causing him to 'yield both purse and body' (III, i, 121). With this reversal of gender roles, Moll calls attention to Laxton's failed masculinity and critiques him for slandering women, declaring 'I scorn to prostitute myself to a man, / I that can prostitute a man to me' (III, i, 110–11). Moll may ultimately be less an integrated character than an assemblage of diverse meanings and epistemological lacunae imposed upon her by a society that struggles to accommodate her difference and, more generally, to discern value within London's increasingly abstract economy.²⁷ Nevertheless, Moll's active chastity and her ability to negotiate the complexities of the early modern economy make her a model for men who face similar, though less immediately recognisable, challenges of identity. Moll ultimately forgives Laxton, rescues the gallants from cozening rogues, and facilitates Sebastian's marriage to Mary Fitzallard. As such, her active chastity functions not only to highlight men's flaws but also to redeem them, in effect teaching men to be more masculine.

Though she herself avoids marriage, Moll endorses Sebastian and Mary's union, suggesting that marriage remains a viable method of managing exchange. Normative characters such as Sebastian and Mary cannot match Moll's intersexual self-completion; for them, marriage remains an alternative, though perhaps less effective, means of neutralising the market's temptations and dislocations. As in *Fair Maid*, stoic integrity proves untenable in early capitalist London, with self-contained autonomy available only to those possessing queer or disabled supplementarity. The plays' definition of marriage in relation to non-normative bodies, however, points toward the compromising and potentially effeminising consequences of using marriage as a means of compensating for the loss of stoic masculinity.

Commoditised Chastity and the Limits of Temperance in Volpone, Epicoene *and* Bartholomew Fair

Throughout his corpus, Jonson engages critically with the city comedy paradigm linking female chastity with male temperance, autonomy and bodily integrity. Seemingly less concerned than his contemporaries with chastity's sociobiological function in securing lineages, Jonson uses female characters to grapple more directly with the problematics of masculinity, and – particularly in *Epicoene* – he is explicit about the allegorical function of female chastity. Like other city dramatists, Jonson expresses doubt that personal integrity can be maintained in commercial London; however, he is more sceptical of marriage as a means of fostering temperance. *Volpone* and *Epicoene* reveal discomfort with the potentially emasculating effects of marriage underscored in *Fair Maid* and *The Roaring Girl* and more generally with the theatrical convention of using women to produce male subjectivity. In *Bartholomew Fair*, however, Jonson reconsiders the potential of chastity for conceptualising subjectivity, attending to its commodity potential as an analogue for bourgeois subjectivity more generally. Here he posits marriage not as a provisional means of containing desire or as a poor substitute for integrated selfhood, but as one of the myriad contracts to which the early capitalist subject must submit.

Jonson most closely follows generic conventions surrounding chastity in *Volpone*, where Celia's chaste, self-contained body contrasts markedly with the open, fragmented and unravelling bodies of male characters whose virtue is compromised by their desire for wealth, luxury and, in Volpone's case, theatricality. Though married, Celia is defined by her vulnerable, virgin-like integrity as she resists her husband's efforts to prostitute her to Volpone. Urging Celia to 'respect [his] venture', Corvino threatens to destroy both her body and her reputation if she disobeys him.[28] He pledges to 'Cry [her] a strumpet through the streets, rip up / [Her] mouth unto [her] ears, and slit [her] nose, / Like a raw rochet!' (III, vii, 97–9), and then to hang her mutilated body from a window, bound to a slave's corpse, a description of a 'monstrous crime' (III, vii, 103) branded in her flesh with 'burning cor'sives' (III, vii, 105). In his violent desire to 'make [her] an anatomy' (II, v, 70), Corvino imagines inscribing her body with the openness typically associated with promiscuous women. Additionally, Corvino's fantasy of mutilation, associated as it is with his own self-cuckolding, reflects the damage that his avarice has inflicted upon his masculinity. In contrast to the majority of the play's male characters, Celia refuses to compromise her integrity, asking whether 'modesty' has been 'an exile made, for money' (III, vii, 138). Although Celia retains her virtue, displaying the autonomous subjectivity associated in *Hymenaei* with virginity, she remains embattled. She and her virtuous male counterpart Bonario are unable to defend themselves successfully, attesting to the vulnerability, and perhaps inadequacy, of centred selfhood in an early capitalist society characterised by artifice, commoditisation, greed and desire. In contrast to *Chaste Maid*, *Fair Maid* and *Roaring Girl*, however, *Volpone* presents marriage as part of the problem of commercial subjugation rather than as part of its solution. Celia is nearly prostituted in marriage, and Lady Would-Be's attempts to seduce Volpone in order to acquire his wealth underscore the financial elements of marriage. Celia's chastity is preserved, and her semi-virginal status reinscribed, only when she is sent back to her father at the close of the play. Sexual and commercial exchange in *Volpone* is always compromising, even within the sanctioned bond of marriage; chaste resistance to this exchange proves largely ineffectual in early capitalist society.

Jonson extends his critique of chastity tropes in *Epicoene*, where he both exposes the implausible fantasy of a perfect woman and reveals the impossibility of maintaining integrated masculinity amidst the tumult of urban, commercial life. Although Jonson begins by establishing the traditional comparison between a chaste woman and dissolute men in order to critique the destabilising effects of urban commerce, he goes on to exploit the representational strategies of the transvestite theatre to show that Epicoene, the chaste silent woman, has been a boy all along. In so doing, he comments metacritically on the use of chastity to address questions of commercial subjectivity, dismantling generic – and cultural – ideals of chaste temperance by showing that the women of the early modern stage are always, in the final instance, men.

Epicoene's male characters struggle to perform the Jonsonian ideal of integrated, autonomous selfhood. This effort is defined in stoic terms, most directly in the case of the misanthropic patriarch Morose, who seeks to 'collect and contain [his] mind, not suff'ring it to flow loosely' by excluding external stimuli, especially noise, and eschewing anything not 'necessary to the carriage of [his] life'.[29] Morose directs much of his antipathy toward London's commerce and entertainment, driving away workmen and musicians and making treaties with fishwives and orange sellers so that they will avoid his house. Despite these efforts, Morose is unable to achieve centred stillness, a failure evident in his prolixity and in his habitual references to impending deluge. In *Epicoene*, stoic selfhood is threatened not only by acquisitive desires and the penetrative noises and odours of the city, but also by conspicuous consumption. Morose's fragmented subjectivity is surpassed, therefore, only by the fabricated identities of the social upstarts John Daw and Sir Amorous La Foole, whose pretentions to learning and nobility reflect the potentiality (and the difficulty) of shaping one's identity through the consumption of products, ideas and affectations. Meanwhile, Morose's nephew Dauphine, whose princely name suggests his proximity to the stoic ideal, attempts to thwart his uncle's attempts to disinherit him and thus strives to preserve the financial basis of his identity.[30] Dauphine's precarious social condition attests to the instability of aristocratic identity in a society marked by unprecedented mobility, both upward and downward, in which commercial dynamics can both buy knighthoods and deplete landed fortunes.

Epicoene charts the effects of early capitalist life on male identity in relation to the relative chastity of the play's female characters, or at least those who present as female: the sexually liberated Collegiates as well as the restrained, silent Epicoene. Consumer artifice is coded as both feminine and effeminising, and this feminine fragmentation is exhibited most graphically in Mistress Otter, a pretentious city wife.³¹ 'A most vile face!' her husband exclaims:

> And yet she spends me forty pound a year in mercury and hogs' bones. All her teeth were made i' the Blackfriars, both her eyebrows i' the Strand, and her hair in Silver Street. Every part o' the town owns a piece of her. [. . .] She takes herself asunder still when she goes to bed, into some twenty boxes, and about next day noon is put together again, like a great German clock. (IV, ii, 83–6, 88–90)

This grotesque blazon, a commercial counterpart to Corvino's verbal slaying of Celia in *Volpone*, encapsulates the dislocating consequences of women's attempts to fashion identities through material consumption.³² Mistress Otter becomes an assemblage of commodities masking an empty, distasteful core. Her promiscuous consumer behaviour, moreover, signals both her sexual liberality and the 'hermaphroditical authority' (I, i, 77) that she and her fellow Collegiates assume as they present themselves as connoisseurs of culture. Though treated with misogynist scorn, the Collegiates embody the commercial forces that challenge male identity. Their derivative, 'pieced' (I, i, 81) identities closely resemble those that Daw and La Foole fashion through their flamboyant attire and intellectual pretentions.

In contrast to the fragmented Collegiates, Epicoene initially appears as an 'exceeding fair' (II, v, 17) Classical beauty, with 'a sweet composition or harmony of limbs' (II, v, 18–19). Her centred subjectivity is reflected in her rejection of consumer goods: she claims to care little for the latest fashions and promises to allow Morose to choose her clothing after they marry. With the word *epicoene* connoting the presence of both genders or lack of fixed gender, Jonson not only hints at Epicoene's mixed gender identity but also indicates that her self-presentation is relevant to both women and men.³³ Her name makes explicit the subtext underlying city comedy's presentation of female characters, which ultimately pertain as much to male as to female forms of subjectivity. Through Epicoene, however, Jonson reveals the limitations inherent to the self-contained ideal, both as an expectation for women and as a model for men. When Epicoene begins to speak after the marriage, she disrupts Morose's building sexual excitement by pointing out the dehumanising aspects of his expectation that women remain silent, asking,

> Why, did you think you had married a statue? or a motion only? one of the French puppets with the eyes turned with a wire? or some innocent out of the hospital, that would stand with her hands thus, and a plaice-mouth, and look upon you? (III, iv, 34–8)

Stoic self-containment here equals both silence and objectification. Epicoene alleges that the chaste, silent woman has become a fetish object to be consumed and controlled. Desire for this object, like the desire for commodities, in turn compromises and further decentres the male subject, who has difficulty controlling his sexual urges in her presence. Morose's assumption that marrying Epicoene will supplement and stabilise his masculine authority only underscores his lacking masculinity, an inadequacy that is later highlighted when he is forced to admit to impotency in order to annul the marriage.

Moreover, Morose's spectacular failure to discern that his new wife is actually a young boy aligns with his broader inability to negotiate London's commercial economies. As Ari Friedlander contends, *Epiocone* evokes the cony-catching practice of cross-biting, in which a male rogue and a female prostitute team up to steal a wealthy man's wallet.[34] Read in this context, the play's epistemological anxieties resonate with those raised in the cony-catching pamphlets about how to discern the proper value of commodities and assess those who vend them. In *Epicoene*, Jonson interrogates the epistemological anxieties surrounding both chastity and commodities (and chastity as commodity), not only exposing the chaste ideal as a theatrical fantasy but also critiquing men's inability to negotiate a commercial marketplace in which gaps between essence and appearance are commonplace. Chastity ceases to be conceived as a potential counterpart to integrated masculinity and is instead understood largely as a commodity to be evaluated.

The revelation that Epicoene is a boy further destabilises conceptions of integrated selfhood by showing that, as with the commoditised identities of the Collegiates, chaste, stoic demeanour can be performed, crafted through costume and social imitation. While this climax affirms stereotypes about women, suggesting that women cannot in fact be temperate, it also destabilises centred masculinity.[35] Even Dauphine's seemingly natural virtue is challenged by the event, as his efforts to secure his inheritance, and thus his personal solvency, depend upon his performative deception of his uncle. *Epicoene* thus not only undermines the fantasy of complete self-containment, masculine as well as feminine, but also suggests that this ideal may be inadequate for early capitalist society, where some embrace of theatrical self-fashioning may be necessary for survival. For this reason, Morose's misanthropic stoicism proves both untenable and anti-social, while Truewit, the satirical connoisseur of consumer culture, drives the plot's comic energy. Although Dauphine declines to trust the verbose Truewit with his plot, he relies on the social knowledge Truewit has acquired by going 'to court, to tiltings, public shows and feasts, to plays, and church sometimes', where women 'come to show their new tires too, to see and to be seen' (IV, i, 54–6). Untutored in the ways of women and gallants, the virtuous Dauphine relies on Truewit's commercial discernment to trick the gulls, to court women, and to reclaim his inheritance.

Whereas *Fair Maid*, *Roaring Girl* and *Chaste Maid* all promote marriage as a means of containing the market's interpenetrative energies, *Epicoene* responds to capitalism's dislocation of masculinity with a vision of homosocial collaboration. In this, *Epicoene* follows the model that Lorna Hutson identifies in Jonson's early comedies in which personal sovereignty arises through eroticised male friendships.[36] With the ideal of chastity deflated, exposed as a masculine fantasy, Jonson concludes his play with the union of the temperate, princely Dauphine and the theatrical, commercially astute Truewit, who join together to negotiate the evolving contours of the early modern marketplace. Invoking his own role as the court poet, Jonson returns to *Hymenaei*'s conception of a subjectivity forged, somewhat traumatically, through service and subjection to the sovereign. *Epicoene*, however, deploys the framework of homosocial friendship to destabilise the absolutist hierarchy implied in the marriage metaphor: although Dauphine has 'lurched [his] friends of the better half of the garland, by concealing this part of the plot' (V, iv, 208–10), Truewit, the theatrical operator, retains some laurels for himself, and his words conclude the play. Here homosocial friendship replaces the heterosexual marriage contract, rendering chastity immaterial in considerations of early capitalist subjectivity, except in so far as it functions as a commodity through which men prove their commercial discernment.

Jonson reconsiders this dynamic in *Bartholomew Fair*, where he presents commoditised chastity not as an object whose essence must be discerned but rather as a subject position. Whereas *Epicoene*'s Dauphine and Truewit combine temperance and masculine wit to thrive in the London marketplace, the most savvy character in *Bartholomew Fair* is arguably Grace Wellborn, who acknowledges her own commodity status and manipulates commercial dynamics to improve her condition and to forge a contingent sense of self. Rather than condemn Grace for this commercial sensibility, *Bartholomew Fair* posits her self-conscious commoditisation as a strategy for navigating commercial markets in which autonomous, temperate selfhood proves impossible to maintain. The subjectivity developed in *Bartholomew Fair* follows the paradigm identified by Kathryn Schwarz, in which the position of the willfully obedient woman within marriage mirrors that of the political subject within the social contract's 'contradictory logic of prescribed choice'.[37] This subject's agency does not arise through autonomous self-control or through absolute submission to a sovereign but rather through skilful negotiation of its always already subjected status. Jonson's emphasis on commoditised chastity signals his adaptation of *Hymenaei*'s model of subject formation to commercial contexts, wherein the bourgeois self emerges in relation not only to state power but also to commercial forces that compromise personal autonomy. Here, Jonson tempers *Epicoene*'s masculinist ethic while also departing from city comedy's generic reliance on marriage as a mode of containing commercial desire and sanctioning exchange. Grace instead acquires agency and social power through her wilful submission to a business-like marriage contract. Her contingent subjectivity proves particularly suited to early capitalist life as it is developed in relation to the commercial strictures that bind her.

Bartholomew Fair showcases the diffuse, penetrating and commoditising powers of early capitalist commerce.[38] As Jean-Christophe Agnew contends, the early modern fair played a central role in the transition from the bounded *agora*, a delimited arena of buying and selling, to a more diffuse market, moving 'transactions outside the purview of manorial and municipal authority and thus [bypassing] the regulative structure of the public market'.[39] As Jonson illustrates in Justice Overdo's failure to regulate Bartholomew Fair, juridical authority was compromised in the fairgrounds, which were generally subject only to the king's Piepower court, a special tribunal called to oversee events such as markets or fairs. In Jonson's play, the fair serves as a microcosm of the London marketplace, in which commoditisation, commerce and artifice are accepted parts of life and in which state power exerts only tenuous control over commercial and personal interactions.

The fair's unruly commercial context highlights women's position as commodities as well as consumers, a duality embodied in Ursla the Pig Woman, whose grotesque, open body has been shaped by twenty-two years of participation in the fair's sexual and gustatory traffic.[40] A former prostitute whose body was once consumed by others, Ursla's corpulence reflects her current consumptive practices as the 'Mother o'the bawds'.[41] A creature of the fair, she caters to consumer desires, and her pig stall, which doubles as a brothel, serves as the fair's central landmark. The brothel, like the fair more generally, calls attention to the commodity potential of women in ways that are often elided in polite middle-class society. The citizens' wives Win and Mistress Overdo inadvertently enter Ursla's employ, seduced first by her pork dishes and then by promises of luxury, freedom and fine clothing. The wives misconstrue the terms 'free-woman' (IV, v, 30) and 'lady' (IV, v, 31), interpreting the bawds' proposition as a chance for social advancement and freedom from patriarchal control – an error that highlights the slippage between prostitution and respectable wifely commoditisation. In the brothel, the women are viewed as chattel, with Win described as a 'delicate, dark chestnut' (IV, v, 19) whose bodily attributes are catalogued at length. The gallants Quarlous and Winwife take advantage of this commercial milieu in their pursuit of wealthy wives. As Quarlous counsels Winwife in his attempt to impose upon the widowed Dame Purecraft, 'You'll never be master of a better season or place. She will venture herself into the Fair, and a pig-box, will admit any assault, be assured of that' (III, ii, 113–15). All women are vulnerable in the fair, their chastity and autonomy threatened either by prostitution or by marriage, institutions that are exposed as strikingly similar in their treatment of women as commodities. This commoditisation manifests itself in a sense that women – and potentially men as well – are interchangeable, reducible to their exchange value. Quarlous underscores this point when, after stealing a licence that will permit him to marry Dame Purecraft, he states, 'I have the licence and all; it is but razing one name and putting in another' (V, ii, 74–5). The fair's commercial dynamics unsettle social hierarchies as well as individuated identities, leaving unsuspecting middle-class characters such as the citizens' wives particularly vulnerable to exploitation and social dislocation.

As in city comedies such as *The Roaring Girl* and *Chaste Maid*, male characters in *Bartholomew Fair* find it difficult to navigate commercial life and, like Win and Mistress Overdo, find themselves undone by the fair's seductions, enticed by the 'hooks and baits, very baits, that are hung out on every side to catch you' (III, ii, 36–7). The men's longings, a term originally associated with Win's pregnant cravings, point to their loss of autonomous selfhood, an insufficiency underscored in the vendor's call, 'What is it you lack?' (II, iv, 3). Bartholomew Cokes, the country fool, epitomises this insufficiency, as he delights in the fair but fails to grasp its inner workings. As his guardian Wasp predicts, 'If he go to the Fair, he will buy of everything to a baby there; and household stuff for that too. If a leg or an arm on him did not grown on, he would lose it i' the press. Pray heaven I bring him off with one stone! And then he is such a ravener after fruit!' (I, v, 98–102). Wasp's language attests to the emasculating effects of consumer desire. Not only does the fair produce in Cokes a desire for dolls and household stuffs commonly associated with women, but it also induces 'longing' such as that associated with women's purportedly volatile physiognomies. As the fair supplements Cokes's inadequate being, it also threatens to dismember him, stripping him of an arm, a leg or a testicle. In addition to fragmenting his body, the fair threatens to relieve Cokes of the funds on which his manhood rests, a parallel drawn in the cutpurse's remark that it would be as easy to gcld Cokes as to steal his purse (IV, iii, 105). Cokes is as susceptible to the craft of the cutpurse as he is to the fair's more 'legitimate' business, causing him to conclude that there's nothing 'but thieving and coz'ning i'this whole Fair' (IV, ii, 59–60), a statement that could apply as well to the early modern economy at large. While the addled Cokes is only mildly fazed by his surroundings, the fair more profoundly destabilises the identities of authority figures such as Zeal-of-the-Land Busy and Justice Overdo, each of whom finds himself confused and in the stocks during the course of the play. Like Cokes, these characters lack the temperance that conduct books encouraged men to cultivate in order to thrive in commercial settings, making them particularly susceptible to the allures of the marketplace and therefore incapable of maintaining either their reputations or their bodily boundaries.

A closer approximation of the temperate ideal is the chaste Grace Wellborn, Justice Overdo's ward, who proves capable of negotiating the fair's sexual and commercial economies. Unlike most city comedy heroines, however, Grace's confidence in her personal integrity arises not from a sense of essential purity or self-containment, but rather from her responsiveness to the commercial dynamics that shape her life. Grace's commodity potential is highlighted by her status as a ward of the court. By royal edict, Justice Overdo has acquired the right to arrange Grace's marriage or, if she refuses the match, to claim her lands or a payment of equal value. He intends to marry her to his brother-in-law, the foolish Cokes. In Grace's words, she came under Overdo's control 'through common calamity: he bought me' (III, v, 255). Grace's calamity is 'common' both because of the rampant commoditisation of women in the fair and because it reflects the dominant experience of marriageable women. However, by arranging her own marriage, Grace manages to manipulate this patriarchal reality, transforming her status as an object of exchange into a performance of chaste, agential selfhood.

Grace's experience is also common because men could become wards of the state as well. In this way, Grace's plight calls attention to the commercial forces shaping men's lives in addition to the lives of wellborn women. As Luce Irigaray contends, the patriarchal economy 'requires that women lend themselves to alienation in consumption, and to exchanges in which they do not participate, and that men be exempt from being used and circulated like commodities'.[42] Yet in *Bartholomew Fair*, as in early capitalist London more generally, men sensed that they were being commoditised as well; their value was being equated to their labour power in ways that resembled the virgin's reduction to pure exchange value. Grace's negotiation of her commodity status thereby informs understandings of masculine subjectivity in *Bartholomew Fair*, and her partial self-extraction from her bonds points to potential modes of subjectivity capable of accommodating commercial realities without fully succumbing to them.

Grace's frank acknowledgement of her commodity status paradoxically permits her to maintain a self-possession lacked by the other characters in the play. Rather than simply resisting the fair's commercial dynamics, as Overdo and Busy purport to do, Grace accommodates herself to them in order to cultivate a contingent autonomy. Conceding that 'they that cannot work their fetters off must wear'em' (III, v, 265), she manipulates her commodity status by allowing herself to be 'stolen' from Overdo by either Winwife or Quarlous, depending on which of the gallants wins a marriage lottery that she orchestrates. To determine the winner, Grace writes down names associated with each man, and asks the first person who walks by – who happens to be the madman Trouble-All – to choose the name that pleases him. A conflict that would have been resolved by duel in the romantic 'sword-and-buckler age of Smithfield' (Induction, 105) is now settled through a lottery-like contract, in which the pursued woman both gains and cedes control over her fate. To Grace, the element of chance imbues her marriage with some legitimacy, as leaving the decision to 'destiny' (IV, ii, 45–6) allows her to avoid selecting between two men whom she has only just met, 'both at one instant, and not yet of two hours' acquaintance, neither of you deserving afore the other of me' (IV, iii, 21–2).[43] Acknowledging her own commodity status as well as the fungibility of her male suitors, Grace's plan affords her more agency than she would have had either in an antiquated duel or as a ward of the state. This plan does not exemplify the brash autonomy of heroines such as Moll in *The Roaring Girl*, nor does it reflect the idealised purity of *Volpone*'s Celia. Instead, it demonstrates an agency formed within tight constraints, constraints that persist for the chaste woman even after she is married and control of her person and property is ceded to her husband.

By arranging the marriage lottery, Grace demonstrates the self-possession and discerning wit commonly associated with Jonson's male characters. Grace is not threatened by Winwife and Quarlous's entreaties, which they worry may cause her 'to doubt [her]self in [their] company' (III, v, 270–1). Indeed, she responds, 'I am so secure of mine own manners as I suspect not yours' (III, v, 273–4). Grace's self-assurance rests not only on her chastity but also on her wit. Explaining why she cannot simply choose between the two men, Grace requests of them, 'If you would not give it to my modesty, allow it yet to my wit; give me so much of woman, and cunning, as not to betray myself impertinently' (IV, iii, 25). As Adam Zucker argues, 'performances of wit, taste, and/or cultural competence are constantly in tension with and made meaningful by a vast field of objects, spaces, and knowledge that produced social power or make status recognizable'.[44] In contrast to plays such as *Epicoene*, the wit of *Bartholomew Fair*'s gallants is shared by that of a chaste woman, who is integral to their manipulation of the social order. Grace's wit differs from that of Quarlous and Winwife, however, because it is defined by her status as a commoditised ward destined to be married against her will.

By focusing on the chaste woman's position in *Bartholomew Fair*, Jonson shifts his emphasis from subjectivity forged through egalitarian male bonds to subjectivity based in the inequality of heterosexual marriage. Grace's status as a commodity is reinscribed at the end of the play, when

Quarlous reveals that he has manipulated Overdo's warrant to make himself Grace's guardian, proclaiming that, while Winwife has won the prize and is 'possessed o'the gentlewoman, . . . she must pay me value' (V, iv, 77–8). Here, as in *Epicoene*, *Bartholomew Fair* presents the triumph of male wit, born of the shared trickery of Winwife and Quarlous, the latter of whom James Mardock considers 'the character who comes closest to inhabiting and interpreting the space of the fair successfully'.[45] Yet this homosocial mastery is tempered in *Bartholomew Fair* by the alternate model presented by Grace, a woman who has chosen to marry a man in whom she has only marginal interest and who now must relinquish her land, or money of equal value, to another man with little legitimate right to it. Grace does not possess the social mastery of the male wits, but instead operates within the narrow confines of the commercial forces that subjugate her.

Grace constructs a contingent agency from within these strictures. She and Winwife forge a workable marriage that acknowledges but attempts to transcend Grace's commodity status. Winwife vows to make Grace 'think that in this choice she had both her eyes' (V, ii, 31–2), while Grace, possessing great faith in her powers of moral suasion, asserts that, 'if fate send me an understanding husband, I have no fear at all but mine own manners shall make him a good one' (IV, iii, 32–4). As this assurance makes clear, Grace retains some agency within the marriage, though it was not freely chosen. This agency arises largely from her intimate understanding of the social codes that shape her existence and which, in this case, will aid her in transforming her husband. Conversely, Winwife's clarity regarding his wife's lack of choice produces in him a desire to compensate for this circumstance and to make her feel as though she has chosen him freely. Grace's marriage thus illustrates the process by which a subject can acquire agency through submission to social forces over which he or she has little control.

Grace's married subjectivity disrupts dominant marital paradigms in which a woman's will is imagined to be fully subsumed by her husband's. By contrast, Grace's will remains distinct from her husband's, as she retains the prerogative to reform his manners. This residual autonomy is rooted in Grace's wilful acquiescence to the marriage that she herself orchestrated, an action that signals not passivity but active choice. Elucidating the problem of obedient female will, Schwarz contends that 'The gap between decree and execution requires an acquiescence that is deliberate and transactional rather than innate', and this 'willful acquiescence confounds the process of objectification as it answers the demand for compliance'.[46] Grace's marriage underscores the potentially transgressive nature of female conformity, as her will permits her to shape the conditions of her submission. Already adept at negotiating commercial strictures, Grace does not submit fully to the possessive bond of marriage; instead, she maintains a sense of her own ability to shape the arrangement.

As in most city comedy, *Bartholomew Fair* revises the subject-sovereign relationship asserted in dominant marriage discourse by presenting marriage as a commercial contract. However, in contrast to *Chaste Maid*, *Fair Maid* and *The Roaring Girl*, this contractual union does not supersede and thus manage other forms of exchange nor does it contain the desires produced by the marketplace. Rather, marriage epitomises the manifold exchanges in which the early capitalist subject must participate. As a subject in the early capitalist economy, Grace selects among subjugations, acquiring contingent agency through her choices and withholding aspects of herself from potentially subsuming bonds. Such a model of agential subjugation is fitting for a play in which state power, represented by Justice Overdo, is critiqued both as overreaching and as inadequately responsive to the complexities of commercial life. As Agnew suggests, '*Bartholomew*

Fair imagined the market as a power capable of generating its own legitimacy through a negotiated process of mutual authorization.'[47] Through Grace's travails, Jonson re-imagines patriarchal marriage in commercial terms, presenting it as an unequal business contract in which the subordinate member retains a degree of control and autonomy. The power of the husband is not absolute, as subjects enter into similar contracts with myriad buyers and sellers, debtors and creditors.

As a commercial subject, Grace acquires agency through her adept social performance and intimate understanding of commodity culture. Rather than insisting on the absolute identity of a chaste woman's essence and appearance, Grace acknowledges and manages potential gaps arising from her commoditised state. In this way, Grace is much like the temperate citizen of Scott's *An Essay of Drapery*, who adopts performative temperance as a means of regulating the relationship between outward appearance and inner essence. Similar to other conduct writers, Scott encourages the cultivation of a modest appearance, asserting that the 'the body, the outward carriage of it covers and uncovers the mind'.[48] Temperance becomes performative in Scott's commercial context, as it moderates the gap between being and seeming. This gap – which is often deemed sinful – is freely acknowledged in Scott's *Essay* as integral to commercial success. For example, in his advice to 'Flatter, but sin not, if that be possible', Scott suggests that 'Dissimulation is a thing more tolerable with a Citizen; it is with him as with one who hath married a wife, whom hee must use well, pretending affection to her, though hee cannot love her: and indeed Divines hold it in some cases lawfull, to pretend one thing and intend an other.'[49] As with the husband who pretends to love his wife, the dissembling merchant must ultimately serve the good, working in the interests of fair and honest trade. Temperance, in this example, not only helps the merchant retain moral integrity (flattering but not sinning), but also shapes his reputation as honest and creditable. Recognising that outward signs will be interpreted as reflecting a merchant's inner essence, Scott explores the ways that temperance may be used to cultivate a performance of self suitable to the London marketplace. In *Bartholomew Fair*'s exploration of commercial subjectivity, Jonson invokes the figure of the marriageable women to emphasise the ways in which the citizen himself resembles the commodities he sells. In so doing, Jonson reconfigures discourses of chastity, making the virtue more flexible, transactional and performative. Grace's chastity, therefore, becomes an active mode of being, a means of managing her own internal fissures and crafting a contingent agency that allows her to negotiate the commercial world around her.

This commercial subject – both in Scott's tract and in *Bartholomew Fair* – is defined not by the aristocratic ideal of absolute integrity but by a critical, discerning sensibility that permits him or her to analyse commercial contexts and to manipulate these contexts to his or her advantage. While this discernment is not dissimilar to that possessed by Jonson's wits, it arises from the subject's selective submission to compromising social forces rather than from a shared, masculine sense of mastery over them. This bourgeois self is more flexible – if ultimately less centred – than the stoic aristocratic self, capable of participating in, and even embracing, early capitalist commercial and social relations. But the bourgeois self is also imperfect, internally divided and therefore distanced from the social world. From this profound alienation, the keen critical sensibility of the commercial subject emerges.

First broached in the 'Articles of Agreement' with which the play begins, the relationship between commercial discernment and artistic evaluation is comically addressed in *Bartholomew Fair*'s puppet play. Like Nightingale's madrigals,

Littlewit's play is unabashedly commercial, with Leatherhead seeking to squeeze as much money from patrons as possible. The puppet play travesties the stories of *Hero and Leander* and *Damon and Pythias*, setting them in commercial London where Leander becomes a 'dyer's son' and Hero 'a wench o'th Bankside' (V, iii, 104–5). In the fair, the ability to assess theatrical quality is conflated with commercial discernment, as both the gullible Cokes and the Puritan Busy prove incapable of distinguishing the representations of the theatre from the events of real life. Ultimately, Grace proves to be the most perceptive interpreter of the puppet play, responding to Busy's accusations that the puppet show is idolatrous with the remark, 'I know no fitter match than a puppet to commit with an hypocrite' (V, v, 40–1).[50] The puppet, a commodity itself marked by a profound disjuncture between its essence and the role it plays, reveals a similar quality in the hypocritical Puritan. Whereas in many city comedies chastity is depicted either as a commodity or as a sign of personal integrity, Grace's commoditised subject status endows her with the critical distance needed to interpret the signs around her, theatrical and social as well as commercial. Those who lack these critical faculties are unable to distinguish signs from reality and are therefore incapable of evaluating products, including artistic productions.

The content of the puppet play – in which Damon and Pythias's homosocial friendship competes with and interrupts Hero and Leander's heterosexual love – comically reconfigures the dynamics of commercial subjectivity explored elsewhere in the play. As Laurie Shannon points out, the legend of Damon and Pythias, in which their unbreakable friendships reforms a tyrant, 'present[s] a humanist fantasy of the highest order and suggest[s] friendship's political sights' as a model of egalitarian personal sovereignty.[51] This fantasy, however, like the high romance of *Hero and Leander*, proves unsuitable in commercial London, where Damon and Pythias first fight over Hero and then, after growing 'friendly together' (V, iv, 227), turn their jealous ire against Leander and anyone who gets in their way, including the puppet master Leatherhead. Their homosocial friendship enjoys a limited triumph but ends in a violent brawl involving not only Leander but also Hero. The consensual sovereignty imagined in ideals of male friendship, so lauded in *Epicoene*, is unsettled in the Bankside, where subjects are always already subjected to commercial desires. Models of sovereignty and subjectivity based in heterosexual marriage are disrupted as well, with Hero gaining sufficient agency to participate in a bar fight. As in the main plot of *Bartholomew Fair*, models of heterosexual and homosocial subjectively coexist but without harmony.

By reflecting on its medium, the puppet play destabilises essentialist understandings of gender and reveals all potential subject positions to be performative. The chaos of the brawl is mediated by the puppet ghost of Dionysius, who arises from the dead to arrest the fighting and to refute Busy's accusations of idolatry. When Puppet Dionysius pulls up his skirts in response to Busy's contention that puppets 'are an abomination' (V, v, 83) because they cross-dress, he comments upon the vexed epistemologies of chastity interrogated in Grace's marriage plot. Here, the puppet satirises the desire to 'know' the essence of sexuality, to pin down chastity, gender or essence. At the same time, he calls attention to the apparent inability of hypocrites such as Busy to discern the basic facts of theatrical commodity culture. *Bartholomew Fair* thus reiterates *Epicoene*'s *coup de théâtre* but takes its critique of essentialised gender a step further: whereas *Epicoene* exposes the performativity of gender, Puppet Dionysius shows that there is literally nothing to see under the performance. In this sense, Puppet Dionysius embodies the performative subjectivity earlier exhibited by Grace. As with the puppet, there is no essential purity undergirding Grace's chastity – cultivated in response to commoditising forces and, in the final instance, called into being by a male actor and playwright.

Because of this reconfigured subjectivity, there is no sense in *Bartholomew Fair*, as there is in plays such as *The Fair Maid of the Exchange*, *The Roaring Girl* and *A Chaste Maid in Cheapside*, that marriage serves a uniquely ameliorative function. Instead, marriage is one contract among many to which Grace and her fellow fairgoers must submit. Rather than containing intemperate bodies in a transcorporeal approximation of stoic integrity, marriage simply leaves its participants to continue negotiating the early modern marketplace. The success of this negotiation depends upon the subject's awareness of his or her own commoditisation and the savvy discernment that permits one to assess and manipulate value in early capitalist London.

Chaste Agency, Commercial Discernment and the Rise of the Playwright as Author

As noted in Chapter 1, playwrights frequently evoke the transition from virginity to chaste marriage as a means of validating the representational and economic exchanges of the theatre and of distancing theatrical work from the taint of prostitution. City comedy alters this paradigm slightly, as playwrights invoke the chastity of figures such as Grace, Phillis and Moll (in her multiple iterations) to explore whether an individual can live in, and even profit from, a commercial society without compromising his or her personal integrity. Interrogations of chastity in these plays focus less on the institution of the theatre itself and more on emerging understandings of the capitalist subject, which was in many ways characterised by a newfound sense of theatrical performativity.

The figure of the chaste woman therefore bears some relation to the playwright, in so far as both capably navigate

London's commercial milieu while managing to remain somewhat above the fray. This parallelism is particularly evident in *The Roaring Girl*, where Moll echoes the protestations of playwrights as she purports to maintain contact with the underworld solely to warn audiences of its dangers. It is Jonson, though, with his metacritical engagement with city comedy and his preoccupation with authorship, who most fully pursues this connection. In *Bartholomew Fair*, I suggest, Grace's contingent agency and resulting critical discernment informs Jonson's presentation of his own role not just as playwright but as theatrical author.

Chastity, as Amy Greenstadt demonstrates, was central to emerging conceptions of authorship. Greenstadt claims that early modern authors often invoked Augustinian discussions of rape to indicate that their intentions remained pure no matter how their texts were treated as they circulated in print. As she contends, 'the notion that the writer's idea pre-exists and is independent of the physical text in which it is expressed closely parallels Augustine's account of the separation between the chaste woman's spiritual "will" and her physical body'.[52] In *Bartholomew Fair*, Jonson amends this model of authorial purity, conceiving of the theatrical author as a commoditised chaste woman, whose agency stems from the negotiation of commercial constraints. In so doing, Jonson does not distance his authorial intention from its material production, as he so frequently does, but instead creates an alternate model of authorial presence forged through selective acquiescence to the commercial dynamics that shape his plays and their reception. Taking seriously Grace Wellborn's complex subjectivity thus shifts our understanding of authorship in *Bartholomew Fair*, complicating Peter Stallybrass and Allon White's suggestion that, 'as "masterpoet" . . . Jonson constituted his identity in opposition to the theatre and the fair'.[53] In this light, the networks of patronage and commerce that Stallybrass and White regard as 'negated or denied elements' in the play become central to Jonson's articulation of early capitalist subjectivity and theatrical authorship.[54] Through Grace, Jonson articulates a performative authorial self that is shaped through commercial constraints rather than in opposition to them.

In both the Induction and the puppet play, Jonson links Grace's performative self to that of the playwright, whose agency similarly arises through his wilful adherence to and manipulation of the social and commercial codes that shape his enterprise.[55] Although the opening Articles of Agreement satirise commercial modes of assessing the theatre with their injunction that patrons may judge the play only according to the price they paid for admission, the articles also concede Jonson's imbrication within the market: 'It is further agreed that every person here have his or their freewill of censure, to like or dislike at their own charge; the author having now departed with his right, it shall be lawful for any man to judge his six penn'orth, so to his eighteen pence, two shillings, half a crown, to the value of his place – provided always his place get not above his wit' (Induction, 77–82). Here, Jonson grudgingly 'depart[s] with his right' to control the play, and transforms judgement into a commodity, a privilege purchased with admission. He attempts to manipulate commercial codes shaping theatrical reception, however, through his stipulation that the above promise holds only so long as a viewer's 'place get not above his wit'. Wit remains a prized quality that is associated with the playwright as much as with anyone else. It is capable of troubling the rigid social hierarchies the articles otherwise suggest, endowing its possessor with the ability to discern and manipulate social and commercial codes. Similar to Grace's assertion of agency in her marriage lottery, Jonson imagines his subjugated, commoditised state as the basis of his authorial agency. From this vantage point, the playwright can critique his society and demonstrate his superiority to it.

In the end, it seems fitting that Jonson, the striving court poet who doubled as a public playwright, should articulate a version of subjectivity suited to a commercial milieu. Even in *Bartholomew Fair*'s closing address to the king, which has been read as placing 'the author in opposition to . . . the theatre audience by an identification of his own judgment with the "power to judge" of the king', Jonson acquires authority through a process of subjugation similar to Grace's.[56] The king, rather than the author, possesses the power to

> tell
> If we have used that leave you gave us well;
> Or whether we to rage or licence break,
> Or be profane, or make profane men speak. (Epilogue, 6–9)

Moreover, Jonson's play as a whole suggests that he, like Grace, is subject to sovereign authority as well as to a range of commercial and social pressures.[57] As with Grace, whose future depends upon her successful negotiation of a fair she has 'no fancy . . . nor ambition to see' (I, v, 113), Jonson acknowledges the playwright's dependence on the market, an admission that contributes to the sense that *Bartholomew Fair* represents the culmination of 'a progressive easing of the unself-conscious disciplinary zeal that pervades [Jonson's] early satires'.[58]

By shifting his focus from homosocial friendship to heterosexual marriage in *Bartholomew Fair*, then, Jonson both negotiates new modes of subjectivity, formed through submission to social and commercial power, and explores new ways of framing relationships among playwrights, plays and audiences. In addition to endowing the playwright with flexible agency, Jonson imagines an ideal audience, a 'Commission of Wit' (Induction, 91), comprised of subjects such as Grace, subjects whose independent discernment parallels that of the author. Yet, as the Articles of Agreement indicate, Jonson suspects that his audience consists not only of apt critical consumers but also of figures such as Cokes and Busy who are liable to misunderstand and therefore to criticise his plays. It is in response to this less than ideal audience that Jonson attempts to circumscribe interpretive freedom, stipulating that audience members must critique not only on levels commensurate with the price of admission but also 'not above [their] wit'. Here, Jonson iterates his model of chaste subjectivity, though with a difference. In so doing, he attempts to tip the balance of power in favour of the theatrical producer. He positions himself not as a chaste, selectively obedient wife, but as a husband, imposing constraints through which audience members must forge their own critical sensibilities.

Notes

1. For a discussion of the disruptiveness of virginity in the masque, see Marie H. Loughlin, '"Love's Friend and Stranger to Virginitie": The Politics of the Virginal Body in Ben Jonson's *Hymenaei* and Thomas Campion's *The Lord Hay's Masque*', *English Literary History* 63.4 (1996): 833–49.
2. Ben Jonson, *Hymenaei, or the Solemnities of Masque and Barriers at a Marriage*, in *The Complete Masques*, The Yale Ben Jonson, ed. Stephen Orgel (New Haven: Yale University Press, 1969), 75–106, esp. l. 654, hereafter cited parenthetically. For discussions of Jonson's ideal of centred masculinity, see Thomas Greene, 'Ben Jonson and the Centered Self', *Studies in English Literature* 10.2 (1970): 325–48; Douglas Lanier, 'Masculine Silence: *Epicoene* and Jonsonian Stylistics', *College Literature* 21.2 (1994): 1–18; and Ann Christensen, 'Reconsidering Ben Jonson and the Centered Self', *South Central Review* 13.1 (1996): 1–17.
3. Greene, 'Ben Jonson and the Centered Self', 326.
4. For a discussion of the misogynist and homophobic basis of Jonsonian masculinity, see Lorna Hutson, 'Civility and Virility in Ben Jonson', *Representations* 78 (2002): 1–27.

5. Victoria Kahn, *Wayward Contracts: The Crisis of Political Obligation in England, 1640–1674* (Princeton: Princeton University Press, 2004).
6. Melissa E. Sanchez, *Erotic Subjects: The Sexuality of Politics in Early Modern English Literature* (New York: Oxford University Press, 2011).
7. See Jean E. Howard, '(W)holesaling: Bawdy Houses and Whore Plots in the Drama's Staging of London', in *Theater of a City: The Places of London Comedy, 1598–1642* (Philadelphia: University of Pennsylvania Press, 2007), 114–61, and Howard, 'Civic Institutions and Precarious Masculinity in Dekker's *The Honest Whore*', *Early Modern Culture: an Electronic Seminar* (2000), http://emc.eserver.org/1-1/howard.html (accessed 29 March 2015).
8. Karen Newman, 'City Talk: Femininity and Commodification in Jonson's *Epicoene*', in *Fashioning Femininity and English Renaissance Drama* (Chicago: University of Chicago Press, 1991), 129–43, esp. 138.
9. Elizabeth Hanson, 'There's Meat and Money Too: Rich Widows and Allegories of Wealth in Jacobean City Comedy', *English Literary History* 72.1 (2005): 209–38, esp. 210.
10. Shannon Miller, 'Consuming Mothers/Consuming Merchants: The Carnivalesque Economy of Jacobean City Comedy', *Modern Language Studies* 26.2/3 (1996): 73–97, esp. 96.
11. For the argument that depictions of women as unruly legitimate patriarchal control, see Gail Kern Paster, 'Leaky Vessels: The Incontinent Women of City Comedy', in *The Body Embarrassed: Drama and the Disciplines of Shame in Early Modern England* (Ithaca, NY: Cornell University Press, 1993), 23–63, and Mario DiGangi, 'Sexual Slander and Working Women in *The Roaring Girl*', *Renaissance Drama* 32 (2003): 147–76.
12. Richard Brathwaite, *The English Gentleman* (London: 1630), Folger copy, 335.
13. Henry Peacham, *Complete Gentleman. With an Introduction by G. S. Gordon*, ed. Henry Frowde (London: The Clarenden Press, 1906), 221.

14. William Scott, *An Essay of Drapery: or The Compleate Citizen. Trading Justly, Pleasingly, Profitably* (London, 1635), 126; 142–3, Folger copy.
15. Scott, *An Essay of Drapery*, 126.
16. Brathwaite, *The English Gentleman*, 316.
17. Brathwaite, *The English Gentleman*, 313.
18. Robert Green, *Penelope's Web* (London, 1601), 23, http://www.oxford-shakespeare.com/Greene/Penelopes_Web.pdf (accessed 11 January 2016).
19. For a Middleton's use of grotesque, open bodies to interrogate the effects of the early capitalist economy, see Seung-Hee Roe, 'The Economy of the Grotesque Body in *A Chaste Maid in Cheapside*', *Feminist Studies in English Literature* 7.2 (2000): 187–219. See also Paster, 'Leaky Vessels', for a discussion of incontinent bodies in *Chaste Maid*. Whereas Paster contrasts this female incontinence to men's more powerful, productive release of semen, I suggest that Middleton draws a parallel between male and female incontinence.
20. Thomas Middleton, *A Chaste Maid in Cheapside*, ed. Alan Brissenden, New Mermaids, 2nd edn (New York: W. W. Norton, 2002), II, i, 8–9, hereafter cited parenthetically.
21. As Douglas Bruster argues, the cuckold myth was central to theorisations of nascent capitalism, as 'the cuckold's patience translated readily into images of commercial investment' ('The Horn of Plenty: Cuckoldry and Capital in the Drama of the Age of Shakespeare', *Studies in English Literature, 1500–1900* 30.2 [1990]: 195–215, esp. 210).
22. Karen Newman, '"Goldsmith's ware": Equivalence in *A Chaste Maid in Cheapside*', *Huntington Library Quarterly* 71.1 (2008): 97–113, esp. 113.
23. [Thomas Heywood], *The Fair Maid of the Exchange*, the Malone Society reprints, prepared by Peter H. Davidson and Arthur Brown (Oxford: Oxford University Press, 1962), 127, hereafter cited parenthetically.
24. For alternate readings of the play's economic themes, see Juana Green, 'The Sempster's Wares: Merchandising and Marrying in the Fair Maid of the Exchange (1607)', *Renaissance Quarterly*

53.4 (2000): 1084–118, and Richard Waswo, 'Crisis of Credit: Monetary and Erotic Economies in the Jacobean Theater', in *Plotting Early Modern London: New Essays on Jacobean City Comedy*, ed. Dieter Mehl, Angela Stock and Anne-Julia Zwierlein (Burlington, VT: Ashgate, 2004), 55–73, esp. 60–4.
25. Thomas Middleton and Thomas Dekker, *The Roaring Girl*, ed. Elizabeth Cook, New Mermaids, 2nd edn (New York: W. W. Norton, 1997), I, ii, 130–1, hereafter cited parenthetically. For a discussion of Moll's complex sexual identity, including her status as a mythically complete hermaphrodite, see Susan E. Krantz, 'The Sexual Identities of Moll Cutpurse in Dekker and Middleton's *The Roaring Girl*', *Renaissance and Reformation* 19.1 (1995): 5–20, esp. 8.
26. Jonathan Gil Harris, *Sick Economies: Drama, Mercantilism, and Disease in Shakespeare's England* (Philadelphia: University of Pennsylvania Press, 2004), 177.
27. See Valerie Forman, 'Marked Angels: Counterfeits, Commodities, and *The Roaring Girl*', *Renaissance Quarterly* 54.4 (2001): 1531–60; Heather Hirschfeld, 'What Do Women Know? *The Roaring Girl* and the Wisdom of Tiresias', *Renaissance Drama* 32 (2003): 123–46; and Ryan Singh Paul, 'The Power of Ignorance and *The Roaring Girl*', *English Literary Renaissance* 43.3 (2013): 514–40.
28. Ben Jonson, *Volpone*, ed. Brian Parker and David Bevington (Manchester: Manchester University Press, 1999), III, vii, 37, hereafter cited parenthetically.
29. Ben Jonson, *Epicoene, or the Silent Woman*, ed. Roger Holdsworth, New Mermaids (New York: W. W. Norton, 1979), V, iii, 48–50, hereafter cited parenthetically.
30. See Mark Albert Johnston, 'Prosthetic Absence in Ben Jonson's *Epicoene*, *The Alchemist*, and *Bartholomew Fair*', *English Literary Renaissance* 37.3 (2007): 401–28, esp. 409, for the links between Dauphine's masculinity and his financial solvency.
31. For the gender coding of commodity culture, see Newman, 'City Talk', and Marjorie Swann, 'Refashioning Society in Ben Jonson's England', *Studies in English Literature* 38.2 (1998): 297–315, esp. 302.

32. For an analysis of the commercial dimensions of the blazon, see Patricia Parker, 'Rhetorics of Property: Exploration, Inventory, Blazon', in *Literary Fat Ladies: Rhetoric, Property, and Gender* (New York: Methuen, 1987), 126–54.
33. For a full discussion of the word *epicoene* as referring not only to a noun that 'can equally and correctly denote something of either sex', but also 'to something or someone lacking fixed gender characteristics, possessing too many gender characteristics, or veering into the wrong gender role', see Mimi Yiu, 'Sounding the Space between Men: Choric and Choral Cities in Ben Jonson's *Epicoene; or, The Silent Woman*', PMLA 121.1 (2007): 72–88, esp. 72.
34. Ari Friedlander, 'Mastery, Masculinity, and Sexual Cozening in Ben Jonson's *Epicoene*', *Studies in English Literature, 1500–1900* 53.2 (2013): 379–99.
35. For critics who read this scene as reflective of *Epicoene*'s conservative gender politics, see Lorraine Helms, 'Roaring Girls and Silent Women: The Politics of Androgyny on the Jacobean Stage', in *Women in Theatre*, ed. James Redmond (Cambridge: Cambridge University Press, 1989), 59–73, esp. 70; Jean E. Howard, 'Crossdressing, the Theatre, and Gender Struggle in Early Modern England', *Shakespeare Quarterly* 39.4 (1988): 418–40, esp. 429; Laura Levine, 'Theatre as Other: Jonson's *Epicoene*', in *Men in Women's Clothing: Antitheatricality and Effeminization 1579–1642* (New York: Cambridge University Press, 1994), 73–88; and Phyllis Rackin, 'Androgyny, Mimesis, and the Marriage of the Boy Heroine on the English Renaissance Stage', PMLA 102.1 (1987): 29–41, esp. 36. For the argument that *Epicoene* destabilises essentialist ideas of gender, see Richmond Barbour, '"When I Acted Young Antinous": Boy Actors and the Erotics of Jonsonian Theatre', PMLA 110.5 (1995): 1006–22, and Yiu, 'Sounding the Space'.
36. Lorna Hutson, 'Liking Men: Ben Jonson's Closet Opened', *English Literary History* 71.4 (2004): 1065–96. For models of personal sovereignty based in male friendship, see Laurie Shannon, *Sovereign Amity: Figures of Friendship in*

Shakespearean Contexts (Chicago: University of Chicago Press, 2002).

37. Kathryn Schwarz, *What You Will: Gender, Contract, and Shakespearean Social Space* (Philadelphia: University of Pennsylvania Press, 2011), 3.
38. For discussions of the fair as encapsulating emerging market dynamics, see Peter Stallybrass and Allon White, 'The Fair, the Pig, Authorship', in *The Politics and Poetics of Transgression* (Ithaca, NY: Cornell University Press, 1986), 27–79, as well as Paul Cantor, 'In Defense of the Marketplace: Spontaneous Order in Jonson's *Bartholomew Fair*', *Ben Jonson Journal* 8 (2001): 23–64.
39. Jean-Christophe Agnew, *Worlds Apart: The Market and the Theater in Anglo-American Thought, 1550–1750* (Cambridge: Cambridge University Press, 1986), 47.
40. For discussions of Ursla's economic dimensions, see Stallybrass and White, 'The Fair, the Pig, Authorship', 63–6.
41. Ben Jonson, *Bartholomew Fair*, ed. G. R. Hibbard, New Mermaids (London: A&C Black, 2007), II, v, 65, hereafter cited parenthetically.
42. Luce Irigaray, *This Sex Which is Not One*, trans. Catherine Porter with Carolyn Burke (Ithaca, NY: Cornell University Press, 1985), 172.
43. Richard Waswo reads this scene as 'explicitly analyz[ing] the interchangeability of suitors, the irrelevance of individual will, and the replacement of reason by chance' ('Crisis of Credit', 64).
44. Adam Zucker, 'The Social Logic of Ben Jonson's *Epicoene*', *Renaissance Drama* 33 (2004): 37–62, esp. 55. For more on the role of wit in *Bartholomew Fair*, particularly in relation to questions of legal judgment, see Andrew Brown, 'Theatre of Judgment: Space, Spectators, and the Epistemologies of Law in *Bartholomew Fair*', *Early Theatre* 15.2 (2012): 154–67.
45. James Mardock, *Our Scene is London: Ben Jonson's City and the Space of the Author* (New York: Routledge, 2008), 105.
46. Schwarz, *What You Will*, 3, 6–7.
47. Agnew, *Worlds Apart*, 120.
48. Scott, *An Essay of Drapery*, 87.
49. Scott, *An Essay of Drapery*, 26–7.

50. Some editions of the play, such as Gordon Campbell, ed., *The Alchemist and Other Plays: Volpone, or the Fox; Epicene, or the Silent Woman; The Alchemist; Bartholomew Fair*, by Ben Jonson (Oxford: Oxford University Press, 1998), follow the Folio in attributing this line to Quarlous. Hibbard joins editors such as Eugene M. Waith (*Bartholomew Fair* [New Haven: Yale University Press, 1963]), Martin Butler (*The Selected Plays of Ben Jonson*, vol. 2 [Cambridge: Cambridge University Press, 1989]), and Michael Jamieson (*Volpone and Other Plays* [London: Penguin, 1966; rprt. 2004]) in attributing the line to Grace, as Quarlous has already left the stage. Hibbard suggests that the compositor may have misread GRA as QVA (Jonson, *Bartholomew Fair*, 180n).
51. Shannon, *Sovereign Amity*, 8.
52. Amy Greenstadt, *Rape and the Rise of the Author: Gendering Intention in Early Modern England* (Burlington, VT: Ashgate, 2009), xi.
53. Stallybrass and White, 'The Fair, the Pig, Authorship', 77.
54. Stallybrass and White, 'The Fair, the Pig, Authorship', 76.
55. For a related argument that Jonson develops a specifically theatrical form of authorship in *Bartholomew Fair*, grounded in the playwright's mastery over geographic and social space, see Mardock, *Our Scene is London*, 95–109.
56. Don Wayne, 'Drama and Society in the Age of Jonson: An Alternative View', *Renaissance Drama* 13 (1982): 103–29, esp. 118. This Epilogue was likely performed at the court performance following *Bartholomew Fair*'s opening night at the Hope Theatre. For further discussion of the play's performance and print history and its bearing on Jonson's representations of authorship and theatre, see Leah Marcus, 'Ben Jonson's Bartholomew Fair: Of Mire and Authorship', in *The Theatrical City: Culture, Theatre, and Politics in London, 1576–1649*, ed. David L. Smith, Richard Strier and David Bevington (New York: Cambridge University Press, 1995), 170–81.
57. Stallybrass and White, 'The Fair, the Pig, Authorship', 74.
58. Katharine Eisaman Maus, *Inwardness and Theater in the English Renaissance* (Chicago: University of Chicago Press, 1995), 155.

CHAPTER 4

CHASTITY AND BLACKNESS: RACIAL VALUE AND COMMODITY POTENTIAL IN *THE FAIR MAID OF THE WEST, PART I* AND *OTHELLO*

Like the chaste female body, the black body becomes a locus of concern regarding commoditisation and subjecthood in early modern England. African slavery contributed to a growing association between blackness and personal commodity potential. England's involvement in the African slave trade, though covert, intensified during the late sixteenth century, as English merchants sought to break Portugal's control over the region.[1] Though English policy officially opposed slavery, Elizabeth I provided material support for John Hawkins's slave-trading voyages in 1562, 1564 and 1567.[2] In addition, a sizeable number of black Africans lived in England around the turn of the seventeenth century, a presence attested to by Elizabeth I's attempts to deport them in 1596 and 1601.[3] Recent scholarship has revealed that many of these black residents were considered property, their condition tantamount to slavery.[4] As Imtiaz Habib has demonstrated, slave ownership was 'informal and surreptitious' in early modern England but became increasingly prevalent between 1550 and 1660.[5] The question of African slavery, then, was not a distant one for the English, even in the nascent stages of the transatlantic slave trade, but was rather a local concern, as Africans laboured in bonded servitude, subject to personal commoditisation more intense than – but still uncomfortably similar to – that facing white English workers. Because they were often regarded as property, blacks in early modern England bore a particular relation to the increasingly powerful commodity form.

Recent scholarship has emphasised the complexity of race in the early modern period and, in doing so, offers a corrective to the view that race as such did not exist prior to the burgeoning of the slave trade and the advent of scientific racism. As Lara Bovilsky contends, 'early modern racial logics have much in common with modern and contemporary ones, including most of all those elements that make racial identities unstable and incoherent'.[6] 'The new emphasis on racial fluidity', according to Ian Smith, 'has not only increased our awareness of multiple sites of racialization, but also underscored the significance of nonbiological or nonphenotypical codes'.[7] Race in the early modern period therefore is defined in relation to categories such as religion, nationality, class, geography and language. In this chapter, I suggest that capitalist forces of commoditisation also inform emerging racial logics, influencing which racial identities are considered indicative of the capacity to attain subject status, often defined in terms of performative, partially commoditised personhood, and, alternately, which identity categories deem one suitable for fully objectified commodity status. On the early modern stage, interrogations of racial subjectivity and commoditisation often occur in relation to representations of chastity, a category with deep racial as well as economic implications.

In discussing his slaving voyages, Hawkins exhibits little worry over African personhood. He largely lumps Africans in with his other goods and reports that he 'had peaceable traffic' in Hispaniola and 'made vent of the whole number of his Negroes, for which he received ... by way of exchange such quantity of merchandise that he did not only lade his own three ships with hides, gingers, sugars, and some quantity of pearls, but he freighted also two other hulks with hides and other like commodities, which he sent into Spain'.[8] Elizabeth I's proclamations expelling Africans from England are somewhat more nuanced than Hawkins's reports and present Africans as occupying a space somewhere between potential subjects and objects of exchange. In her 1596 letter to the Lord Mayor of London, Elizabeth complains that 'there are of late diverse blackamoors brought into this realm, of which kind of people there are already here too many, considering how God hath blessed this land with great increase of people of our own nation as any country in the world, whereof many want of service and means to set them work for idleness and to great extremity'.[9] Although Elizabeth presents the Africans as lacking agency, having been 'brought into this realm' rather than coming of their own accord, they are also revealed to fulfil service roles as capably as their English counterparts, who are left in 'idleness' and 'extremity'. In contrast to the English servants, however, the Africans are presented as suitable for slavery if they are not already slaves. Elizabeth requests that Englishmen possessing Africans relinquish them to the German merchant Caspar van Senden, who had recently rescued eighty-nine prisoners from Spain, in exchange for which 'he only desireth to have license to take up so much blackamoors here in this realm and transport them into Spain and Portugal'.[10] The queen 'doubts not' that Englishmen possessing Africans 'shall do charitably and like Christians rather to be served by their own countrymen then with those kind of people, will yield those in their possession to [van Senden]', whereupon the Africans will presumably be sold into slavery in Spain and Portugal.[11] This arrangement not only attests to the racist and xenophobic objectification of Africans, also present in Hawkins's report, but also points toward the potential adequation of Africans both to English servants, with whom they complete for employment, and to English soldiers, who are in a sense traded for Africans in what Elizabeth describes as a 'a very good exchange'.[12]

Concern over emerging capitalist labour relations underlies Elizabeth's deportation of Africans and informs English discussions of slavery more broadly, as capitalism disrupted traditional networks of service and obligation and seemed to commoditise the labour and bodies of all workers. As David Hawkes contends, early moderns were influenced by the Classical perspective in which 'the condition of a wage worker had been regarded as comparable, and if anything inferior, to that of a slave. Both groups were sold for money – slaves in their entirety, proletarians piecemeal – and both consequently suffered a degrading legal and psychological reification.'[13] Drained of their civic value and individuality by commoditisation, slaves were considered more thing than person, associated with bodily labour rather than with mental capacity. Early moderns identified and were troubled by a similar reification in the wage labourer. Writing in 1656, for example, John Moore complains that 'inclosers' purchase 'the poore for silver . . . make chaffer and merchandize of them for gain and profit: they use them as they doe their beasts, keep them or put them off for advantage: then buy them, and sell them, as may best serve their turns to get by them'.[14] The exploitation of labour, Moore's statement indicates, leads to the broader objectification and bestialisation of the workers themselves. Comparisons between slaves and wage labourers thus provide a means of thinking through capitalism's objectifying effects. They also inform early modern ideas of racial difference, as the English attempt to establish an ontological difference between black slaves and white wage labourers.

Female chastity factors into the theatre's presentation of racial difference, functioning both as a symbol of purity and as a commoditised form of personhood. As Kim Hall demonstrates, early modern racial thinking was conducted in gendered terms, with anxieties about foreign contamination often expressed through portrayals of black men having or pursuing sexual relationships with white women.[15] In this context, women's chaste fairness becomes associated with racial whiteness. Noting that the racial implications of the word 'fair' arise in concert with England's colonial expansion, Hall argues that depictions of interracial desire negotiate questions of sexual and commercial intercourse.[16] As such, she contends, 'women's bodies become the site of struggle between, on the one hand, the need for both colonial trade and cultural assimilation through union and, on the other, the desire for well recognized boundaries between self and other'.[17] Chastity's commodity status informs this question of cultural and mercantile exchange due to its potential to operate as an object to be traded cross-culturally, while also maintaining its status as a sign of racial and national purity. As a form of commoditised personhood, moreover, chastity informs emerging racial taxonomies emerging out of the institutions of slavery and wage labour.

This chapter examines Thomas Heywood's *The Fair Maid of the West, Part I* and William Shakespeare's *Othello* (both written between 1601 and 1604), two plays that situate female chastity within multiracial Mediterranean environments characterised by commercial and cultural traffic, including traffic in human bodies.[18] Whereas the plays I have discussed until this point invoke chastity to interrogate English male value, *Fair Maid* and *Othello* turn their gaze toward assessments of foreign men, juxtaposing black masculinity with female chastity as a means of weighing black men's commodity potential against their subject potential. Reading *Othello* in conjunction with *Fair Maid*, I argue, illuminates how conceptions of chastity-as-subject and chastity-as-object converge in English assessments of racial value, and how, ultimately, white workers' displacement of their own commodity status onto black men and white women contributes to the formation of the racist ideologies that justified the slave trade.

Drawing on the paradigm dominant in city comedy, *Fair Maid* depicts female chastity as an agential subject position suited for negotiating a commercial milieu. By translating this paradigm to the context of international trade, *Fair Maid* renders chastity a more overtly white, English virtue, with the protagonist Bess, who is named after Elizabeth I, representing the power and purity of the nation state. In this setting, the failings of the lascivious Moors mirror the lack of personal integrity exhibited by English men in the international marketplace, and, like the English men, the Moorish Mullisheg is redeemed by Bess's mystical chastity. As such, Mullisheg is given the opportunity to assimilate, at least partially, into the English cultural sphere on the condition that he serve the economic interests of the state. With its comparison between chaste and racialised commercial subjectivity, I argue, *Fair Maid* anticipates a liberal cosmopolitanism in which racialised men are accepted as people rather than as objects but are afforded only provisional subject status.

Othello interrogates the relationship between chastity and blackness to expose the vulnerable position of black men within this model. Drawing on his own status as a commoditised worker, Iago supplants *Fair Maid*'s assimilationist paradigm, which might permit a Moor to rise to high standing and even marry a white woman, with an alternate discourse that emphasises chastity's commodity status and then assesses racialised men in similar terms. In this model, racialised 'others' do not acquire agency through their subjugation to the economic interests of the state, but are instead assessed as commodities. As such, they are deemed incapable of attaining the flexible, commercial subjectivity available to white men and are instead conceived as objects, defined by their black bodies and assumed to possess little interiority. In this way, *Othello* dramatises the logic by which commercial ideologies disrupt claims to intrinsic personal virtue and by which external traits – not only of blackness but also of whiteness – are transformed into signifiers of essential racial value.

Chaste Ventures and Liberal Multiculturalism in The Fair Maid of the West, *Part I*

The Fair Maid of the West, Part I, subtitled *A Girl Worth Gold*, follows the city comedy convention in which the protagonist's chastity allows her to navigate commercial contexts without compromising her personal integrity. Reminiscent of her namesake Elizabeth I, Bess's self-contained, virginal body endows her with the autonomy necessary to navigate the economic sphere – first as a tavern maid and then as a ship captain on the high seas. Her ability to retain her chastity counters the aristocratic allegation that involvement in commerce sullies one's character and inspires sexual promiscuity. Early in the play, patrons marvel that Bess remains chaste despite her job as a barmaid. As one gentleman asks, 'Honest, and live there? / What, in a public tavern, where's such confluence / Of lusty and brave gallants?'[19] Bess attends to her patrons, many of whom have travelled great distances to witness her beauty, joking with them and even kissing them, but she goes no further. In short, Bess conforms to Donald Lupton's description of a barmaid in *London and the Country carbonadoed and quartered into several characters*: 'Shee must bee Courteous to all, though not by Nature, yet by her Profession; for shee must entertaine all, good and bad.'[20] As Lupton advises, the barmaid who 'will kisse handsomely at parting' provides 'a good shooing-Horne or Birdlime to draw the Company thither againe the sooner'.[21] Though a sexually attractive character, Bess remains virtuous, drawing a firm line between her professional obligations and her personal sexual commitments. Because of this exceptional ability, Bess's chastity is fetishised as immensely powerful; as Jean Howard observes, 'Bess emerges as an exception to her sex, a paragon of modesty and faithfulness. As such she functions as a unifying symbol of the nation and as a catalyst to transform and perfect the men around her.'[22]

As in many city comedies, Bess's sexual temperance is linked to her prudent financial sensibility, particularly her ability to guard money. Sexual and financial economies converge in the pact she makes with her truelove, Spenser, who declines to marry her because of her low class status but who nonetheless entrusts her with his wealth and his tavern before departing for sea (after killing a man who questions Bess's honour). Following Spenser's advice that she 'join to

[her] beauty virtue' (I, iii, 56), Bess agrees to guard Spenser's possessions, including her chastity, vowing:

> Let me recollect myself
> And what he left in charge, virtue and chastity;
> ... All these will I conserve
> And keep them strictly as I would my life.   (I, iii, 85–9)

An impenetrable fortress, Bess's self-contained body operates as a kind of vault, protecting Spenser's wealth. Rather than cloister herself, however, Bess engages in financial, personal and cultural exchange in her new occupation as a tavern mistress. Her virtue and beauty engender profits; as she sums up her situation, 'For money flows / And my gain's great' (II, i, 148–9). As a chaste entrepreneur, Bess embodies the bourgeois ethos that virtue can be profitable and, alternately, that business can be virtuous. As such, she serves as a model of masculine integrity, showing men how to behave if they hope to protect their personal and national assets.

As the plot progresses, *Fair Maid* extends this paradigm to explore the function of chaste subjectivity in international contexts, where chastity serves not simply as an analogue to English, masculine selfhood but also as a repository of English national and racial purity. These racial and nationalistic elements are highlighted when Bess buys a ship, evocatively named the *Negro*, and heads to sea, mistakenly believing that Spenser has died and hoping to avenge his murder. The ship's name, as Howard argues, not only evokes that of a slave ship but also 'suggests that the construction of Englishness depends on the simultaneous construction of what is non-English'.[23] Bess's chastity becomes the locus of this national identity, allowing her to successfully pilot the *Negro*. With her purity affirmed after she resists the attempts of Spenser's friend Goodlack to seduce her, Bess navigates Spanish and Eastern climes considered hostile to English femininity, showing that she can resist sexual, economic and cultural corruption. On the high seas, Bess's chastity works not only in her own personal financial interests but also in the economic interests of the English nation, blending piracy with more accepted commercial practices.[24] When she conquers Spanish and Turkish ships, for example, their captains willingly submit to her authority and by extension to the authority of the English monarch, under whose auspices she operates.

The play's racial investments become most clear when Bess arrives at the court of the Moorish King Mullisheg, where her adventures culminate after she learns that Spenser has been captured by a Spanish sailing ship en route to Barbary. The residents of Mullisheg's court universally respect Bess's chaste authority, economic as well as moral, and, upon seeing her, Mullisheg exclaims, 'Ay, there's a girl worth gold' (IV, v, 19). His words are telling, as Bess acts as a standard throughout the play, delimiting value, and, more literally, procuring gold on behalf of the English nation. Presented as subordinate allies, less evil than the Spanish but perhaps less sophisticated as well, the Moors in *Fair Maid* conform to depictions of Moorish trading partners in travel narratives.[25] From this perspective, Moors appear not simply as agreeable partners but also as incompetent businessmen willing to submit uncritically to English dominance.

Having gained Mullisheg's favour, Bess uses the opportunity to negotiate provisions for her men and her ship. When asked to preside over trials of international merchants accused of breaking trade laws, she effectively opens Barbary's markets to English merchants. Prior to that point, Mullisheg had hoped to replenish his public treasury, which had been depleted by war, by taxing foreign merchants, forcing 'Those Christians that reap profit by our land' to 'contribute unto so great a loss' (IV, iii, 25–6). To remedy this imbalance, the Moors demand that Christian merchants who conceal any portion of the custom 'Shall forfeit ship and goods' (IV, iii, 19). Rather than upholding these laws, which work to balance power between Moors and Europeans, Bess asks for clemency for Christian merchants and rescues a preacher who has been attempting to convert Muslims. Advocating specifically for England's national interests, moreover, Bess secures exclusive trading rights for the English in Barbary on the grounds that they are morally superior to the Spanish.

Bess's dealings with the Moors provoke anxieties about cross-cultural intercourse. As Daniel Vitkus contends, 'Her exchange with Mullisheg is a microcosmic version of England's trade with Barbary and with Muslims, and thus the text indicates England's newly promiscuous status in the Mediterranean economy.'[26] Bess's compliance with Mullisheg's request for a kiss raises similar anxieties as did her kisses with English patrons, but with an added racial dimension. Her servant, Clem, dwells on Mullisheg's dark skin, citing the fabled impossibility of washing an Ethiop white in his comment, 'May'st thou never want sweet water to wash thy black face in, most mighty monarch of Morocco' (V, ii, 64–5). When Mullisheg kisses Bess, Clem recoils, asking, 'Must your black face be smooching my mistress's white lips with a Moorian? I would you had kiss'd her a–' (V, ii, 80–1). Clem's anxiety suggests that Bess's congeniality has exceeded the bounds of propriety and that free cultural exchange may lead to racial contamination.[27] Redirecting Clem's racist xenophobia, however, Bess emphasises the possibility of chaste, controlled exchange with Barbary, insisting, ''Tis no immodest thing / . . . for Bess to kiss a king' (V, i, 65–6). Like the virgin Queen for whom she is named, Bess maintains her sexual integrity but extends her blessings to men of all countries, deploying these interactions for her nation's gain.

In addition to serving as a metonym for her country's impenetrable integrity, Bess acts as a model for English men who find it difficult to manage the temptations and dangers of international exchange. In *Fair Maid*, as Barbara Sebek notes, Barbary is presented 'as a place of dangerous eroto-commercial, cross-cultural commerce' where 'men's bodies are potentially as commodifiable and woundable as those of women'.[28]

The compromising, effeminising threat of Eastern trade is graphically illustrated in the Moors' castration of Clem and their attempt to castrate Spenser, a fate from which Bess saves him. Bess is once again figured as preserving England's wealth from acquisitive foreigners who wish 'to rob a man of his best jewels' (V, ii, 127), but her literal protection of Spenser's bodily integrity also points to her broader role in redeeming British masculinity and differentiating it from the sexual – and racialised – perversity of Eastern trading partners.[29]

In many respects, then, *Fair Maid* follows the conventional course of city comedy, invoking militant female chastity to model idealised English masculinity and to reform the many men who fail to reach this ideal. Where *Fair Maid* departs from this traditional paradigm is in its suggestion that black men may be similarly reformed by Bess's influence and that they therefore may be assimilated into England's socio-economic sphere so long as they serve English interests.[30] Although Mullisheg transforms into an evil, monstrous Moor in *Fair Maid of the West, Part II*, written significantly later, his failings in *Part I* are less severe than those of the malicious Spaniards and hardly more grievous than those of the English, who show themselves to be at various times lustful, weak and effeminate.[31] Like the English men, Mullisheg is reformed by Bess's chastity, and he ultimately becomes an ally to England. As such, Mullisheg is ostensibly offered access to an English masculine subjectivity, formed through submission to chaste national power. He shows himself to be amenable to this paradigm by bestowing treasure on Bess and Spenser, a tangible representation of the mercantile wealth the English will gain through trade with pliable Eastern partners. Marvelling at Bess and Spenser's constancy, Mullisheg prepares them a wedding so extravagantly gilded that 'wheresoe'er [Bess's] fame shall be enroll'd, / The world report thou art a girl worth gold' (V, ii, 152–3). Mullisheg's response to Bess's chastity thus mitigates fears about the loss of English bullion in overseas ventures, ensuring that monetary value returns to

England, where the 'streets / Glister with gold' (I, i, 11–12). Mullisheg is only marginally accepted as an English ally, however, allotted provisional subject status, and he is thereby removed from sexual exchange. Bess's proven chastity – by this point unambiguously coded as white – ensures that she and Spenser will produce English heirs, who will presumably carry on their nation's economic pursuits. With the proper balance of restraint and exchange, Bess's adventure indicates that sexual and economic wealth will return to England, its yields multiplied. Bess, the girl worth gold, becomes the transcendental signifier of proper conduct, to which men from all nations must aspire.

With this arrangement, *Fair Maid* sets forth a proto liberal, multiculturalist paradigm in which non-white men (the play ignores non-white women) may be assimilated on the condition that they serve the interests of the state. These men thus occupy a vulnerable and marginal position, both within English culture and as trading partners, as any perceived transgression warrants their exclusion. In this, their position resembles that of the black labourers whose continued residency in England depends upon sustained demand for their work.[32] They also resemble the women to whom they are continually compared on the early modern stage, accepted only as unequal members of society and denied full subject status. Nonetheless, the threatening possibility that black men might fully assimilate and gain equality with white men lurks behind *Fair Maid*'s interracial kiss, and Mullisheg is embraced only to the extent that he respects the sacred chastity of English women and imposes on himself a similar restraint, at least where white English women are concerned. It is this anxiety, engendered by an assimilationist model of racial subjectivity, to which Shakespeare's *Othello* responds, as it interrogates the tenuous position of the assimilated black man as well as the discursive links between female chastity and black male value upon which his marginal subject status depends.

Chastity and Racial Objectification in Othello

A similar paradigm of racial inclusion permits Othello's incorporation into Venetian life, as the dominant society values his service to the state and accepts him as long as he follows expected codes of behaviour. As Habib argues, Othello's status is dependent upon the need for his labour, and in this sense he resembles the black Africans that Elizabeth I sought to deport.[33] The animosity directed at Othello may therefore result less from his status as an outsider as from the prospect that he may gain insider subject status, a possibility made more likely by his desired union to Desdemona.[34] *Othello*, in this sense, begins where *Fair Maid* leaves off by testing the effects of miscegenation on an assimilationist model that purports to embrace cultural and racial diversity. Although *Fair Maid* authorises casual contact between the English and black foreigners, the spectre of miscegenation troubles the play's assertion that the power of English chastity can reform and even assimilate black men. This spectre is unleashed in *Othello*, as Othello's interracial relationship with Desdemona compromises his tenuous subject status, unleashing the Venetians' racism.

Desdemona initially adopts a perspective influenced by the international romance tradition of which *Fair Maid* is a part, arguing that her chaste love may mirror, legitimate or even create a similarly virtuous subjectivity in Othello. Adhering to this framework, Desdemona insists that her love confirms Othello's worth, corroborating the Duke's assessment that he 'is far more fair than black' within a racist moral binary.[35] As she makes known her desire to accompany Othello to Cyprus, she explains,

> My heart's subdued
> Even to the very quality of my lord:
> I saw Othello's visage in his mind,
> And to his honours and his valiant parts
> Did I my soul and fortunes consecrate.   (I, iii, 251–5)

Desdemona submits herself to Othello's entire person, his blackness as well as his military status. Yet her location of his 'visage' in his 'mind' suggests that his intellect and virtue override his black face, permitting her to dedicate herself not only to his 'honours' but also to his 'valiant parts', a category that encompasses his physical as well as moral qualities. Desdemona's use of the word 'consecrate', moreover, associatively suggests that her soul may make sacred those qualities in Othello that would otherwise be considered abject. Attempting to subvert a narrative in which interracial intercourse warrants Othello's exclusion from Venice, Desdemona suggests that their marriage redeems him. As such, her chastity – a quality already called into question by her choice of mate – becomes integral to Othello's continued status as a Venetian subject, a point that Othello makes explicit in his ill-fated proclamation, 'My life upon her faith' (I, iii, 295).

In the beginning of the play, Othello implicitly trusts both his own noble persona and Desdemona's chastity, and he resists discourses that threaten to commoditise either of them. He believes his own merits, like Desdemona's virtue, to be transparent, confidently asserting to the Senate that 'my demerits / May speak unbonneted to as proud a fortune / As this that I have reached' (I, ii, 22–4). With the term 'unbonneted' linking his honour to a virgin's evident purity, Othello assumes that one's 'complement extern' (I, i, 62), to use Iago's phrase, corresponds to one's intrinsic virtue and that this virtue is readily accessible. As he asserts, 'My parts, my title and my perfect soul / Shall manifest me rightly' (I, ii, 31–2). Othello's discursive association with maidens, however, unwittingly recalls the trials of 'unbonneted' women such as Desdemona whose external appearances are scrutinised for potential signs of unchastity. In addition, as Sandra Fischer points out, a 'bonnet' is a type of coin, and Othello's use of the word 'unbonneted' inadvertently points to commercial dynamics informing assessments of his own value as well as that of Desdemona.[36]

In contrast to Othello, Iago approaches the world in economic terms.[37] He thinks about his own value in terms of his service to the state, comparing himself to Cassio with the comment, 'I know my price, I am worth no worse a place' (I, i, 10). His status as a military labourer shapes his own personal commoditisation, and his self-presentation reflects the commodity's disjuncture between external appearance and interior essence, as he refuses to align his 'outward action' to the 'native act and figure of [his] heart' (I, i, 60–1). This personal commoditisation results in the self-alienation expressed in his enigmatic statement, 'I am not what I am' (I, i, 64). As such, Iago recoils at the noble, aristocratic bearing of Othello, who, as Janet Adelman states, 'is everywhere associated with the kind of interior solidity and wholeness that stands as a reproach to Iago's interior emptiness and fragmentation'.[38] Jean Feerick demonstrates that modern understandings of race emerge out of older class-based distinctions and that in plays such as *Othello* 'differences of colour emerge, as it were, in dialectical relation to social rank, allowing social tensions originating with the difference of rank to be resolved, mitigated, or exploited with reference to this emerging difference of colour'.[39] Iago's racism thus emerges from his class-based resentment, and he draws on the discourses of commoditisation that shape his own experience to dismantle Othello's sense of self. In particular, he imposes racist and misogynist modes of evaluating black male subjectivity in relation to white female chastity, a virtue upon which Othello has buttressed his own identity. Iago's incessant harping on chastity's potential as an alienable commodity, I suggest, in turn influences Othello's own objectification, placing him within racist discourses related to African slavery.

Whereas Othello initially regards Desdemona, somewhat like Bess in *Fair Maid*, as an active agent capable of negotiating intercultural exchange, Iago insistently reinforces her status as a commodity, as he seeks to transform Othello and Desdemona's marriage into 'a frail vow betwixt an erring

Barbarian and a super-subtle Venetian' (I, iii, 356–7). He presents Desdemona as a possession that has been stolen and illicitly circulated when he warns her father, 'Zounds, sir, you're robbed' (I, i, 84). Barbantio responds in kind, averring that Desdemona must have been 'abused, stolen from me and corrupted / By spells and medicines bought of mountebanks' (I, iii, 61–2). Barbantio's language suggests not only that Othello is a 'thief' (I, ii, 57, 62), but also that Desdemona has been turned into a debased, adulterated commodity, no longer worth its original value. Given the association between chastity and national purity, Barbantio's animosity stems in part from the fear that Desdemona's riches, sexual and financial, may be lost to the community, as she has tied her 'duty, beauty, wit and fortunes / In an extravagant and wheeling stranger / Of here and everywhere' (I, i, 133–5). Desdemona's 'gross revolt' (I, i, 132) is therefore national as well as familial, as she has committed her personal virtues, her 'fortunes', and her reproductive potential to a Moor possessing only tenuous status as a Venetian. This transfer of value to a stranger is sufficiently disturbing for Barbantio to wish that the lacklustre Roderigo 'had had her' (I, i, 173), a sentiment that intensifies the impression that Desdemona, a valuable piece of property, should have been bestowed upon one of 'The wealthy, curled darlings of our nation' (I, ii, 68).

When confronted by the Senate, Othello attempts to resist this commoditising discourse. Although he concedes 'That [he has] ta'en away this old man's daughter' (I, iii, 79), he modifies these terms, saying, 'It is most true; true, I have married her' (I, iii, 80). Refuting imputations of kidnapping and rape, Othello insists that their affection is mutual and tells the story of 'How [he] did thrive in this fair lady's love / And she in [his]' (I, iii, 127–8). His tale exceeds the framework of property and possession suggested by his statement that he 'won' Desdemona (I, iii, 95), demonstrating instead that the marriage arose, in the words of one of the senators, 'by request and such fair question / As soul to soul affordeth'

(I, iii, 114–15). This formulation emphasises Desdemona's wilful consent, with the mention of souls reflecting the intrinsic humanity of both members of the couple. Although Barbantio grudgingly accepts Desdemona's participation in the marriage contract, he re-imposes the language of possession by belatedly bestowing his 'jewel' (I, iii, 196) on Othello with the words, 'I here do give thee that with all my heart / Which, but thou hast already, with all my heart / I would keep from thee' (I, iii, 194–6). As he disposes of the possession that has already escaped his grasp, Barbantio underscores Desdemona's potential falseness with his warning, 'She has deceived her father, and may thee' (I, iii, 294). To Barbantio, Desdemona resembles an 'evil object', an unlicensed commodity that was considered 'false and deceitful' as well as 'unwholesome, inferior in quality and generally unsatisfactory and defective', its depravity 'frequently associated with the "faults" of womankind'.[40] Iago underscores the thin line between true and false commodities when he observes that Othello 'hath boarded a land carrack: / If it prove lawful prize, he's made for ever' (I, ii, 50–1). By evoking epistemological anxieties pertaining to the inscrutable value of commoditised chastity, Iago and Barbantio position Othello not only as a usurper and thief, stealing property that does not belong to him, but also as a potentially unsavvy consumer.

Both Iago and Barbantio draw parallels between Desdemona's commodity status and Othello's own potential commoditisation as a black slave. The monetary terms used to assess Desdemona resonate with Othello's own experience 'Of being taken by the insolent foe / And sold to slavery' (I, iii, 138–9), and Barbantio references this history when he warns that, if transgressions such as Othello's 'may have passage free / Bond-slaves and pagans shall our statesmen be' (I, ii, 98–9). Exhibiting the fear that Africans may become naturalised citizens through marriage, Barbantio dismantles Othello's subject status as a Venetian general and, by recalling his former position as a bond slave, attributes to him the object status that he also confers onto women. Black slavery, in turn, informs Barbantio's vision of female subordination, as he pledges that, had he additional daughters, Desdemona's 'escape would teach me tyranny / To hang clogs on them' (I, iii, 198–9). The image of clogs fastened to human bodies, moreover, echoes the bestial imagery used by Iago. By casting Othello as an 'old black ram' (I, i, 87) and a 'Barbary horse' (I, i, 110), Iago simultaneously positions Desdemona as a 'white ewe' (I, i, 88) and one half of 'the beast with two backs' (I, i, 115). This animalisation is, of course, only a cruder articulation of Barbantio's reaction to Desdemona's departure – 'O heaven, how got she out?' (I, i, 167) – as though she were escaped livestock.

Reinforcing Barbantio's warning against Desdemona's deceptiveness, Iago emphasises her status as property that can be stolen or inaccurately evaluated. Iago's repeated use of the word 'purse', a slang term for vagina, highlights women's status as sexual and economic prizes. While most evident in his refrain to Roderigo, 'put money in thy purse', Iago directly compares Desdemona to a purse when he reminds Othello, 'Who steals my purse steals trash – 'tis something-nothing, / 'Twas mine, 'tis his, and has been slave to thousands' (III, iii, 160–1). As a purse, Desdemona – or her vagina – can be stolen and circulated among thousands of owners; it serves the purposes of others, rendering it a slave. The theft of Desdemona would in turn damage Othello's reputation, the very quality Iago lauds as constitutive of personal value, potentially stripping him of his subject status.

For this reason, Othello's jealousy grows as he comes to regard Desdemona as a potentially alienable commodity. He first uses the language of commoditisation to describe the pending consummation of their marriage, stating, 'The purchase made, the fruits are to ensue: / That profit's yet to come 'tween me and you' (II, iii, 9–10). He later fixates on the horror of sharing this purchase, raving, 'I had rather be a toad / And live upon the vapour of a dungeon / Than keep a corner in the thing I love / For others' uses' (III, iii, 274–7). Othello's value as a person comes to rest on his ability to control his possessions; without it, he becomes bestial, something more lowly than a toad confined to a dungeon. As Natasha Korda has argued, 'women and Africans were linked, within the cultural imaginary, by their purportedly skewed relations to material objects'.[41] From this perspective, Othello's inability to properly assess and exert ownership over his possessions signals his failure to achieve possessive individualism, an emerging concept 'whose foundational precept of "property in the person" ... excludes certain categories of subjects from the prerogative of possession due to their supposed inability to recognize value'.[42]

Iago's conflation of chastity, vaginas and women, and his categorisation of them all as commodities, informs the overdetermined significance of Desdemona's handkerchief. Resisting commodity discourse, Desdemona contrasts her 'first remembrance from the Moor' (III, iii, 295) with her purse, lamenting, 'I had rather have lost my purse / Full of crusadoes' (III, iv, 25–6). Despite her desire to elevate the handkerchief's affective powers above monetary exchange, Desdemona's words inadvertently remind audiences of the purported accessibility of her own vaginal purse, which might be circulated among thousands. She also hints at a metonymic connection between the handkerchief and her chastity/vagina, a linkage that Iago solidifies in his comment that the handkerchief is 'hers ... and being hers / She may, I think, bestow't on any man' (IV, i, 12–13).[43] Drawing on the handkerchief's prior associations, including the design evoking spotted wedding sheets, Iago intensifies the handkerchief's metonymic relationship to Desdemona's body and chastity, with the overall effect of literalising them both as jointly owned entities that can be stolen or given away. In this way, Othello's belief that Cassio 'had my handkerchief' (IV, i, 22) comes to indicate that Cassio has also had Desdemona. The handkerchief, initially depicted as a mystical African fetish, thus acquires traits associated with the commodity fetish, reflecting the supernatural aspect of commodities that, divorced from their origins, seem to acquire a power of their own. As fetish, the handkerchief functions as supplement, replacing chastity's inscrutable origin with its tangible presence.

Iago's tendency to view people in terms of commodities informs his privileging of appearance over internal essence. As Hawkes suggests, commodification leads to a privileging of the sense of sight because 'the imposition of exchange-value obtruded a mere image – which thus became an "idol" – between the subjective observer and the object observed'.[44] Iago assumes a discontinuity between internal and external value and also recognises that visible, external signs – which can be manipulated or misinterpreted – shape one's perceived value in society. Iago faults Othello largely for improper visual perception in selecting a lieutenant, even when his 'eyes had seen the proof' (I, i, 27) of Iago's military superiority. Othello's inability to correctly interpret external appearances, Iago intimates, allowed him to be duped by Cassio, whom he believes 'put[s] on the mere form of civil and humane seeming' (II, i, 236–7). Punishing Othello for this failure of both vision and interpretation, Iago forces Othello to think more critically, and suspiciously, about external appearances. As an expert in the commodity form, moreover, Iago – the ensign who will show Othello 'a flag and sign of love, / Which is indeed but sign' (I, i, 154–5) – educates Othello in a system of commercial semiotics in which the outward signs of commodities paradoxically obscure but also illuminate interior corruption or debasement. As he leads Desdemona to 'undo her credit with the Moor' (II, iii, 354), causing Othello to view her as a false commodity, Iago simultaneously encourages Othello to assess his own personal value in similarly commercial terms. Drawing on the corollary between Desdemona's chastity and Othello's masculine subjectivity, Iago eats away at Othello's belief in both his and Desdemona's intrinsic virtue, virtue which may have been reflected in her whiteness but which overrode his blackness, making him 'far more fair than black' (I, iii, 291). As Iago turns Desdemona's 'virtue into pitch' (II, iii, 355), therefore, he also recodes the meaning of Othello's dark skin, casting it as an irredeemable mark of abjection.

To enforce this commercial mode of thinking, Iago recasts the signs of Cassio's and Desdemona's courtliness – the very indicators of rank that advanced Cassio over Iago – into signs of adultery. Depicting Cassio as one who 'hath a person and a smooth dispose / To be suspected, framed to make women false' (I, iii, 396–7), Iago strives to 'gyve [him] in [his] own courtisies' (II, i, 170), using Cassio's courtly banter and stylised kisses to 'strip [him] out of [his] lieutenantry' (II, i, 171–2). He then similarly depicts Desdemona as 'paddl[ing] with the palm of his hand' (II, i, 252). Contradicting Roderigo's suggestion that the action 'was but courtesy' (II, i, 254), Iago expounds that it is 'an index and obscure prologue to the history of lust and foul thoughts' (II, i, 255–6), insisting that Desdemona's actions both signal and prefigure 'the master and main exercise, th'incoporate conclusion' (II, i, 260–1). In conversation with Cassio, Iago casts Desdemona's attributes in a similar light. Whereas Cassio draws on the courtly love tradition to call Desdemona 'exquisite' (II, iii, 18), 'a most fresh and delicate creature' (II, iii, 20), 'right modest' (II, iii, 23), and 'perfection' (II, iii, 25), Iago counters by describing her as 'sport for Jove' (II, iii, 17) and 'full of game' (II, iii, 19) and by referring to her eye as 'a parley to provocation' (II, iii, 21–2). Iago gradually trains Othello to interpret Desdemona's signs in a similar manner, causing him to regard her moist hand, for example, as indicative of a 'fruitfulness and liberal heart' that 'requires / A sequester from liberty, fasting and prayer, / Much castigation, exercise devout' (III, iv, 38–41). External signs become paramount from this perspective, as they both cover and reveal hidden truths.[45]

Iago further baits Othello into distrusting initial appearances by suggesting that he himself possesses interior thoughts that he does not wish to reveal; his oblique comments cause

Othello to suspect that 'there were some monster in [Iago's] thought / Too hideous to be shown' (III, iii, 110–11) and that he has 'shut up in [his] brain / Some horrible conceit' (III, iii, 117–18). Othello reaches these conclusions by interpreting Iago's measured speech and verbal halts, deciding that these mannerisms are 'close delations, working from the heart, / That passion cannot rule' (III, iii, 126–7). As a result, Othello becomes convinced that he can access a deeper layer of truth and pleads with Iago, 'If thou dost love me / Show me thy thought' (III, iii, 118–19). After using himself as a model, Iago encourages Othello to view Desdemona and Cassio in a similar manner, as possessing secrets that can be uncovered only through penetrating perception. Ostensibly considering his own soul, Iago asks,

> Who has a breast so pure
> But some uncleanly apprehensions
> Keep leets and law-days and in session sit
> With meditations lawful? (III, iii, 141–4)

The pure breast, of course, recalls Desdemona, and Iago's protestation that he is 'not bound to that all slaves are free to' (III, iii, 138), and therefore will maintain his private thoughts, reminds Othello that even slaves – and by extension wives – keep secrets from their masters. By recalling Othello's own history of bondage and rebellion, Iago intensifies Othello's distrust of Desdemona and, in the process, further debases Othello's sense of his own noble integrity.

Iago grows increasingly direct in applying this paradigm to Desdemona, noting that Venetian women 'do let God see the pranks / They dare not show their husbands' (III, iii, 205–6) and suggesting that Desdemona had been dishonest when Othello was courting her: 'She did deceive her father, marrying you, / And when she seemed to shake, and fear your looks, / She loved them most' (III, iii, 209–11). From this insight, Othello concludes that Desdemona, like Iago, possesses hidden depths, and he becomes obsessed with what Cassio and Desdemona might do in private, away from his sight. Although Othello briefly recalls his former image of Desdemona as a woman 'of so high and plenteous wit and invention' (IV, i, 186–7), he settles on a view of her as a commodity whose inner value is unknowable and thus suspect. She becomes 'a subtle whore, / A closet, lock and key, of villainous secrets' (IV, ii, 21–2). Closed off to him, Desdemona becomes an impenetrable closet, hiding her inner corruption.

Despite his disruption of the link between a person's outward appearance and inner value, Iago paradoxically reinforces the specular field as the only available means of interpreting inner motives, as rank and reputation cease to be reliable guides. As a result, Othello begins to emphasise sight in statements such as 'she had eyes and chose me' (III, iii, 192), and 'I'll see before I doubt' (III, iii, 193). As his need for 'ocular proof' (III, iii, 363) grows, Othello more intently scrutinises the significance of his own blackness within early modern racial hierarchies. As Arthur Little argues, Othello's 'examination of [Desdemona's] unseen body simulates the play's interrogations of Othello's own metaphorical black body, unseen and missing despite his physical black presence'.[46] Just as he scrutinises Desdemona's chastity, Othello begins to interrogate his own blackness, emphasising the 'ocular proof' of his own black body and thus his assumed inferiority.[47] Othello begins to worry that his own embodiment has caused Desdemona to be unfaithful, wondering,

> Haply for I am black
> And have not those soft parts of conversation
> That chamberers have, or for I am declined
> Into the vale of years.   (III, iii, 267–70)

Contributing to this focus on Othello's body, Iago glosses Othello's appearance and actions in terms of barbarous blackness, reading his epileptic fit, for example, as a precursor to a more animalistic outburst in which 'he foams at mouth, and by and by / Breaks out to savage madness' (IV, i, 54–5). Othello's blackness ceases to be an incidental veil over his 'fair' (I, iii, 291) virtue and instead becomes an indicator of his innate depravity and savage irrationality.

Here, *Othello* captures the paradox of personal commoditisation as it intersects with race. The partial commoditisation of white men, often articulated through reference to female chastity, leads to new models of performative, capitalist selfhood, defined by the productive management of the disjuncture between interior essence and exterior appearance. By contrast, when black men are commoditised, external appearance – of blackness – takes precedence, overriding any potential interiority. This corporeality is associated with slavery. Observing that in the Classical world the slave is defined in terms of body rather than mind, Jennifer Glancy notes that the Greek word *soma*, or body, was also used colloquially to refer to a slave.[48] Blackness, inscribed on the body, negates the performativity often associated with commoditised subjectivity. The common proverb about the impossibility of 'washing an Ethiope white' attests to the indelible nature of a blackness that cannot be altered through conversion, citizenship or performance; the convertability considered central to emerging conceptions of *homo economicus* is thus denied to black people.[49]

Adding to this increasing sense of racial abjection, Othello comes to regard his own personal value as marred by the corruption of his wife, on whose virtue he had previously staked his honour. The textual crux in which Othello bemoans that either '*Her* name' (in the Quarto) or '*My* name' (in the Folio) 'that was as fresh / As Dian's visage, is now begrimed and black / As mine own face' (III, iii, 388–91, emphases added) illuminates the extent to which Othello's reputation is bound up with Desdemona's.[50] The phrase 'Dian's visage' recalls Desdemona's chastity, the loss of which has ruined either his name or her own. In either case, external blackness is transformed into a sign and cause of internal depravity, 'begrim[ing]' (III, iii, 390) that with which it comes in contact. Othello's personal value thus begins to correspond to his racialised exterior. As his doubts about Desdemona's fidelity intensify, Othello figuratively expunges her from his soul and body, pledging, 'All my fond love thus do I blow to heaven: / 'Tis gone! / Arise, black vengeance, from the hollow hell' (III, iii, 448–50). In so doing, Othello replaces Desdemona's purifying whiteness, once lodged with him, with black vengeance, embracing Iago's view of him as a black savage.[51] Desdemona, in turn, is imagined as sullied by her association with his blackness and becomes, as Iago contends, 'that cunning whore of Venice / That married with Othello' (IV, ii, 91–2). As he reinterprets the signs of white femininity, Othello simultaneously reassesses the sign of his own blackness, leading him to discover an identity based in stereotypes of savage black masculinity – an identity that appears essential but which has been fashioned by Iago's machinations.

Within this increasingly essentialised racial framework, Desdemona's white beauty comes to represent an essential chastity that Othello believes can be redeemed in death and that the audience associates with Desdemona's innocence.[52] *Othello* thus dramatises the radical abstraction that Richard Dyer identifies as central to delineations of racial difference: when humans are divided into the categories of black and white, a range of varied skin tones becomes reified into symbolic categories of race, representative of moral lightness and darkness.[53] Having embraced this racist moral binary, Othello comes to regard Desdemona's whiteness as incommensurate with her presumed transgression. His rhetorical question, 'Was this fair paper, this most goodly book / Made to write "whore" upon?' (IV, ii, 72–3), suggests that her sexual transgression mars both her beauty and her whiteness. Momentarily exhibiting a desire to make her sin visible, Othello vows that, if he kills her with a sword, '[Her] bed, lust-stained, shall with lust's blood be spotted' (V, i, 36), an option that depicts the consummation of their marriage as the violent rape it was initially assumed to be. When Othello decides instead not to 'shed her blood' (V, ii, 3) but to preserve 'that whiter skin of hers than snow / And smooth as monumental alabaster' (V, ii, 4–5), he articulates a desire to purify Desdemona so that her interior reality may correspond to her outward whiteness. Here, Othello transforms the presumed rape into a sacrifice, purifying Desdemona and, on a larger scale, the body politic.[54] He also reifies racial whiteness. As Dyer argues, 'Whiteness as an ideal can never be attained, not only because white skin can never be truly white, but also because ideally white is an absence: to be really, absolutely white is to be nothing.'[55] As the image of 'monumental alabaster' suggests, Othello hopes to transform Desdemona into this pure, white nothingness; death will purify her, leaving her 'Pale as [her] smock' (V, ii, 271) and 'cold ... / Even like [her] chastity' (V, ii, 273–4). In the process, death will eradicate any unknowable internal reality that may complicate this vision of whiteness. Having killed Desdemona, Othello may 'love [her] after' (V, ii, 19), as he finally possesses a commodity whose internal essence is knowable because it no longer exists. In death, with her innocence finally revealed, Desdemona's whiteness is reinscribed as an unambiguous sign of her virtue, a sign that Othello tragically misinterpreted.

Othello's blackness is similarly reified in the killing of Desdemona, an act which not only damns him but which also expunges any remnant of Desdemona's fairness remaining within him. Emilia's reaction to the murder, 'O, the more angel she, / And you the blacker devil!' (V, ii, 128–9), encapsulates this racial dynamic in which Othello grows more black and Desdemona more white as a result of the murder, with each character's physical colouring aligning with its received moral implications. Having murdered virtue, in Desdemona and in himself, Othello is left with nothing but essentialised, abject blackness, wherein internal and external realities are collapsed. This absence of internal reality is confirmed by

Iago's enigmatic closing statement, 'Demand me nothing. What you know, you know' (V, ii, 300). Although Othello had earlier associated his own, perhaps fearsome, interiority with Iago's secret depths, this potential for sophisticated interiority is closed off at the end of the play. By this point, Othello is defined by what he knows – that he has killed Desdemona, an act that seals his own all-encompassing blackness. Iago, the commoditised worker, has ideologically distanced himself from Othello. Having conferred his commodity status onto the Moor, he employs racist discourse to transform commoditisation from a state of flexible, if amoral, performativity to one of depraved objectification.

These reified racial categories come to define Othello's personal value in a manner that aligns with the emerging commoditisation of black bodies in the African slave trade. As Emilia rebukes Othello for killing Desdemona, she reinforces his quantifiable value, stating, 'This deed of thine is no more worthy heaven / Than thou wast worthy her' (V, ii, 156–7). Induced by Iago, and then by Emilia, to think of people as quantifiable commodities, Othello reverts to an image of himself as a slave when he realises his tragic error, chastising himself with,

> O cursed, cursed slave!
> Whip me, ye devils,
> From the possession of this heavenly sight!
> Blow me about in winds, roast me in sulphur,
> Wash me in steep-down gulfs of liquid fire!   (V, ii, 274–8)

Though these tortures accord with conventional depictions of hell, Othello's curse also alludes to the horrors of chattel slavery. Othello imagines the sight of Desdemona – and his life more broadly – as a possession that can be stripped from him, whipped out of him by devils, just as it was once stolen by slave owners. His life, like Desdemona's chastity and Iago's labour, becomes an alienable commodity. Subsequently, in his more frequently analysed final speech, Othello depicts himself as a heathen unable to properly value his possessions, who, 'Like the base Indian, threw a pearl away / Richer than all his tribe' (V, ii, 345–6). He further describes himself as an internally divided citizen, simultaneously the 'turbanned Turk' (V, ii, 351) who 'traduced the state' (V, ii, 352) and the military defender of Venice who 'smote him – thus!' (V, ii, 354). But these illustrations of his incomplete subject status are informed by his prior allusion to himself as a slave, an instance that represents the culminating triumph of Iago's commercial discourse. As a slave, a nonperson, Othello is incapable either of accessing possessive individualism or of negotiating his vexed cultural position.[56] Lodivico, the voice of the Venetian state, affirms Othello's trajectory from partially assimilated subject to abject nonperson, marvelling that he 'that wert once so good' has 'Fallen in the practice of a cursed slave' (V, ii, 288–9).

Othello thus interrogates the assimilationist model of racial subject formation proffered in *The Fair Maid of the West, Part I*. It elucidates the limitations of this model for achieving anything approximating racial equality and shows how it collapses in the face of the objectification of black bodies inherent both to informal slave ownership and to the nascent transatlantic slave trade. Chastity remains central to *Othello*'s revised mode of assessing black value, however, and the play's conclusion moves toward removing chastity from the commodity sphere, showing it to be a property of inestimable value. Still believing that Desdemona was unfaithful, Othello laments,

> Had she been true,
> If heaven would make me such another world
> Of one entire and perfect chrysolite,
> I'd not have sold her for it.   (V, ii, 139–42)

Recalling Desdemona's earlier assertion that she would not be unfaithful for all the world, Othello esteems this alternate, unadulterated and soon to be reconstructed Desdemona as the most valuable possession, her value so great that it cannot be monetised. As I have argued, Iago dismantles Othello's subjectivity by denying that either chastity or blackness can be subject positions – the central premise of *The Fair Maid of the West* – and instead by viewing both gendered and racialised bodies as commodities. As such, these bodies are drained of interiority and are defined by their external characteristics – the only available means, according to Iago's market epistemology, of assessing exchange value. Iago fails, however, to fully equate chastity and blackness; instead, when Desdemona is proven innocent, her chastity is ideologically divorced from blackness and transformed into its polar opposite. Chastity, as I discuss more fully in the following chapter, thus becomes a repository of racial whiteness, the commodity potential of which must not be named within emerging regimes of white supremacy. This ideological perspective emerges in response to Iago's conception of chastity as commodity, as it works to elide the still present commoditisation of chastity within European kinship structures, leaving only black bodies openly and irredeemably commoditisable.

Fissures in this reconfigured understanding of race, however, are particularly evident in the figure of Bianca, the working-class prostitute who lacks access to the unmarked, racial whiteness that Desdemona comes to embody – a lack perhaps indicated by the very marked whiteness of her name. Bianca's profession renders her somewhat less white than Desdemona, troubling the play's racial binaries and indicating that Iago's machinations have failed to fully displace the taint of labour onto black bodies. As both prostitute and seamstress, moreover, Bianca complicates the play's depiction of early capitalist labour and personal commoditisation. Given that portrayals of prostitutes often stood in for labourers more generally, Bianca should presumably mirror Iago's empty, depraved, commoditised subjectivity, with her commoditisation rendering her the whore that Iago believes all women – and perhaps all men – to be. Yet Shakespeare deviates from this common analogy by making Bianca's work visible and, in doing so, calling attention to the labour of women that underlies the production of many commodities as well as the production of women as commodities. By manually copying the design on Desdemona's handkerchief, Bianca reiterates the labour of the African woman who originally produced the artefact, invoking a set of racial, gendered and transnational relations otherwise elided as the handkerchief accrues meaning as a symbol either of white chastity or of black masculinity. As she embroiders the handkerchief for Cassio, her lover/customer, she reminds us that the value of an object resides in the complex web of social relations that produced it, social relations that are elided in the commodity form, leaving an aporia that may be supplemented, but never filled, by unstable, fetishised meanings. Analogously, as 'A housewife that by selling her desires / Buys herself bread and clothes' (IV, i, 95–6), Bianca makes legible the traffic in women that gives chastity its value, and she calls attention to patterns of labour and consumption in early modern England. Whereas both Desdemona and her handkerchief come to be treated as commodity fetishes, so much so that their fetishised significance occludes their very status as commodities, Bianca exposes the labour that produces such commodities as well as the social hierarchies that deem her inferior because she must work. Bianca's labouring body, finally, brings into relief *Othello*'s portrait of slavery, reminding audiences that slavery is not simply a metaphorical analogue to commoditised chastity, but is rather a set of exploitative labour relations, shaped by expanding international markets, that denied personhood to African men and women.

Notes

1. For a discussion of England's support for the slave trade, see Kim Hall, *Things of Darkness: Economies of Race and Gender in Early Modern England* (Ithaca, NY: Cornell University Press, 1995), 19–21.

2. Hall, *Things of Darkness*, 21; See also Ania Loomba and Jonathan Burton, eds, *Race in Early Modern England: A Documentary Companion* (New York: Palgrave, 2007), 125.
3. For a thorough documentation of this black presence, see Imtiaz Habib, *Black Lives in the English Archives, 1500–1677* (Burlington, VT: Ashgate Publishing, 2008).
4. See Tom Earle and Kate J. P. Lowe, eds, *Black Africans in Renaissance Europe* (New York: Cambridge University Press, 2005); Habib, *Black Lives*; Habib, 'The Black Alien in *Othello*: Beyond the European Immigrant', in *Shakespeare and Immigration*, ed. Rubin Espinosa and David Rutter (Burlington, VT: Ashgate, 2014), 135–58; and Peter Erickson, 'Race Words in *Othello*', in *Shakespeare and Immigration*, ed. Espinosa and Rutter, 159–76.
5. Habib, 'The Black Alien in *Othello*', 154.
6. Lara Bovilsky, *Barbarous Play: Race on the English Renaissance Stage* (Minneapolis: University of Minnesota Press, 2008), 3.
7. Ian Smith, *Race and Rhetoric in the Renaissance: Barbarian Errors* (New York: Palgrave Macmillan, 2009), 4.
8. John Hawkins, 'The first voyage of the right worshipful and valiant knight, Sir John Hawkins, now treasurer of Her Majesty's navie Royall, made to the West Indies, 1562', in *Race in Early Modern England: A Documentary Companion*, ed. Ania Loomba and Jonathan Burton (New York: Palgrave, 2007), 125–6, esp. 126.
9. Queen Elizabeth I of England, 'An open letter to the Lord Maiour of London and th'Aldermen his brethren' (1596), in *Race in Early Modern England: A Documentary Companion*, ed. Loomba and Burton, 135–6, esp. 136.
10. Queen Elizabeth I of England, 'An open warrant to the Lord Maiour of London' (1596), in *Race in Early Modern England: A Documentary Companion*, ed. Loomba and Burton, 136.
11. Queen Elizabeth I of England, 'An Open warrant', 136.
12. Queen Elizabeth I of England, 'An Open warrant', 136.
13. David Hawkes, *Shakespeare and Economic Theory*, The Arden Shakespeare (New York: Bloomsbury, 2015), 91.

Hawkes also draws on David Graeber's insight that wage labour is intimately connected to chattel slavery and may even arise from it. See Graeber, 'Turning Modes of Production Inside Out: Or, Why Capitalism is a Transformation of Slavery', *Critique of Anthropology* 26 (2006): 61–85, and Graeber, *Lost People: Magic and the Legacy of Slavery in Madagascar* (Bloomington: Indiana University Press, 2007).

14. John Moore, *A Scripture-word against Inclosure* (1656), quoted in Hawkes, *Shakespeare and Economic Theory*, 94.
15. Hall, *Things of Darkness*, 9.
16. Hall, *Things of Darkness*, 3.
17. Hall, *Things of Darkness*, 125.
18. For the dating of *Othello* and *Fair Maid*, see the Introduction to *Othello*, ed. A. J. Honnigmann (London: The Arden Shakespeare, 2002), 1–111, esp. 1, and the Introduction to *The Fair Maid of the West, Parts I and II*, ed. Robert K. Turner, Jr. (Lincoln: University of Nebraska Press, 1967), ix–xx, esp. xii–xiii. For the ways in which slavery emerges from Mediterranean trade, see Daniel Vitkus, 'The Circulation of Bodies: Slavery, Maritime Commerce, and English Captivity Narratives in the Early Modern Period', in *Colonial and Postcolonial Incarceration*, ed. Graeme Harper (London: Continuum, 2001), 23–37. For a discussion of the Mediterranean, particularly Italy, as a more racially diverse and commercially vibrant analogue to England, see Erickson, 'Race Words in *Othello*', 164; David C. McPherson, *Shakespeare, Jonson and the Myth of Venice* (Newark: University of Delaware Press, 1990); and Graham Holderness, *Shakespeare and Venice* (Burlington, VT: Ashgate, 2010).
19. *The Fair Maid of the West, Parts I and II*, ed. Robert K. Turner, Jr. (Lincoln: University of Nebraska Press, 1967), I, i, 24–6, hereafter cited parenthetically.
20. Donald Lupton, *London and the Country carbonadoed and quartered into several characters* (London: Printed by Nicholas Okes, 1632), Folger Copy 1, 128.
21. Lupton, *London and the Country*, 128.
22. Jean Howard, 'An English Lass Amid the Moors: Gender, Race, Sexuality, and National Identity in Heywood's *The*

Fair Maid of the West', in *Women, 'Race', and Writing in the Early Modern Period*, ed. Margo Hendricks and Patricia Parker (London: Routledge, 1994), 101–17, esp. 104.

23. Howard, 'An English Lass', 110. Anthony Gerard Barthelemy suggests that the name of the ship indicates the English desire to dominate non-white people (*Black Face, Maligned Race: The Representation of Blacks in English Drama from Shakespeare to Southern* [Baton Rouge: Louisiana State University Press, 1987], 165).

24. Jonathan Gil Harris argues that *The Fair Maid of the West* 'articulates a recognizably bullionist fantasy in which piracy, privateering, and merchant venturing are all instruments of the nation-state' ('Hepetitis/Castration and Treasure: Edward Misselden, Gerard Malynes, *The Fair Maid of the West, The Renegado*', in *Sick Economies: Drama, Mercantilism, and Disease in Shakespeare's England* [Philadelphia: Pennsylvania University Press, 2004], 136–62, esp. 157). For more on piracy in the play, see Barbara Fuchs, 'Faithless Empires: Pirates, Renegadoes, and the English Nation', *English Literary History* 67 (2000): 45–69.

25. Emily C. Bartels notes that the Moors in Richard Hakluyt's *Navigations* are presented as agreeing amicably with Elizabeth I's promotion of English trade in Barbary, including her prohibition that excluded Moors from importing their goods, thus forbidding reciprocal exchange ('Making More of the Moor: Aaron, Othello, and Renaissance Refashionings of Race', *Shakespeare Quarterly* 41.4 [1990]: 433–54, esp. 441–2).

26. Daniel Vitkus, *Turning Turk: English Theater and the Multicultural Mediterranean, 1570–1630* (New York: Palgrave, 2003), 133.

27. Alternately, Howard contends that anxieties about female power, embodied in Bess, are displaced onto the Moor, who becomes 'the chief figure of sexual danger' ('An English Lass', 116). Claire Jowitt extends the argument that 'sexual anxieties concerning female rule are focused on Mullisheg's eroticized court' in 'East versus West: Seraglio Queens, Politics, and Sexuality in Thomas Heywood's *Fair Maid of the West, Part I and II*', in *Roxolana in European Literature, History*

and Culture, ed. Galina I Yermolenko (Burlington, VT: Ashgate Publishing, 2010), 58–70, esp. 58.

28. Barbara Sebek, '"Strange Outlandish Wealth": Transglobal Commerce in *The Merchant's Mappe of Commerce* and *The Fair Maid of the West, Parts I and II*', in *Playing the Globe: Genre and Geography in English Renaissance Drama*, ed. John Gillies and Virginia Mason Vaughan (Madison, NJ: Fairleigh Dickinson University Press, 1998), 167–202, esp. 178, 189.

29. Jonathan Gil Harris discusses castration in *The Fair Maid of the West* in relation to anxieties about piracy, 'namely, that bullion flows are not unidirectional, and treasure (or "best jewels") can be expropriated from England as much as appropriated by it' (*Sick Economies*, 156).

30. Here I differ from Howard, who argues that blacks in *Fair Maid* are represented 'not so much as potential fraternal rivals but as potential slaves' ('An English Lass', 117).

31. For a discussion of the political and economic contexts that shape the relatively favourable depiction of the Moors as compared to the Spanish, see Jesus Lopez-Pelaez Casellas, 'Building an English (Early Modern) Identity: "Race" and Capitalism in Heywood's *The Fair Maid of the West, or A Girl Worth Gold*', *Revista Canaria de Estudios Ingleses* 54 (2007): 55–68.

32. Habib, 'The Black Alien in *Othello*', 136–45.

33. Habib, 'The Black Alien in *Othello*', 148–9.

34. Habib, 'The Black Alien in *Othello*', 148. In 'Making More of the Moor', Bartels reads Othello as more fully an insider in Venetian society, but like Habib, she suggests that it is this insider status that most perturbs Iago.

35. William Shakespeare, *Othello*, ed. A. J. Honnigmann, The Arden Shakespeare, Third Series (London: Thompson, 2002), I, iii, 291, hereafter cited parenthetically.

36. Sandra Fischer, *Econolingua: A Glossary of Coins and Economic Language in Renaissance Drama* (Newark: University of Delaware Press, 1985), 22.

37. On Iago's penchant for economic language and the significance of economic imagery in the play more generally, see Robert B. Heilman, 'The Economics of Iago and Others',

PMLA 68.3 (1953): 555–71, and Patricia Parker, 'Cassio, Cash, and the "Infidel 0": Arithmetic, Double-entry Bookkeeping, and *Othello*'s Unfaithful Accounts', in *A Companion to the Global Renaissance*, ed. Jyotsna Singh (London: Blackwell, 2009), 223–41.
38. Janet Adelman, 'Iago's Alter Ego: Race as Projection in Othello', *Shakespeare Quarterly* 48.2 (1997): 125–44, esp. 127–8. Mary Floyd-Wilson relates this integrated self to the 'naturally dry and fixed composition' attributed to Africans in Classical geohumoral models ('Othello's Jealousy', in *English Ethnicity and Race in Early Modern Drama* [New York: Cambridge University Press, 2003], 132–60, esp. 147).
39. Jean E. Feerick, *Strangers in Blood: Relocating Race in the Renaissance* (Toronto: University of Toronto Press, 2010), 5.
40. Natasha Korda, 'Vicious Objects: Staging False Wares', in *Masculinity and the Metropolis of Vice, 1550–1650*, ed. Amanda Bailey and Roze Hentschell (New York: Palgrave, 2010), 161–83, esp. 161–2.
41. Natasha Korda, *Shakespeare's Domestic Economies: Gender and Property in Early Modern England* (Philadelphia: University of Pennsylvania Press, 2002), 113.
42. Korda, *Shakespeare's Domestic Economies*, 113.
43. Since Lynda Boose's essay, 'Othello's Handkerchief: "The Recognizance and Pledge of Love"', *English Literary Renaissance* 5 (1975): 360–74, critics have assumed a metonymic connection between the red and white handkerchief and Desdemona's body. More recently, Ian Smith has suggested that the handkerchief, dyed in mummy, may be black and therefore representative of Othello's body ('Othello's Black Handkerchief', *Shakespeare Quarterly* 64.1 [2013]: 1–25). In my view, the slippery signifying function of the handkerchief reflects its status as an alienable commodity. For a fuller analysis of the handkerchief as 'a cardinal signifier of the operation of signs in the play', see David Schallwyk, 'Othello's Consummation', in *Othello: The State of the Play*, ed. Lena Cowen Orlin (New York: Bloomsbury, 2014), 203–33, esp. 224.
44. Hawkes, *Shakespeare and Economic Theory*, 122.

45. For more on Iago's process of identifying and then rhetorically making visible hidden (un)truths, see Michael Neill, 'Unproper Beds: Race, Adultery, and the Hideous in Othello', *Shakespeare Quarterly* 40.4 (1989): 383–412; Patricia Parker, 'Fantasies of "Race" and "Gender": Africa, *Othello*, and Bringing to Light', in *Women, 'Race', and Writing in the Early Modern Period*, ed. Hendricks and Parker, 84–100; and Katharine Eisaman Maus, 'Proof and Consequences: Othello and the Crime of Intention', in *Inwardness and Theater in the English Renaissance* (Chicago: University of Chicago Press, 1995), 104–27.

46. Arthur L. Little Jr., *Shakespeare Jungle Fever: National-Imperial Re-Visions of Race, Rape, and Sacrifice* (Stanford: Stanford University Press, 2000), 74.

47. I am indebted to Peter Erikson's discussion of the effect that this emphasis on ocular proof has on the understanding of Othello's blackness ('Images of White Identity in Othello', in *Othello: New Critical Essays*, ed. Philip C. Kolin [New York: Routledge, 2002], 133–45, esp. 140).

48. Jennifer Glancy, *Slavery in Early Christianity* (New York: Oxford University Press, 2002), 14.

49. For a discussion of this trope in *Othello*, see Karen Newman, '"And wash the Ethiop white": Femininity and the Monstrous in *Othello*', in *Shakespeare Reproduced: The Text in History and Ideology*, ed. Jean E. Howard and Marion F. O'Connor (New York: Methuen, 1987), 143–62. For more on race and conversion in the period, see Dennis Austin Britton, *Becoming Christian: Race, Reformation, and Early Modern English Romance* (New York: Fordham University Press, 2014).

50. For the differences between the Quarto and the Folio texts, which may suggest a growing racial awareness in England, see Leah Marcus, 'The Two Texts of *Othello* and Early Modern Constructions of Race', in *Textual Performances: The Modern Reproduction of Shakespeare's Drama*, ed. Lucas Erne and Margaret Jane Kidnie (Cambridge: Cambridge University Press), 21–36.

51. For Othello's internalisation of racist Venetian attitudes, see Edward Berry, 'Othello's Alienation', *Studies in English Literature, 1500–1900* 30 (1990): 315–33.

52. This dichotomy is enhanced by Dympna Callaghan's observation that whiteface was the primary means of designating femininity on the early modern stage ('"Othello Was a White Man": Properties of Race on Shakespeare's Stage', in *Alternative Shakespeares*, vol. 2, ed. Terence Hawkes [New York: Routledge, 1996], 192–215).
53. Richard Dyer, 'Coloured White, Not Coloured', in *White* (London: Routledge, 1997), 41–81.
54. Drawing on Stephanie H. Jed, *Chaste Thinking: The Rape of Lucrece and the Birth of Humanism* (Bloomington: Indiana University Press, 1989), Arthur Little argues that race and rape are closely intertwined and that the sacrifice of a chaste woman often acts as a corrective to the contaminating miscegenational rape (*Shakespeare Jungle Fever*, 4).
55. Dyer, 'Coloured White, Not Coloured', 78.
56. For the idea of the slave as a nonperson, see Orlando Patterson, *Slavery and Social Death: A Comparative Study* (Cambridge, MA: Harvard University Press, 1982).

CHAPTER 5

MEDITERRANEAN MARKETS, COMMODITISED MASCULINITY AND THE WHITENING OF CHRISTIAN CHASTITY IN *THE MERCHANT OF VENICE* AND *THE RENEGADO*

English plays and travel tracts evince anxiety that participation in overseas trade, especially with the East, may expose Western Christians to objectifying commoditisation. The expansion of Mediterranean trade following the founding of the Levant Company in 1581 allowed merchants to more easily exchange English cloth and other goods for luxury items such as cotton, wine, silk and spices attained in ports throughout Italy, Greece, Turkey, Persia, Africa and the East Indies.[1] Travel and trade not only brought the English into contact with other cultures but also introduced them to competing *regimes of value*, defined by Arjun Appadurai as cultural categories determining exchange potential.[2] Intercultural exchange, as Appadurai explains, provides 'contexts for the commoditization of things that are otherwise protected from commoditization'.[3] The commodity potential of Western bodies, sexuality and sacred items in particular becomes vividly apparent in the intensely commercial, multicultural contexts of Mediterranean trade. English concern with personal commoditisation in the Mediterranean centres on the institutions of slavery and the harem, often with the effect of displacing antisocial commoditising impulses onto Easterners despite England's own investment in pursuing profits in expanding markets. The early modern theatre mediates these concerns, and its embodied mode of representation heightens the travel tracts' focus on the commoditising subjugation of Eastern captivity and the attendant fungibility of identity in multicultural commercial environments.

In recounting the horrors of captivity, English travel writers depict slavery as a sign of Easterners' inappropriate willingness to commoditise people and as a threat to the personal and cultural integrity of Westerners. In his *Relation of a Journey*, George Sandys registers disgust at slave markets where Christians are 'sold as horses in Faires; the men being rated according to their faculties, or personal abilities; as the women for their youths and beauties'.[4] John Rawlins similarly emphasises the treatment of people as chattel as he recounts his own experience of slavery in Algiers in *The Famous and Wonderful Recovery of a Ship of Bristol*, relating that 'many came to behold us, sometimes feeling our brawns and naked arms, and so beholding our prices written in our breasts, they bargained for us accordingly, and at last we were all sold'.[5] This objectification often leads, in the travel tracts, to both sexual subjugation and religious conversion. Slavery threatens the chastity of Christian women, whose masters, Sandys explains, are free to 'lie with them, chastise them, exchange or sell them at their pleasure'.[6] Christian men are exposed to similar sexual exploitation, which is presented as effeminising. Thomas Sanders, for example, recounts a story, printed in Hakluyt's *Principal Navigations*, in which two members of a French crew are 'condemned slaves perpetually unto the great Turke' and are asked to convert to Islam by the king's son who 'was very desirous to have them to turn Turkes' and for them to be circumcised.[7] The text is replete with homoerotic suggestion, and the men are 'violently used' even though they refuse to convert.[8] Rawlins similarly associates slavery with conversion, noting that many of his companions, 'even for fear of torment and death, make their tongues betray their hearts to a most fearful wickedness and so are circumcised with new names and brought to confess a new religion'.⁹ Homoerotic emasculation is embodied most fully in the figure of the eunuch, whose castration (often conflated with circumcision) functions as a sign of conversion.¹⁰ Making an explicit connection between castration and the commoditisation of slavery, Sandys writes, 'Many of the children that the *Turkes* do buy (for the markets do afford of all ages) they castrate, making all smooth as the backe of the hand.'¹¹ In *A true and strange discourse*, Henry Timberlake expresses the common view that Eastern men display their lasciviousness through their maintenance of eunuchs, whom they 'keep openly, and shame not to let them at their doors to show which of them hath the fairest'.¹² As a result, slavery is rendered a specifically Muslim threat to Christian sexual and religious identity, causing Christians 'to marry their children very young, yea, even at ten years of age for fear least the Turkes should defile or alter them'.¹³ Eastern slavery, for the English, thus vividly epitomises what John Wheeler calls in his *Treatise of Commerce* the ability of traffic to make 'merchandise of mens soules' and also of their bodies.¹⁴

As Nabil Matar and Daniel Vitkus have demonstrated, white enslavement constituted a legitimate threat during the late sixteenth and early seventeenth centuries, as a substantial number of Europeans were captured by Barbary pirates and sold into slavery throughout the Mediterranean.¹⁵ This problem attracted sufficient attention in England that in 1621 James I sent an ultimately unsuccessful armada to free thousands of English and Spanish slaves from *bagnios* in Algiers.¹⁶ While English travel narratives reflect this historical reality, they also register broader anxieties about the commoditising and contaminating effects of international trade and about England's own mercantile practices. Although the English worried about preserving their national and religious integrity, they also hoped to profit in Eastern markets and promoted systems of capitalist exchange that tended, as Vitkus maintains, 'to break down all boundaries that separated nation, creed, or race and to replace them with the universal logic of capital'.[17] The travel narratives manage these conflicting impulses in part by displacing disconcerting commoditising impulses – and the purportedly debased sexual proclivities associated with them – onto the Turks. In her discussion of the coarticulation of racial difference and compulsory heterosexuality, Carmen Nocentelli argues that it is in the imperial periphery 'that some sociosexual practices and arrangements ceased to function as mere confirmations of a shared human weakness and took on an identitarian valence, becoming markers of an alterity increasingly conceived of as ontological'.[18] By figuring eunuch slaves as symbols of emasculating commoditisation, English merchants link Eastern regimes of value with the East's reputed homoeroticism, endowing both with racial significance. This racialisation of sexual behaviour, as Roderick A. Ferguson's queer of colour critique demonstrates, arises from the disruptive effects of capitalism. Ferguson contends that, in its unending search for expendable labour, capital 'often violated ideals of racial homogeneity held by local communities' and 'also inspired worries that such violations would lead to the disruption of gender and sexual proprieties'.[19] Aberrant sexual practices are thus associated with non-white groups, even – and especially – when these practices are brought into existence by Western capitalism. Accordingly, the travel narratives blame contact with East, rather than the logic of capitalism, for compromising both Christian masculinity and Christian female chastity.

In this chapter, I focus on William Shakespeare's *The Merchant of Venice* (1596) and Philip Massinger's *The Renegado; or The Gentleman of Venice* (1624), which extrapolates upon many of the themes raised in Shakespeare's play. Both *Merchant* and *Renegado* respond to the dynamics established in the travel narratives, interrogating the interplay of race, religion, sexuality and commerce in international trading ports. Both also register anxieties about Eastern slavery, through *Renegado* references slavery more overtly; in particular, they engage with the questions of human commoditisation that constitute the focus of the English travel narratives. The concern that people can be commoditised, and in the process drained of personal essence, informs the plays' mutual interest in what Vitkus terms 'turning', a trope with religious, sexual and economic implications that encapsulates the volatility of identity in international markets.[20] *Merchant* and *Renegado* emphasise the sexual consequences of personal commoditisation in culturally diverse environments, suggesting that commoditisation leads to effeminised subjugation in men and exposes women to interracial and inter-religious intercourse, with the effect not only of compromising their individual chastity but of diluting the religious and racial purity of English national identity.

Both plays, I argue, respond to crises of personal commoditisation – and to the sexual, religious and racial ramifications of these crises – through idealised representations of female chastity. Jonathan Burton has observed that early modern Turk plays substitute vulnerable women for the enslaved, sexually subjugated men of the travel tracts as a means of effacing the homoerotic dynamics of captivity and of reframing Christian men as empowered saviours.[21] *Renegado* adheres to this model, as threats to Vitelli's masculinity are overshadowed by his sister's captivity, which endangers her religious and sexual integrity. Even though *Merchant* vividly illustrates the emasculating effects of international trade, attention shifts away from Antonio's plight toward Portia's potentially commoditised chastity. The tragicomic turn in both *Merchant* and *Renegado*, I contend, is enabled by the extraction of chastity from the economic realm and the disavowal of its commodity status.[22] *Merchant* accomplishes this transformation by repositioning chastity within an emerging bourgeois domestic sphere, while *Renegado*, alternately, reifies chastity as an embodied Christian virtue. By the end of each play, chastity is endowed with intrinsic racial and religious value that, once conferred upon European Christians more broadly, exempts them from the degrading effects of personal commoditisation in an international marketplace. This renewed emphasis on chastity as an embodied, spiritual essence, moreover, informs the plays' respective articulations of racial whiteness, which, both *Merchant* and *Renegado* suggest, emerges as an ideological means of protecting upper- and middle-class Christian Europeans from the commoditising forces of the global marketplace.

Domestic Chastity and the Articulation of Racial Whiteness in The Merchant of Venice

Set in Venice, which Geraldo U. de Sousa calls 'a commercial and cultural center for the whole world' and 'a place where East meets West', *The Merchant of Venice* explores the fraught dynamics of Eastern trade elucidated in the travel tracts.[23] *Merchant* reflects the English desire, in the wake of the founding of the Levant Company, to usurp Italy's dominant role in the Mediterranean, but it also registers profound anxiety about the ethical and cultural consequences of this advancement in global trade.[24] Anxieties about Eastern slavery are manifested in the contract at the heart of the play: that Shylock will give Antonio a loan of 3,000 ducats to finance Bassanio's pursuit of Portia on the condition that, if he is not repaid by the agreed upon date, Antonio will forfeit a pound of his flesh. As both Vitkus and Burton note, Jews were closely associated with Muslims in the period because they often facilitated trade between Europe and the Ottoman Empire and sometimes served as middlemen between Barbary pirates and those who sought to buy their captives and stolen goods.[25] Complicating the play's treatment of slavery is Amanda Bailey's observation that the debtor is 'the heretofore unacknowledged precursor of the African slave', as 'the singular innovation of debt bondage was its unleashing of the law's ability to transform the human of debt bondage into a new species of money'.[26] Although Shylock does not seek to use Antonio's body as a form of credit in the manner developed by the transatlantic slave trade, he calls overt attention to the institution of slavery when he asserts that he may use Antonio's forfeited body as he pleases. He reminds the Christians,

> You have among you many a purchased slave,
> Which, like your asses, and your dogs and mules,
> You use in abject and in slavish parts,
> Because you bought them.[27]

Critiquing the Christians' economic hypocrisy, Shylock draws a parallel between their slaves and the pound of flesh, asserting that because the flesh is 'dearly bought' (IV, i, 99), he may do with it as he wishes. In particular, he maintains the right to subjugate a white Christian body in a manner that, from a Christian perspective, was deemed appropriate only for racialised others. The questions of property and personhood raised in the debt bond are thus complicated by the play's multicultural commercial setting.

As Shylock's critique suggests, *Merchant* complicates the travel narratives' clear division between Eastern and Western regimes of value. Despite their tendency to project commoditising impulses onto others, the Christian characters' own rejection of usury leads them to advocate for the contract that prices Antonio's flesh, and hence his life, at 3,000 ducats.[28] With their Aristotelian view that money can signify value but not constitute it, the Christians are more comfortable with the bond than they are with usurious transactions in which money reproduces of its own accord. For this reason, they permit Antonio's body to stand as surety for his debts and collude with a commercial logic that reduces people to their exchange value. This comfort with the commodity potential of people conflicts with English travel writers' promotion of what Igor Kopytoff calls the cultural imperative of 'singularization', a process that removes certain entities from the market, endowing them with unique spiritual or affective value.[29] Sandys complains in his narrative, for example, that the Turks charge admission to see the Holy Sepulchre, turning it into a tourist attraction: 'O who can without sorrow, without indignation, behold the enemies of Christ to be the Lords of his Sepulcher! Who at festival times sit mounted under a Canopie, to gather many of such as do enter: the profits arising thereof being farmed at eight thousand Sultanies.'[30] The commoditisation of Christian sacra, Sandys implies, accords with the Turks' practice of enslaving Christians. *Merchant* troubles this common presumption that it is only Christians who properly honour personal and sacred value. Shylock's demand for a pound of flesh forces the Christians to confront the implications of their own regimes of value, which often conflate the personal and the economic, a tendency encapsulated in Antonio's offer to Bassanio, 'My purse, my person, my extremest means, / Lie all unlocked to your occasions' (1.1.138–9). This alignment of purse and person is problematised as the play explores the troubling possibility that a person's monetary worth may constitute the entirety of his or her value.

In contrast to the Christians' economic friendships, Shylock attempts to cordon off the affective sphere, deigning to do business with the Christians but refusing to dine with them. His moneylending rests on this distinction between the economic and the affective, which is built into the Jewish interpretation of Deuteronomy 23:20 that 'unto a stranger thou mayest lend upone usury; but unto thy brother thou shalt not lend upon usury'.[31] This separation of spheres lends an air of impersonality to Shylock's economic relations that contrasts markedly with the Christian's affective networks, and he deconstructs the Christians' identification of morality with credit, remarking that Antonio is a 'good man' only in so far as his financial standing renders him 'sufficient' (I, iii, 24). Because he distinguishes between economic and affective ties, Shylock is less ready than are the Christians to attach economic value to people and to items of sentimental value. He reflects his commitment to the principle of singularity when he laments Jessica's willingness to sell his wife's ring for a pet monkey: 'It was my turquoise: I had it of Leah when I was a bachelor. I would not have given it for a wilderness of monkeys' (III, i, 109–11). Similarly, despite reports of Shylock shouting 'My daughter! O my ducats!' (II, viii, 15) throughout the streets, his comment that he wishes that his daughter were dead with 'the ducats in her coffin' (III, i, 82) suggests that no amount of money would compensate for the shame of losing Jessica to a Christian. Shylock's emphasis on singular value belies Salanio's anti-Semitic accusation, common in Christian theological writing, that Jews confused sacred items with goods that could be sold, a confusion epitomised in the sin of simony.[32] Shylock's tendency to separate forms of value shapes his understanding of slavery and the debt bond as well. Although he assumes ownership of Antonio, Shylock is generally less comfortable than are the Christians with the commercial logic that reduces people to the cash nexus, confirming Marc Shell's observation that, while Christian moral codes accommodate the use of money to represent value, 'In Jewish law there is no commensuration between human life and money.'[33] Rather than considering Antonio's body to be worth 3,000 ducats, Shylock comes to regard the bond as an opportunity to exact retribution for Antonio's anti-Semitic attacks and for the loss of his daughter. He readily admits that a pound of flesh will yield no profit, and he rejects the large sums of money offered in its place; according to Jessica, Shylock 'would rather have Antonio's flesh / Than twenty times the value of the sum / That he did owe him' (III, ii, 285–7).

Merchant's debt bond thus crystallises tensions between the economic imperative of commoditisation and the countervailing desire to maintain singular, affective value. In the play's culturally diverse setting, competing regimes of value reflect ethnic and religious differences. Shylock is thus paradoxically depicted as both a stereotypically greedy Jewish moneylender and a pagan whose emphasis on singularity borders on fetish worship and human sacrifice. Antonio, Bassanio and Portia are similarly conflicted, as they seek to maintain the intrinsic, singular value of individual Christian souls even as they show themselves to be more ready than is Shylock to commoditise human life in general. These anxieties regarding personal commoditisation, I suggest, are tenuously resolved in the domestic plot, where Portia asserts the intrinsic value of her chastity and discursively extracts it from the economic sphere. Chastity functions as a safeguard of Christian personal value in the play even as Portia defends and reinforces the law of exchange value in the Venetian economy.

Jyotsna Singh argues that *Merchant* illuminates interconnections between commercial and sexual economies and 'Portia's courtship and generosity . . . suggest a telling correlation of the "traffic in women" through marriage in Belmont and the "traffic in merchandise" in Venice.'[34] As Morocco's pursuit of Portia makes clear, the commoditisation of chastity threatens not only to adulterate European bloodlines but also to transport Portia's sexual and monetary wealth away from Europe. Portia begins the play as an internationally renowned treasure, pursued by men of many countries who attempt the challenge orchestrated by her dead father. She is, as Bassanio explains, like the mythological 'golden fleece', and 'many Jasons come in quest of her' (I, i, 170–2). This ostensibly open access to Portia's body raises cultural fears about miscegenation, a trope that was often associated with cross-cultural merchandising.[35] These fears converge around Morocco, the only African suitor and the one who most explicitly acknowledges Portia's commodity status; as he explains,

> all the world desires her.
> From the four corners of the earth they come
> To kiss this shrine, this mortal breathing saint.
> The Hyrcanian deserts and the vasty wilds
> Of wide Arabia are as thoroughfares now
> For princes to come view fair Portia.   (II, vii, 38–43)

The routes Morocco mentions mirror those likely travelled by merchants to Venice, and this image of Africans flocking to Italy underscores anxieties about foreign competition and cultural contamination. He figures Portia as an object of devotion, a 'mortal breathing saint' that inspires pilgrimages; but – like the sacred objects of the Holy Land whose commoditisation English travellers abhor – her sacred status has been compromised by commercial dynamics. Unlike an icon that is observed and worshiped, Portia will be possessed in marriage and potentially removed to a foreign locale.

Although the casket test advertises Portia as a prize, its rhetoric asserts the singularity of white female chastity – an entity that cannot be fully commoditised without dismantling traditional kinship structures – to extract Portia from the commodity sphere, thus limiting access to her body and her wealth. As de Sousa contends, 'The Venice of the play reflects not only networks of mobility and a sense of global interconnectedness but also attempts to safeguard itself from the forces associated with foreign influence and migration.'[36] The casket test serves this safeguarding function, as it rewards suitors who retain a traditional Christian distinction between internal worth and external appearances and who thus understand the motto found in the gold casket that 'All that glisters is not gold' (II, vii, 65). In this way, the test 'is meant to ensure', as Craig Muldrew argues, that Portia 'is not sought solely for the monetary value of her dowry, represented by the chests of gold and silver, but is rather trusted so that her wealth can be spent ethically'.[37] Morocco, like the Turks in the travel tracts, is inappropriately concerned with economic exchange and is incapable of distinguishing between external representation and inner value.[38] Mistakenly considering the former to reflect the latter, he regards lead as too common to represent Portia, asking 'Is't like that lead contains her? 'Twere damnation / To think so base a thought' (II, vii, 49–50). Not fluent in the Christian discourse of intrinsic value, Morocco misses the test's ideological point: that the human prize at its centre cannot be reduced to her external trappings of wealth, popularity or beauty.[39] The test's discourse of intrinsic value thus diffuses fears about miscegenation by eliding Portia's commodity status, paradoxically ensuring that her riches – sexual as well as monetary – are retained for European use.

This privileging of intrinsic value, moreover, informs the play's articulation of racial whiteness, as such value does not extend to Morocco. Despite Morocco's claim that his blood is as red as that of 'the fairest creature northward born' (II, i, 4), his skin colour prohibits him from being a suitable match for Portia, who quips, 'If he have the condition of a saint and the complexion of a devil, I had rather he should shrive me than wive me' (I, ii, 124–6). Morocco's assertion that his dark skin hides a fair interior reverses Bassanio's racist metaphor for false representation, a 'beauteous scarf / Veiling an Indian beauty' (III, ii, 98–9), which connects dark skin to abjection. Portia further highlights the cultural exclusivity of discourses of intrinsic value with her racist dismissal, 'A gentle riddance. Draw the curtains, go. / Let all of his complexion choose me so' (II, vii, 78–9). With his skin colour trumping his soul, Morocco is barred from Christian kinship structures and, by the terms of the casket test, from all sexual reproduction (a stipulation waved for Arragon). He can continue to trade with the Christians, but he cannot access the domestic realm that privileges intrinsic value. Morocco's ostracism thus exposes the cultural limits of the doctrine of intrinsic value, for which the casket test serves as a metonym. Not only does the test reveal that the doctrine pertains unequally to Europeans and to non-Europeans, but it also points to the limits of the doctrine even within Christendom: that it does not apply equally to women and to men and that it does not adequately account for the complex ways in which people are interpolated into commercial transactions.

Even Bassanio struggles to decode the casket test's meaning, demonstrating the extent to which market values have eroded Christian humanist sensibilities. To keep his monetary preoccupations at bay, Portia prepares him with her romantic song (with its initial lines rhyming with lead). Once primed, Bassanio correctly chooses the lead casket by recalling humanist platitudes, dismissing the silver and gold caskets because 'The world is still deceived with ornament' (III, ii, 74). Despite his earlier excitement about pursuing 'a lady richly left' (I, i, 161), Bassanio purports to reject monetary pursuits by choosing the lead casket, exclaiming 'Therefore, then, thou gaudy gold, / Hard food for Midas, I will none of thee' (III, ii, 101–2). He suggests that gold, like silver, that 'pale and common drudge / 'Tween man and man' (III, ii, 103–4), alienates people from one another, prohibiting the intimacy necessary for companionate marriage. Sentiments such as these occlude the commoditisation inherent in the patriarchal casket test, instead emphasising Portia's singular virtues and ostensibly removing her from market exchange.

Moreover, like the test's protection of Portia's chastity, Bassanio's success informs the play's production of racial whiteness. Kim Hall argues of Shakespeare's sonnets that 'Heterosexual social order is literally re/produced in a context that responds to new social pressures that force fairness/whiteness into visibility.'[40] The same can be said of the casket test in *Merchant*, where the backdrop of international trade puts pressure on sexual exchange. In this context, national as well as racial differences are emphasised. Portia characterises her other suitors with a litany of ethnic stereotypes: Arragon is bombastic and arrogant, the German is drunk, the Scotsman oppressed, and the Neapolitan Prince is so enamoured with his horse that Portia fears 'his mother played false with a smith' (I, ii, 41–2). The Englishman, interestingly, strives for unmarked, cosmopolitan status but instead appears 'oddly ... suited', as though he 'bought his doublet in Italy, his round hose in France, his bonnet in Germany, and his behaviour everywhere' (I, ii, 69–71). Although these characterisations do not rely on skin colour as does Portia's rejection of Morocco, Morocco's presence endows them with additional racial significance, underscoring Hall's observation that Africans serve 'to create a value for whiteness' and structure degrees of relative distance from a white ideal.[41] Portia's purified racial identity thus emerges not only in relation to Morocco's blackness but in relation to the marked national identities of the European suitors. Her white chastity confirms Hall's contention that '"white" is attached to values – purity, virginity, and innocence – represented by (or notably absent in) women'.[42] Portia's selection of Bassanio helps to confer onto him a similar whiteness, and with her help he emerges as an unmarked humanist subject, a status that occludes his national identity and renders him more transcendently white than the other suitors. Although he arrives bearing 'Gifts of rich value' (II, iv, 90), Portia and Nerissa judge him not by the superficial trappings of wealth, language, skin colour or cultural custom but rather by a presumed inherent value that renders him 'the best deserving a fair lady' (I, ii, 113–14). Intrinsic personal value thus comes to be associated with unmarked racial whiteness.

Throughout the play, Portia endeavours to protect her chastity and the racial whiteness adhering to it from potentially compromising commoditisation in the international marketplace. In her conditions for marriage, Portia even more forcefully dissuades Bassanio from the economic worldview that assesses women in terms of their wealth and beauty. Using language common to discourses of Eastern trade, she initially presents her marriage as a form of conversion, economic as well as personal, proclaiming:

> Myself, and what is mine, to you and yours
> Is now converted. But now, I was the lord
> Of this fair mansion, master of my servants,
> Queen o'er myself; and even now, but now,
> This house, these servants and this same myself
> Are yours, my lord's.   (III, ii, 166–71)

Portia converts herself from maid to wife, ostensibly subsuming her identity within Bassanio's and transferring authority over her person and her property to her husband. Her servants are similarly converted as they are submitted to mechanisms of market exchange, regarded more as commodities than as individual subjects. Portia's use of the rings, however, mitigates this sense of total transformation as well as the implication that Portia has been willingly objectified in marriage, made comparable to her house, her servants and her moveable property. Adopting Shylock's semiotics of rings as tokens of singular value, Portia collapses both her personal and economic value into the physical ring she gives Bassanio and she associates both forms of value with her chastity. Rather than simply transfer her person and her possessions to Bassanio, she does so 'with this ring, / Which', as she warns him, 'when you part from, lose or give away, / Let it presage the ruin of your love, / And be my vantage to exclaim on you' (III, ii, 171–4). In doing so, she reifies the commercial dynamics of marriage, encasing them within the love token, which she imbues with affective value. With her conditional offer, moreover, Portia shapes the rules by which Bassanio must treat her, insisting that the intrinsic value of her person and her chastity must be honoured above any potential exchange value they may possess.[43] Although the monetary significance of Portia's ring persists – and Bassanio knows that his personal solvency depends on it – Portia works throughout the remainder of the play to ensure that her own chaste value transcends the systems of homosocial exchange in which both she and Bassanio are implicated. As she does, she delineates a racially exclusive domestic sphere in contradistinction to the objectifying and multicultural marketplace, ultimately fulfilling the European desire to limit the sexual circulation of Christian women and reinforcing the discursive association between whiteness and intrinsic personal value.

In her attempt to remove herself from economic circulation, Portia delineates a revised relationship between the public and private spheres suitable for a world increasingly shaped by Europe's intensifying mercantile and imperial ventures. In its dramatisation of this process *Merchant* participates in what Ann Christensen calls the 'uneven transition toward the spatial and ideological separation of the spheres engendered in part by the advent of capitalism'.[44] Although the private sphere existed more as ideological ideal than as material reality during the late sixteenth century, it came to be seen as a space in which affective bonds were nurtured and in which men could seek refuge from an impersonal marketplace.[45] As Wendy Brown contends, once conceived as a 'separate sphere', the family 'becomes available for sentimentalism, for reification as a naturalized haven in a heartless world'.[46] The household functions for men as 'a place to retreat *to* and emerge *from* rather than a place to *be*; it is a "man's castle" in an oddly instrumental, compensatory, and transitional sense'.[47] Buttressed by the Reformation's emphasis on companionate marriage as the foundation of family life, the home is depicted as a feminine space in which men can heal from injuries to both body and soul inflicted by public life.[48] This conception of home, Christensen demonstrates, arises in dialectical relation to the expansion of overseas trade, which both redefines business as something that happens far away from home and inspires nostalgia in merchants who were away from home for long period of time.[49] With its emphasis on the bodily and spiritual wounds inflicted by trade, *Merchant* indicates that anxieties about personal commoditisation in international markets also contribute to sentimental portrayals of the home as a redemptive, nurturing space. These domestic ideologies, Portia's machinations demonstrate, have the attendant effect of occluding the commodity potential of female chastity, recasting it as the spiritual foundation of the Christian home.

As Portia aggregates intrinsic personal value and affective relations within the domestic sphere, she simultaneously configures the public sphere as a realm dominated by the principle of exchange value. Portia enforces this distinction at the trial, imposing impersonal laws of exchange as she thwarts Shylock's desire for singular, specific revenge. Despite her seemingly mystical benevolence, Portia admits that people's lives can be adequated to monetary sums when she offers to buy Antonio's life for many times the amount of the bond. When Shylock rejects this offer – and with it the abstraction of exchange value – she forces him to comply with dominant market principles and deems his affective desire for revenge inappropriate for the commercial realm. In addition to prohibiting Shylock from accessing his fleshly purchase, Portia's verdict requires him to relinquish all his money, a punishment he insists is akin to death: 'You take my life', he claims, 'When you do take the means whereby I live' (IV, i, 372–3). Despite his efforts to divorce his economic and personal affairs, Shylock is finally forced to admit that, like the Christians, his person depends upon his purse. The court's ruling forces him to comply with an emerging regime of value that prohibits the violent possession of European Christian bodies but which instead, in the nascent logic of chattel slavery, permits other bodies to be turned into commodities.

As with the casket test, Portia's legal manoeuvring sustains 'the commodity that strangers have ... in Venice' (III, iii, 27–8) while also ensuring that Venetian Christians retain their dominant status and are protected from potentially threatening aspects of international trade. In one sense, Shylock's forced conversion strips him of his cultural specificity and its attendant economic privileges, rendering him a malleable, commercial subject who is in some sense indistinguishable from other Christians. Conversion was often associated with performative, commoditised subjectivity, reflecting the ways in which the principles of exchange value emptied people of their intrinsic natures and transformed them to match new circumstances.[50] However, as Vitkus maintains, it is precisely this sense that humans were interchangeable and that one could therefore adopt another's cultural identity that 'generated the need for a rigidly defined discourse of racial alterity'.[51] The remainder of Shylock's punishment marks him as culturally and racially foreign by restricting his participation in the domestic sphere; not only is his daughter taken from him, but Antonio is named the guardian of the estate that will be transferred to Jessica. Shylock, who once viewed his home as a respite from anti-Semitic society, is, like Morocco, barred from the private sphere that mitigates the commoditising effects of the economy. He is thus forced to conform to the Christian stereotype of the usurious Jew, the embodiment of monetary, rather than sexual, reproduction.[52]

Portia's enforcement of the law of exchange value in the public sphere coincides with her purging this realm of affective relationships that rely on notions of intrinsic, singular personal value. Such relationships, she suggests, are suitable only for the heterosexual domestic sphere. This aggregation of affect within the domestic realm renders inappropriate not only Shylock's vengeful financial practices but also Antonio and Bassanio's homoerotic friendship, which Portia recasts as transgressively sodomitical. Bassanio himself suggests that his loyalty to Antonio may compromise his marriage when he promises him that 'life itself, my wife and all the world / Are not with me esteemed above thy life' (IV, i, 280–1).[53] In order to privilege her marriage, Portia depicts this homoerotic impulse as a symptom of an international market in which foreigners have subjected Christian men to the personal commoditisation associated with Eastern slavery. When she feigns a willingness to enforce the literal terms of the contract, informing Antonio that he 'must prepare [his] bosom for [Shylock's] knife' (IV, i, 241), she literalises the vulnerability of male bodies in the international economy. Beyond the vulnerability brought about by the bond, Antonio is also at the mercy of mercurial markets as far away as Tripoli, Mexico and India. This subjugation, as Shylock's potentially castrating cut suggests, is depicted in sexual terms. When Antonio refers to himself as the 'tainted wether of the flock' (IV, i, 113), he recalls the eunuchs who symbolise the emasculating effects of Eastern trade in the travel tracts.[54] After she has reframed homoerotic affection as castrating subjugation, Portia absolves the debt that binds Antonio to her husband, loosening the men's ties to one another and freeing Bassanio to commit fully to his marriage. As she reconfigures the relationship between the public and private spheres, Portia illustrates the subjugating, emasculating effects of the law of exchange value that she herself promotes as proper to the economic sphere. The heterosexual domestic sphere, grounded in reified female chastity, emerges as the antidote to such subjugating personal commoditisation, as least for those whose racial and sexual identities grant them entrance. Although he is physically liberated, Antonio remains tainted by his homoeroticism, which relegates him to the margins of domestic life at Belmont. In addition to excluding Antonio from heterosexual reproduction, his homoeroticism, which as James L. O'Rourke and Anthony G. Barthelemy have argued was associated specifically with Italy, marks him with ethnic Italianness as well as with the taint of purportedly Eastern forms of sexuality, with the effect of distancing him from Portia and Bassanio's more cosmopolitan whiteness.[55] In its treatment of homoeroticism, *Merchant* anticipates the capitalist state's tendency to, as Ferguson argues, pathologise and racialise aberrant forms of sexuality produced by capitalist development and to reinforce the normativity of heteropatriarchal relations, which finds its apotheosis in the white nuclear family.[56] *Merchant* thus illuminates the function of the emerging domestic sphere as a means of regulating sexual behaviour as well as defining racial hierarchies.

Like Antonio, Shylock's daughter Jessica attains only marginal access to the domestic sphere. As M. Lindsay Kaplan has shown, her conversion reflects the fantasy and the difficulty of submerging religious and cultural difference within a Christian totality.[57] In contrast to Morocco's failed pursuit, Jessica's entrance into Christian kinship structures carries with it financial advantages. Whereas the marriage of Portia to Morocco would have drained Italy of its wealth, placing it under foreign control, Jessica transports Shylock's ducats with her, almost as part of the costume that constitutes her 'exchange' (II, vi, 36).

As she promises Lorenzo, 'I will make fast the doors and gild myself / With some moe ducats, and be with you straight' (II, vi, 50–1). Jessica's conversion is figured in terms of her willingness to convey wealth to the Christians: for her, this willingness is a source of guilt (a resonance of 'gild' in the above quotation), while for the Christians it authenticates her conversion. Lorenzo exclaims, 'Now, by my hood, a gentle, and no Jew' (II, vi, 52), as though Jessica's willingness to steal her father's money signals her Christian nature. In contrast to Portia, who defends her own intrinsic value even as she is 'converted' (II, ii, 167) in marriage, Jessica is exchanged, submitted to market mechanisms and ostensibly emptied of her former personal – and racially legible – value.

Jessica's experience, however, illustrates the ways in which racial difference impinges upon the transformative power of conversion. As Dennis Austin Britton has shown, scenes of conversion figure centrally within early modern portrayals of race, reflecting the ways in which the Church of England's baptismal theology, in rejecting Catholic miracles, 'transformed Christians and "infidels" into distinct races'.[58] Jessica's conversion reflects this more sceptical approach to the powers of conversion. Whereas in the Catholic romance tradition, Britton argues, infidels could be miraculously converted by love, 'English responses to the infidel-conversion motif will often reject the romance telos (the transformation and incorporation of the other) and thereby reinforce a theological view that religious identity is largely fixed and racial. A byproduct of this theological view is that racial purity helps to assure salvation.'[59] Whereas Jessica regards her conversion as an act of faith and love, asserting that she 'shall be saved by [her] husband' who has 'made [her] a Christian' (III, v, 5.17–18), the Christians cast it in racial terms, associating her potential conversion with her fair skin. Lorenzo, for example, characterises her as both white and chaste in his analysis of her handwriting, claiming "tis a fair hand, / And whiter than the paper it writ on / Is the fair hand that writ' (II, iv, 13–15), while Salarino draws a racial distinction between Jessica and her father, saying that 'There is more difference between thy flesh and hers than between jet and ivory, more between your bloods than between red wine and Rhenish' (III, i, 34–6).⁶⁰ Whereas blackness functions as a sign of unalterable identity, captured in the proverb that you cannot wash an Ethiop white, Jessica's whiteness, Lorenzo and Salarino suggest, renders her a candidate for complete conversion, of the sort that empties entities of their intrinsic value by abstracting them to the common denominator of exchange.⁶¹ Jessica's conversion fails to have this fully transformative effect, however, as she remains marked by a Jewishness, that, surviving exchange, approximates racial rather than religious difference. Even after her marriage, for example, Gratiano refers to her as Lorenzo's 'infidel' (III, ii, 217), reinforcing what Janet Adelman calls 'the indelible attachment of Jewishness to Jewish bodies'.⁶² Jessica's residual Jewishness is rooted in her personal history as well as in her body, causing her to recall her betrayal of Shylock in her wistful comment,

> In such a night
> Did Jessica steal from the wealthy Jew,
> And with an unthrift love did run from Venice
> As far as Belmont. (V, i, 14–17)

Although Jessica has enriched the Christians with her patrimony, her cultural foreignness remains a source of concern, as does her willingness to flout patriarchal norms. Jessica's hold on both chastity and racial whiteness thus remains tenuous; she may be more white than Morocco, but, despite Lorenzo's protestations, she fails to attain Portia's transcendent whiteness, as she remains marked by Jewish specificity. Jessica's presence in Belmont, therefore, serves as a reminder of the porous boundaries of the domestic sphere and of racial whiteness, both of which must be continually reaffirmed through violent acts of exclusion and, in her case, inclusion.

As an easily exchanged entity, moreover, Jessica lacks the apparently self-evident intrinsic personal value that Portia associates with the domestic sphere. In contrast to her imposition of exchange value in the Venetian courtroom, Portia appropriates Shylock's notion of intrinsic, singular value for the domestic realm, thus adopting forms of value associated with cultural outsiders even when those outsiders themselves are demonised. She enforces this reconfigured regime of value when she wrests her own ring from Bassanio and shames him for having exchanged it at Antonio's behest. When Bassanio returns to Belmont, Portia illustrates the consequences of treating his wife's chastity – and her other property – in such a careless manner. She reasserts the equation of the ring with her own value and with Bassanio's honour, admonishing him,

> If you had known the virtue of the ring,
> Or half her worthiness that gave the ring,
> Or your own honour to contain the ring,
> You would not then have parted with the ring.
> (V, i, 199–202)

She further chastises Bassanio by threatening to treat her own figurative ring of chastity with similar carelessness, exchanging it with the young lawyer as she sees fit: 'I will become as liberal as you', she taunts, 'I'll not deny him anything I have, / No, not my body nor my husband's bed' (V, i, 226–8). Emphasising chastity's limited exchange potential, Portia demonstrates that Bassanio's disregard for the ring's unique affective qualities could result in the failure of their marriage; when dealing with women, she implies, free market exchange is tantamount to cuckoldry. Such cuckoldry would undo the ideological work of the casket test, leaving women to dispense with their bodies and their riches at their own discretion, perhaps with the result of racial mixing. This fear resonates in Gratiano's closing quip, 'while I live, I'll fear no other thing / So sore as keeping safe Nerissa's ring' (V, i, 306–7).

Critics frequently maintain that *Merchant*'s comic conclusion, especially the miraculous arrival of Antonio's ships, obscures contradictions within early capitalism. Mark Netzloff argues, for instance, that *Merchant* 'elide[s] the preconditions of capital, effacing the processes of abstraction and limitless circulation upon which capitalist value production depends, and instead conceptualize[s] a manageable realm of exchange in which capital always returns to and reinforces the domestic sphere'.[63] Similarly, Singh contends that 'the spirit of the gift' with which the play ends 'offers a rhetorical cover or a mystification of the transactions of global capital and trade'.[64] At the same time, however, this domestication of commercial dynamics exposes the process by which the private sphere is constructed as a means of managing the effects of international trade on upper- and middle-class Christians such as Portia and Bassanio. In doing so, *Merchant* also illuminates the constructedness of racial whiteness, demonstrating its emergence in dialectical relation to capitalist forces that threaten to commoditise the bodies, labour and sexuality of European Christians. Although Portia and Nerissa remain confined within the patriarchal family structure, the affective ideologies of the domestic sphere ensure that they will be shielded from the overt commoditisation associated both with the Venetian economy (where Leah's ring now circulates) and with Eastern harems and slave markets. As such, they are also restricted from interracial sexual encounters, embodied in the play by the Moor whom Launcelot has impregnated and who, as presumably 'less than an honest woman' (III, v, 38), cannot be incorporated into Christian kinship structures. With their chastity secured, Portia and Nerissa become repositories of racial whiteness, imbuing their lineages with an inherited intrinsic value. By establishing a racially exclusive domestic sphere, *Merchant* tenuously fulfils the desire expressed in the travel tracts to expand trade into foreign markets while simultaneously inoculating the English from the effects of international exchange. The material foundation of this domestic sphere, buttressed by overseas trade, Portia's fortune and the expropriation of Shylock's wealth, is obscured by its humanist ideologies of intrinsic value and affective familial intimacy.

Catholic Semiotics and Embodied Chastity in The Renegado

The Renegado, like *Merchant*, takes place in an international trading port in which commercial dynamics spin out of control, compromising Europeans' racial and religious integrity. Set in Tunis, *Renegado* reflects concerns about the capture and potential conversion of English merchants in Barbary.[65] The plot centres on the plight of the enslaved Italian maiden Paulina and her brother Vitelli, the 'Gentleman of Venice', who poses as a merchant as part of a plot to save her and, in so doing, exposes himself to the seductions of the Mohametan princess Donusa.[66] The subplot involves the treachery and redemption of the eponymous renegado Grimaldi, who has 'turned Turk' and is responsible for selling Paulina to the Mohametan viceroy. *Renegado* thus foregrounds the discursive matrix of slavery, conversion and sexual subjugation that informs *Merchant*'s central conflict. In various registers the play explores the problematics of conversion, a trope that, as in *Merchant*, possesses significance that is sexual, economic and racial as well as religious. *Renegado* asks how conversions of all sorts can be managed in a tumultuous commercial environment that encourages exchange, and, in particular, the play confronts the imperialist problem of how to promote Mohametan conversion to Christianity while avoiding conversion in the opposite direction.

As in *Merchant*, *Renegado*'s tragicomic resolution is enabled by the removal of chastity from the commodity sphere, a discursive trajectory that tenuously resolves anxieties regarding the personal commoditisation of European men and women in multiracial environments and that informs the play's imperialist articulation of Christian exceptionalism. In contrast to *Merchant*, however, this reification of chastity occurs not through recourse to an emerging domestic sphere but rather through the use of Catholic semiotics that cast chastity as a spiritual yet embodied possession of Christians.

Aided by the force of miraculous relics and sacraments, chastity comes to be conflated with Christian faith and functions as a safeguard against conversion that adheres to white European bodies but, paradoxically, can be conferred to eligible Christian converts. Even as *Renegado* presents a vision of a Christianity that purports to incorporate social difference, it increasingly aligns Christianity with whiteness. In addition, the disparate modes of Christian selfhood made available to Vitelli, Paulina and Donusa, and the denial of this identity to Mohametan men, point toward an emerging imperialist paradigm that trumpets the virtues of freedom and liberal individualism but in which temperate, male subjectivity depends upon the subjugation of women and people of colour.

Although Vitelli and his fellow Christians have been promised 'free trading' and 'safety' in Tunis, traffic with Eastern cultures poses a threat to Christians' bodily and spiritual integrity in *Renegado*.[67] This threat is most acutely manifested through depictions of slavery, as over 'a thousand slaves' are assumed to reside in 'the Turkish galleys' (II, vi, 32–3). As in the travel narratives, slavery, the most extreme form of Eastern commoditisation, is associated with both conversion and sexual subjugation. This matrix is embodied in the figure of Grimaldi, whose willingness to turn Turk accords with his practice of selling 'ravished virgins', including Vitelli's sister Paulina, 'To slavery ... for coin to feed [his] riots' (I, iii, 74–5). Grimaldi's actions endanger Paulina's faith as well as her virginity, as it is assumed that her captor, the viceroy Asambeg, will 'compel[] her / To yield her fair name up to his foul lust / And after turn apostata to the faith / That she was bred in' (I, i, 136–9). Sexual and religious registers are intertwined in the play, with sexual activity leading to religious conversion. Despite depicting slavery as a consequence of Eastern tyranny, *Renegado* makes clear that personal commoditisation and the related processes of sexual subjection and religious conversion are consequences of participation in the market economy more generally, and are a threat to both masculine integrity and female chastity. In this way, *Renegado* reflects the anxiety that, in Vitkus's words, the English 'would somehow be 'converted' or contaminated by the new economic conditions produced by the obsession with "making merchandise"'.[68]

The emasculating aspects of commercial exchange are figured in the play in terms of castration, which was considered a consequence of Mohametan conversion and captivity. Merchants are depicted as willing to convert – and potentially undergo castration – for pecuniary motives. Vitelli's servant Gazet, for example, considers dissembling a beneficial business practice and avers that he will pose as a member of any religion (excepting Mohametanism at first) if it profits him. In addition to recalling Grimaldi's actual conversion, Gazet's mercenary approach to religion informs his later misinformed interest in becoming a eunuch at the Mohametan court as a form of social advancement. Castration functions as a metaphor for the loss of personal value that a man undergoes in the process of conversion, and frequent puns on 'jewels' and 'stones' reflect the East's dual threat to Western wealth and masculinity. As Carazie, an English eunuch employed at Donusa's court, puts it, castration is 'but parting with / A precious stone or two. I know the price on't' (III, iv, 51–2). As Barbara Fuchs contends,

> by entering the realm of metaphor male potency also becomes oddly unstable: stones can be lost, stolen, or foolishly bartered away. The resulting relation of castration to commerce, and the description of the castrated eunuch Carazie as the sole English character in the play, suggest a troubling connection between England's trade and its vulnerable masculinity.[69]

Jonathan Gil Harris argues, moreover, that *Renegado*'s references to castration reflect anxieties about the loss of the nation's bullion to Eastern pirates.[70] Even in the absence of direct Mohametan threats, however, masculinity is subject to enervating commoditisation in the play's market society. Gazet explains his initial unwillingness to convert to Mohametanism, for example, by saying that his testicles are the property of his lover Doll: ''Tis her venture / Nor dare I barter that commodity / Without her special warrant' (I, i, 40–2). When manhood is figured as a commodity, it can be alienated from its possessor and subjugated either to foreign or feminine ownership.

Borrowing from the generic conventions of city comedies, *Renegado* draws on intertwined discourses of sex and economics to suggest that both male temperance and female chastity are compromised in market contexts that elicit uncontrollable desire. The familiar vendor's call 'What do you lack?' (I, iii, 1) attests to the ways in which desire for commodities arises from an insufficiency in the subject. The cheap commodities for sale in the market, described as 'brittle as a maidenhead at sixteen' (I, i, 2), reflect the failure of overvalued products to adequately redress this insufficiency. As an aristocrat disguised as a merchant, Vitelli's manhood is shaken in this commercial Eastern environment, first when his anxiety over Paulina's fate causes him to lose his 'manly patience' (I, i, 80) and, later, when he falls prey to Donusa's seduction. The market proves similarly compromising for women, but in *The Renegado*, it is Eastern rather than Western women who show themselves to be most vulnerable to this threat. Mirroring Vitelli's experience, Donusa's foray into the market exposes her to desires that compromise both her sexual integrity and her class status, as she is considered too highborn to mingle with common people. Her fall from grace is precipitated by her desire to see the market, as she

> feel[s] a virgin's longing to descend
> So far from [her] own greatness as to be,
> Though not a buyer, yet a looker on
> Their strange commodities. (I, ii, 114–17)

Her commercial desire quickly turns sexual when her encounter with Vitelli compels her to 'buy' and not just 'look'. At Vitelli's stall, Donusa presents herself as a commodity by comparing her own person to the images painted on Vitelli's wares, purportedly of the 'rarest beauties of the Christian world' (I, iii, 137) though Gazet suspects them to be 'figures / Of bawds and common courtesans in Venice' (I, i, 12–13). Averring that she 'instantly could show [him] one to theirs / Not much inferior' (I, iii, 140–1), she unveils herself, thus transgressing Mohametan gender conventions and asserting her worth in a sexual marketplace. Formerly known for her 'frozen coldness which no appetite / Or height of blood could thaw' (III, iii, 3.69–70), Donusa is undone by the enticements of the cultural, commercial and sexual marketplace. This commercial power remains mystified, however, and Donusa is left wondering, 'What magic hath transformed me from myself? / Where is my virgin pride? How have I lost / My boasted freedom?' (II, i, 23–5).

Donusa's susceptibility to the market's seductions stems from her subjugation to Eastern tyranny, which impedes temperance. Although Donusa conceives of her virgin self-sufficiency as freedom, she has been unable to exercise this freedom within the confines of Eastern patriarchy, as 'jealous Turks / Never permit their fair wives to be seen / But at the public bagnios or the mosques – And even then veiled and guarded' (I, ii, 18–21). This cloistered life engenders a lack of self-control. As Francisco warns Vitelli,

> these Turkish dames –
> Like English mastiffs that increase their fierceness
> By being chained up – from the restraint of freedom,
> If lust once fire their blood from a fair object,
> Will run a course the fiends themselves would shake at
> To enjoy their wanton ends.   (I, iii, 9–14)

Never having had to grapple with the responsibilities of liberty, Francisco suggests, Mohametan women wantonly pursue the first object of their passion. Given that Donusa is considered 'the wonder and amazement of / Her sex, the pride and glory of the empire' (III, iii, 66–7), her fall points to the moral frailty of all Mohametan women, who lack the guidance of Christian teachings as well as the apparently Western virtue of self-possession. Donusa's desire to see the marketplace also reflects her curiosity about Western liberty, however, as well as a latent desire to possess herself rather than to remain a possession of her male relatives. She inquires about rumours that 'Christian ladies live with much more freedom / Than such as are born here' and asks Carazi, 'what's the custom there / Among your women?' (I, ii, 17–18, 22–3). In dealing with her own servants and lovers, moreover, Donusa explicitly disavows Turkish tyranny, and she refuses to participate in a ceremony in which her father would present her suitor Mustapha 'for [her] slave' because 'Such tyranny and pride agree not with / My softer disposition' (I, ii, 95, 98–9). Donusa's desire for freedom thus informs her infatuation with Vitelli and marks her as a candidate for conversion. As Donusa's experience attests, *Renegado* begins to present a reformed view of the market not just as a dangerous and seductive site of intercultural mixing and potential sexual and religious subjugation, but also as an integral component of liberal Western society. Only temperate Christians, who have attained the power of possessive individualism, are capable of navigating these commercial environments without compromising their personal integrity.

In the beginning of the play, neither Donusa nor Vitelli possesses such integrity, and their relationship is presented in commercial terms that reflect the depravity of unregulated intercultural intercourse. Donusa debases herself as she continues to employ the economic discourse she used in the market when she meets Vitelli at her palace under the pretence that she would like to repay him for a mirror she has broken. Calling herself his 'debtor' (II, iv, 15), she compensates him first with 'bags stuffed full of . . . imperial coin' (II, iv, 83) and 'gems for which the slavish Indian dives / To the bottom of the main' (II, iv, 85–6). Donusa's claim to chastity, from the Christian point of view, is undermined by her association with luxury, as her palace is lavishly decorated and her body adorned with ornament. She further compromises her chastity by associating her own person with these material treasures, offering Vitelli 'The tender of / Myself' (II, iv, 101–2). Her commoditised sexuality predictably destabilises Vitelli's aristocratic integrity, and he describes his desire as a form of possession, a self-alienation akin to forced conversion. 'What unknown desires', he asks, 'Invade and take possession of my soul, / All virtuous objects vanished?' (II, i, 26–8). This transformation is emasculating, though it does not involve literal castration. Vitelli proves unable to practise 'manly patience' (I, i, 80), and instead exclaims, 'I am ravished' (II, iii, 12). As a result, he succumbs to the 'base desires' (I, iii, 21) of interfaith attraction, as Donusa's proposition shakes his 'constant resolution' (II, iv, 109) and 'beat[s] all chaste thoughts from [him]' (II, iv, 129).

Whereas both Donusa and Vitelli undergo predictably negative transformations in the intercultural marketplace, Paulina is protected from this fate by the magic of a Christian 'relic' (I, i, 147) that the Jesuit Francisco promises will 'keep the owner free from violence' (I, i, 149). The relic blends Catholic and Protestant religious semiotics, functioning as both a miraculous charm and a sign of Paulina's inner fortitude. It protects her only so long as 'she fall not by her own consent' (I, i, 152), and she 'does preserve / The virtue of it by her daily prayers' (I, i, 150–1). Jane Hwang Degenhardt connects *Renegado*'s use of Catholic semiotics to its portrayal of Islam as an embodied threat to English racial identity and argues that, 'Because this threat of conversion exceeded the realm of spiritual faith, it demanded physical and material countermeasures in order to believably enact its resistance or reversal.'[71] Christian chastity is thus presented both as inherently stronger than Mohametan chastity, as Paulina refuses to consent to her captor Asambeg's wishes, and as physically protected by divine powers. Counteracting the vulnerability of Christian bodies in multiracial climates, the relic renders Paulina's chastity miraculous. It transforms Asambeg, 'rob[bing] [him] of the fierceness [he] was born with' (II, v, 107). Even her name functions as 'a charm' that 'choke[s] [his] fury' (II, v, 110-11). 'There is something in you', he tells Paulina, 'That can work miracles' (II, v, 149-50). Although Paulina is enslaved, her person having literally been sold to Asembeg, her chastity is longer subject to commoditising market forces or to corruption at the hands of foreign men. As a result, common comparisons between chastity and commodities no longer apply. As Asambeg himself recognises in his ode to Paulina,

> Any simile,
> Borrowed from diamonds or the fairest stars
> To help me to express how dear I prize
> Thy unmatched graces, will rise up and chide me
> For poor detraction. (II, v, 120-4)

Asambeg suggests that Paulina's miraculous chastity transcends the framework that Donusa established when she literalised the association between her person and her jewels by presenting her body as an alternate form of 'tender' (II, iv, 101). Although Asambeg's compliment bears some relation to conventional depictions of chastity as an inestimable jewel, his rejection even of any similes to this effect indicates that economic chastity discourse itself is inadequate to encapsulate the worth of Paulina's Christian virtue.

Chastity ceases to function as a commodity and becomes a reified virtue inherent to Christian women and buttressed by the power of a Christian God. The play's Catholic modes of representation facilitate this shift, as the magical power of the relic closes gaps between reality and representation, between intrinsic and extrinsic value, to imagine chastity not as performative or commoditisable but as an inherent, embodied Christian quality. In contrast to Portia's ring, the relic worn on Paulina's neck does not simply represent her chastity, as such materialised metaphors inadvertently call attention to chastity's commodity potential. Instead, the relic actively protects chastity. By invoking Catholic semiotics,

Renegado bypasses *Merchant*'s focus on the domestic sphere as a means of protecting the personal value of Christians and instead asserts that Christian faith itself – associated with the miraculous chastity of the relic – renders one intrinsically valuable and impervious to the commoditising, corrupting forces of the international marketplace. Degenhardt rightly notes that *Renegado* genders its treatment of chastity, as men prove capable of cultivating spiritual fortitude while women need the aid of magical relics; the play thus reveals 'a collusion of racial and patriarchal logic in which the female body is susceptible to racial reinscription in ways that the male body is not'.[72] This division is not absolute, however, as Paulina's divinely aided chastity informs the modes of virtue adopted by Vitelli and Donusa; though achieved through conversion or recommitment to Christianity, their reclaimed virtue is imagined in similar terms as the embodied personal property of Christians.

Christianity, then, rather than the domestic sphere, provides an alternative to the market's commoditising energies. In the aftermath of his sexual encounter with Donusa, Vitelli discovers that he cannot redeem himself through the market logic of exchange. In an attempt to regain his former identity, which has been 'strangely metamorphosed' (II, vi, 20), Vitelli attempts to reverse his earlier transaction with Donusa. Lamenting 'At what an overvalue [he has] purchased / The wanton treasure of [her] virgin bounties' (III, v, 41–2) and hoping to 'Redeem [his] forfeit innocence' (III, v, 45), he returns the casket of jewels Donusa had given him, symbolically 'deliver[ing] back the price / And salary of [her] lust!' (III, v, 48–9). He initially assumes that he can return the riches (and perhaps even the 'virgin bounty' with which they are associated) in exchange for his virtue. Donusa reveals a flaw in Vitelli's calculation, however, when she reminds him that 'a loss to you, mine equals, / If not transcends it' (III, v, 57–8). The transaction has resulted in a net loss for both of them. Donusa has not gained by Vitelli's loss as the market principle would have it; rather, as a woman, her loss of chastity promises to be even more disastrous than his loss of masculine honour. Donusa's comparison also points to the inherent problem in chastity-as-commodity discourse: that chastity can be lost but never recovered through exchange. Vitelli's honour is now subject to the same principle; his sexual sin cannot be erased by returning the jewels, nor can another transaction recover his lost identity.

Whereas conversion to Mohametanism is depicted as a market-based form of exchange that depletes personal value, conversion or commitment to Christianity – aided by the divine power that infuses the play's Catholic symbolism – constitutes a rejection of the market forces with which the East is associated. Vitelli therefore achieves chaste temperance only when he abandons this commercial register and embraces his role as a Christian martyr, ready to die at the hands of his Mohametan captors. Faced with persecution, Vitelli achieves a Christian stoicism he once found elusive, proclaiming, 'What punishment / Soe'er I undergo, I am still a Christian' (III, v, 95–6) and asserting that ''Tis not in man / To change or alter me' (IV, iii, 53–4). Vitelli's pledges echo Paulina's faith in her 'chastity, built upon / The rock of my religion' (IV, ii, 29–30). Though Vitelli's virtue is performative rather than achieved by means of a relic, its connection with his sister's miraculous chastity enhances the sense that virtue is intrinsic to devout Christians, and this enhanced virtue subsequently permits him to resist Donusa's attempts to convert him to Mohametanism. The spiritual force of Vitelli's renewed embrace of Christian virtue, moreover, has imperialistic implications, as it surpasses anything comparable in Mohametan men. Vitelli's 'manly patience' and 'all-commanding virtue' (IV, ii, 55–6) astonish his captors, who were 'never witness / Of such invincible fortitude as this Christian' (IV, ii, 45–6). Christians, *The Renegado* suggests, possess a spiritual fortitude that not only protects them from conversion but also attracts the admiration of Mohametans, suggesting that Christianity is the one true religion.

Donusa's conversion therefore confers upon her intrinsic personal value, which, as in *Merchant*, is associated with whiteness as well as with Christianity. Like many Eastern beauties in early modern drama, Donusa occupies a racially ambiguous position, as her relatively fair skin makes her a candidate for potential incorporation into Western society while her dark hair and eyes mark her as different. The tenuousness of Donusa's claim to whiteness is evident in Vitelli's belief that she has been darkened by her sexual encounter with him. '[T]he sating of [her] lust', he avers, 'hath sullied / The immaculate whiteness of [her] virgin beauties' (III, v, 4–5). Her conversion reconstitutes her whiteness, allowing her to 'Look truly fair, when [her] mind's pureness answers / [her] outward beauties' (IV, iii, 146–7). Before her conversion, Donusa had been characterised by the disjuncture between her outward beauty and her inner depravity, and, as Vittelli alleges when she attempts to convert him, her words are like 'sugared pills' containing 'strong poison' (IV, iii, 73–4). This disconnect between exterior appearance and inner reality opens space for deceit, aligning Donusa with her servant Manto, who claims to have 'passed / For current' (III, i, 14–15) many years after she lost her virginity. Donusa's conversion makes her whole again, bringing her 'mind's pureness' into accordance with her 'outward beauties'. Associated with both chastity and whiteness, this wholeness signals Donusa's capacity to be integrated into Western culture. Conversion to Christianity is thus figured not simply as one more form of exchange, as it is largely in *Merchant*, but rather as a transformation that reverses the commoditising and alienating effects of the market.

Just as Paulina's chastity is reinforced by the relic, Donusa's conversion is solidified through Catholic rituals, both the sign of the cross, 'the sacred badge [God] arms his servants with' (IV, iii, 142), and the sacrament of baptism. '[A] perfect sign / Of innocence' (V, iii, 111–12), the baptism completes the reconstruction of Donusa's chastity, as it 'purge[s] those spots that cleave upon the mind / If thankfully received'

(V, iii, 115–16). The baptism also cleanses Donusa of her cultural history, 'wash[ing] off' her Mohametan 'Stains and pollutions' (V, iii, 113). It also frees her from the sexual tyranny of Mohametan men such as Asambeg, as it causes her to 'with scorn look down upon / All engines tyranny can advance to batter / Your constant resolution' (IV, iii, 143–5). In the process, she is transformed into 'another women' (V, iii, 121) who is ready to die a Christian martyr and submissive wife. Though still invested in a Protestant belief that sacramental signs must align with internal states of being, *Renegado*'s theatrical use of Catholic signifiers works to close the gap between being and seeming, distancing assessments of personal value from the commercial thinking that characterises Vitelli and Donusa's relationship in its initial stages. As Britton argues, *Renegado* further shores up Donusa's conversion by combining it with a discourse of martyrdom, which 'is powerful for purging the infidel-conversion motif of the concupiscence so closely associated with romance' and for transforming a 'tragic . . . racialized object to redeemed Christian'.[73] The Catholic sacraments also work to differentiate Christian conversion from 'turning Turk', showing that only the former aligns with divine truth. Baptism now becomes the 'choicest jewel' that Donusa will wear 'On her fair forehead' (V, i, 25–6), a spiritual alternative to the material jewels she once wore and an analogue to the relic that permits Paulina's 'chastity [to be] preserved by miracle' (V, ii, 69). Although the language of jewels persists, serving as a reminder of chastity's origins as commodity, it now appears residual and is no longer interrogated for its potentially unsettling ramifications.

Donusa's transformation attests to the power of Christianity to incorporate foreign women in particular. Although *The Renegado* reconceptualises chastity as a virtue that may be conferred onto foreign women, this virtue does not extend as far as foreign men, who, as in *Merchant*, are barred both from entrance to the domestic sphere and from assimilation into Western society. In fact, as Donusa's conversion marks the beginning of her welcomed turn toward European values, it simultaneously causes her to reject Mohametan men. This rejection assumes a racial dimension, as she insults the 'wainscot face' (III, i, 48) and 'grim aspect or tadpole-like complexion' (III, i, 49) of her former suitor Mustapha, and she advises him to have his 'barber wash [his] face' because he looks 'like a bugbear to fright children' (III, i, 59–60). *Renegado*, like *Merchant*, thus aligns blackness with unconvertability, revealing that, as Burton suggests, 'skin prejudice and religious difference . . . operate according to similar and mutually informing imperatives, particularly in regard to questions of gender'.[74] Unlike Donusa who is endowed with both whiteness and chastity when she converts, the Mohametan men never achieve the forbearance they admire in Vitelli, and their mercurial temperaments remain associated with Eastern tyranny. As such, they show themselves to be unfit husbands for either Donusa or Paulina, both of whom prefer Westerners' presumably more liberal treatment of their wives. As Britton states, 'racialized male bodies resist the transforming impulses of not only comedy but also of romance'.[75] The women's preference for Christians is a source of shame and disgust for the Mohametan men, and they are particularly offended that Donusa would 'Basely descend to fill a Christian's arms / And to him yield her virgin honour up' (III, iii, 73–4). The triumph of the Christian men in this homosocial competition ultimately proves the superiority of their virtue and their masculinity and associates both with an emerging ideology of white supremacy.

Although it cannot convert Mohametan men, Christian faith, supplemented by the binding force of Catholic semiotics, does have the power to redeem even the most treacherous of renegades. Grimaldi, who formerly 'ha[d] no compunction' (I, iii, 76) about the suffering he caused with his privateering and slave trading, undergoes a divine transformation at the hands of the Jesuit priest Francisco. Grimaldi's initial conversion to Mohametanism resulted from spiritual despair after a moment of crisis in which, during mass, he 'snatched from' Francisco 'the sanctified means' and 'Dashed it upon the pavement' (IV, i, 32–3). When Grimaldi loses favour with Asambeg and his ships and goods are confiscated, he falls deeper into despair in the absence of faith, wealth and advancement. Grimaldi's counter conversion, like Donusa's, is confirmed by nearly magical Catholic rituals. Desiring to 'teach the desperate to repent' (III, ii, 104), Francisco dons the bishop's vestments he was wearing at the time of Grimaldi's sacrilegious act and pardons him using the authority of the Bible and several Latin phrases, therefore complying with the stipulation that Grimaldi can be redeemed only by the same priest whom he offended. Though suspiciously Popish from an English perspective, this spectacular ritual both confirms and enacts Grimaldi's true penance. As Francisco insists, 'This penitence is not counterfeit' (IV, i, 128). Whereas Grimaldi's conversion to Mohametanism stemmed from purely commercial motivations and instantiates the emptying process of exchange, his reclamation of Christianity reverses this process. He, like Donusa, is made whole.

The Renegado's turn away from commoditised chastity discourse thus facilitates a broader embrace of intrinsic virtue. With his rejection of Mohametanism, even Grimaldi learns that actions should arise from intrinsic motivations, and he embraces the idea that helping Vitelli, Donusa and Paulina escape 'shall reward itself in the performance, / And that's true prize indeed' (V, ii, 40–1). This emphasis on intrinsic value nonetheless accrues material wealth for the Christians. With Francisco and Grimaldi's help, Vitelli, Donusa and Paulina escape with 'choicest jewels' (V, viii, 27) in tow. This wealth, however, has largely been divorced from Christian bodies, which are endowed with inherent worth and are no longer subject to the horrors of slavery, the harem or Mohametan conversion. Despite this assurance, however, the ultimate return of the Christians to Europe evinces some anxiety that Christian fortitude may be better preserved in

Western environments. This is the same anxiety that necessitated the play's reliance on Catholic semiotics, as spiritual fortitude seems inadequate in commercial Eastern climates and needs extra protection, whether this protection is magical, theatrical or divine. Nonetheless, the play's Catholic semiotics, the relic in particular, transforms the relationship between female chastity and masculine integrity. As neither a commodity nor a simple intrinsic virtue, chastity becomes a divinely inspired trait possessed by white Christian women that can be conferred, albeit in less material form, onto those European men and foreign women whose racial characterisation allows them to embrace Christianity.

Toward Liberal Individualism and Whiteness as Property

Renegado's treatment of chastity reflects its relative comfort with mercantile activity. Jonathan Gil Harris contends that the play's conclusion embraces free trade, imagining 'a transnational community of Christian venturers liberated not only from Islamic masters but also from the emasculating sway of the state in general'.[76] Valerie Forman similarly argues that the play employs religious discourse to present trade as redeemed, 'taking the first step toward naturalizing profit and thus effacing the need to ask about its source and the loss elsewhere that would be necessary to counterbalance it'.[77] Free trade, in contrast to Islamic tyranny, becomes integral to Western Christian identity rather than a source of ethical and spiritual anxiety. The play's depiction of chastity reflects this shift. Whereas *Merchant*, written twenty-eight years earlier, retains a significant focus on the potential commoditisation of both Christian men and women and dramatises the process by which intrinsic chastity is constructed in order to mitigate this threat, *Renegado* naturalises chaste virtue, presenting it not as a social construction forged in relation to market dynamics but as a miraculous byproduct of conversion and, by extension, a property inherent in European Christians. By the end of *The*

Renegado, chastity has been largely divorced from its material underpinnings; as such it remains a coveted sign of virtue but no longer presents intense semiotic, economic and ethical challenges. This chastity is neither a market-based commodity nor an intrinsically valuable antithesis to the market, but rather a virtue that adheres within European Christian bodies and is extended provisionally to those who embrace their way of being. If *Merchant* employs economic chastity discourse to negotiate an emerging capitalist economy, *Renegado* extends this project for a society that has more fully integrated the principles of market exchange.

Accordingly, whereas *Merchant* expresses openly discriminatory attitudes toward racial and religious others, *Renegado*'s conclusion gestures toward an emerging liberal paradigm that ostensibly endows all people with equal liberty but in fact grants full subject status only to white, Christian men. Although *Renegado*'s proto-imperial politics purport to make chaste virtue available to anyone who embraces Western values, only Vitelli attains the self-possession that liberal individualism requires. Donusa's conversion transforms her into a submissive wife, prepared to be Vitelli's 'humble shadow' (V, iii, 85), while Paulina's fetishised chastity remains outside of her control, owing less to her powers of self-possession than to the miraculous power attributed to virginity in Catholic mythology. The servant Gazet remains inordinately enthralled to commerce, while Mohametan men display tyrannical understandings of possession that make them unsuited to Western subjectivity. *Renegado* thus extends *Merchant*'s nascent vision of a social contract, implicit in Hobbesean formulations but developed more fully by Locke, that relies upon sexual and racial subordination in order to sustain the liberal subject. As theorists such as Carole Pateman, Charles Mills and Wendy Brown have shown, this contract relocates patriarchalism to the private sphere, building white male agency upon the subordination of women in marriage as well as the exploitation of people of colour, excluding both groups from full subjecthood.[78] To establish the autonomous subject, liberalism claims equality for all people, 'produc[ing] abstract, genderless, colorless sovereign subjects ... whose sovereignty and abstract equality contend uneasily with the discourses marking relative will-lessness and inferiority according to socially marked attributes'.[79] We see this process at work in *Merchant*, where Portia builds her domestic sphere in part by marginalising those deemed racially, religiously or sexually unfit and displaces inappropriately commercial sensibilities onto these marginalised groups. In *Renegado*, the backdrop of Muslim tyranny establishes the conditions against which a European Christian man might assert possessive individualism; despite Paulina's and Donusa's stated desire for liberty and self-possession, these ideals apply to them only catachrestically, as the women remain subordinate to Vitelli. Muslim men, by contrast, function as the antithesis of the Western individual and are therefore incapable even of any such limited transformation.

By aligning whiteness, Christianity, intrinsic value and possessive individualism, both *Merchant* and *Renegado* participate in the prehistory of whiteness-as-property, a phenomenon whose apotheosis David R. Roediger locates in the nineteenth century whereby racial whiteness serves as 'a way in which white workers responded to a fear of dependency on wage labor and to the necessities of capitalist work discipline'.[80] Whiteness becomes an object of value even, or especially, in exploitative or commoditising environments. Both *Merchant* and *Renegado* evince a desire to make whiteness matter, to assert its value in multiracial commercial environments in which everything appears subject to the endless conversions of the cash nexus. The plays also – at the commencement of England's involvement in the African slave trade – begin to formulate an obverse logic by which the bodies and labour of marginalised others may be made subject to the full extent of the market's commoditising energies. When defined against commercial exchange value, whiteness comes to be associated not simply with Europeanness or with Christianity, but also with the presence of intrinsic personal value; that is, with humanity. In *Merchant* and *Renegado*, then, we begin to glimpse the Enlightenment's understanding of whiteness as universal, a formulation in which, as Warren Montag states, whiteness becomes 'the very form of human universality itself' so that '[t]o be white is to be human, and to be human is to be white'.[81] Although, as critics such as Mary Floyd-Wilson and Jean Feerick have argued, pan-European whiteness had not yet solidified in the late sixteenth and early seventeenth centuries, *Merchant* and *Renegado* reflect an aspirational English desire to join such a racial category.[82] *Merchant* presents whiteness as multiple and malleable, and it evinces significant anxiety about England's distance from pan-European whiteness, emblematised in the figure of Lord Falconbridge who arrives 'oddly . . . suited' (I, ii, 69) to the casket test and is dismissed in the same manner as Portia's other ethnically marked suitors. *Renegado* presents whiteness more confidently and simplistically, cathecting it to the Christian chastity that is reified in Paulina's relic. Whiteness literally becomes property that can be transported, along with the 'choicest jewels' (V, viii, 27), out of the East. In both plays, articulations of whiteness arise from and seek to mitigate anxieties about personal commoditisation – in particular the commoditisation of female chastity – in volatile international markets.

Notes

1. For a discussion of the expansion of Mediterranean trade, see Daniel Vitkus, '"The Common Market of All the World": English Theater, the Global System, and the Ottoman Empire in the Early Modern Period', in *Global Traffic: Discourses and Practices of Trade in English Literature and Culture from 1550 to 1700*, ed. Barbara Sebek and Stephen Deng (New York: Palgrave, 2008), 19–37.
2. Arjun Appadurai, 'Introduction: Commodities and the Politics of Value', in *The Social Life of Things* (New York: Cambridge University Press, 1986), 3–63, esp. 15.
3. Appadurai, 'Commodities and the Politics of Value', 15.

4. George Sandys, *A relation of a iourney begun an: Dom: 1610 Foure bookes. Containing a description of the Turkish Empire, of AEgypt, of the Holy Land, of the remote parts of Italy, and ilands adioyning* (London: Printed by Richard Field for W. Barrett, 1615), British Library Collection, 69, EEBO.
5. John Rawlins, *The Famous and Wonderful Recovery of a Ship of Bristol, Called the Exchange, from the Turkish Pirates of Argier, with the Unmatchable Attempts and Good Success of John Rawlins, Pilot in Her, and Other Slaves* (1622), in *Piracy, Slavery, and Redemption*, ed. Nabil Matar and Daniel J. Vitkus (New York: Columbia University Press, 2001), 103.
6. Sandys, *A relation*, 70.
7. Richard Hakluyt, *Principal Navigations, Voyages, Traffiques and Discoveries of the English Nation* (1589), 12 vols (Glasgow: James MacLehose and Sons, 1904), 5:197, quoted in Jonathan Burton, *Traffic and Turning: Islam and English Drama, 1579–1624* (Newark: University of Delaware Press, 2005), 97.
8. Burton, *Traffic and Turning*, 97.
9. Rawlins, *The Famous and Wonderful Recovery*, 102–3.
10. For a discussion of circumcision as 'the consummate mark of the apostate', see Burton, *Traffic and Turning*, 100.
11. Sandys, *A relation*, 70.
12. Henry Timberlake, *A true and strange discourse of the trauailes of two English pilgrimes what admirable accidents befell them in their iourney to Ierusalem, Gaza, Grand Cayro, Alexandria, and other places* (London: Thomas Archer, 1603), Folger Collection, 24.
13. Timberlake, *A true and strange discourse*, 24.
14. John Wheeler, *A Treatise of Commerce* (London, 1601; repr., New York: Columbia University Press, 1931), 6.
15. See Nabil Matar and Daniel J. Vitkus, eds, *Piracy, Slavery, and Redemption* (New York: Columbia University Press, 2001), and Vitkus, 'The Circulation of Bodies: Slavery, Maritime Commerce, and English Captivity Narratives in the Early Modern Period', in *Colonial and Postcolonial Incarceration*, ed. Graeme Harper (London: Continuum, 2001), 23–37.
16. Stephen Clissold, *The Barbary Slaves* (Totowa, NJ: Rowman and Littlefield, 1977), 136.

17. Vitkus, '"The Common Market of All the World"', 31. For a discussion of the Western imposition of exchange value in Eastern countries, see Jyotsna Singh, *Colonial Narratives / Cultural Dialogues: 'Discoveries' of India in the Language of Colonialism* (New York: Routledge, 1996), esp. 32–3.
18. Carmen Nocentelli, *Empires of Love: Europe, Asia, and the Making of Early Modern Identity* (Philadelphia: University of Pennsylvania Press, 2013), 8.
19. Roderick A. Ferguson, *Aberrations in Black: Toward a Queer of Color Critique* (Minneapolis: University of Minnesota Press, 2004), 15.
20. Daniel Vitkus, *Turning Turk: English Theater and the Multicultural Mediterranean, 1570–1630* (New York: Palgrave, 2003), 107.
21. Burton, *Traffic and Turning*, 126.
22. For other readings that treat *Merchant* and *The Renegado* as tragicomedies, see Valerie Forman, *Tragicomic Redemptions: Global Economics and the Early Modern Stage* (Philadelphia: University of Pennsylvania Press, 2008), 27–63, 146–85, and Dennis Austin Britton, *Becoming Christian: Race, Reformation, and Early Modern English Romance* (New York: Fordham University Press, 2014), 142–72.
23. Geraldo U. de Sousa, '"My hopes abroad": The Global/Local Nexus in *The Merchant of Venice*', in *Shakespeare and Immigration*, ed. Ruben Espinosa and David Ruiter (Burlington, VT: Ashgate, 2014), 37–58, esp. 40. For Venice's more general significance, see David C. McPherson, *Shakespeare, Jonson and the Myth of Venice* (Newark: University of Delaware Press, 1990); Leo Salinger, 'The Idea of Venice in Shakespeare and Ben Jonson', in *Shakespeare's Italy: Functions of Italian Locations in Renaissance Drama*, ed. Michele Marrapodi et al. (New York: Manchester University Press, 1993), 171–84; and Graham Holderness, *Shakespeare and Venice* (Burlington, VT: Ashgate, 2010).
24. For English desire to surpass the Italians as dominant players in the Mediterranean, see Vitkus, '"The Common Market of All the World"', 21.
25. Vitkus, *Turning Turk*, 178; Burton, *Traffic and Turning*, 206.

26. Amanda Bailey, *Of Bondage: Debt, Property, and Personhood in Early Modern England* (Philadelphia: University of Pennsylvania Press, 2013), 25, 146.
27. William Shakespeare, *The Merchant of Venice*, ed. John Drakakis, The Arden Shakespeare, Third Series (London: Methuen, 2010), IV, i, 89–92, hereafter cited parenthetically.
28. For further discussions of economic value, commoditisation, debt and bondage in *Merchant*, see Amanda Bailey, 'Shylock and the Slaves: Owing and Owning in *The Merchant of Venice*', *Shakespeare Quarterly* 62.1 (2011): 1–24; Walter Lim, 'Surety and Spiritual Commercialism in *The Merchant of Venice*', *Studies in English Literature, 1500–1900* 50.2 (2010): 355–82; William O. Scott, 'Conditional Bonds, Forfeitures, and Vows in *The Merchant of Venice*', *English Literary Renaissance* 34.3 (2004): 286–305; Charles Spinosa, 'The Transformation of Intentionality: Debt and Contract in *The Merchant of Venice*', *English Literary Renaissance* 24.2 (1994): 370–409; and Marc Shell, 'The Wether and the Ewe', in *Money, Language, and Thought: Literary and Philosophic Economies from the Medieval to the Modern Era* (Berkeley: University of California Press, 1985), 47–83.
29. Igor Kopytoff, 'The Cultural Biography of Things', in *The Social Life of Things*, ed. Appadurai, 64–91, esp. 73–4, 88. For a discussion of this Western imposition of exchange value, see Singh, *Colonial Narratives / Cultural Dialogues*, esp. 32–3.
30. Sandys, *A relation*, 161.
31. *The Holy Bible*, King James Version (New York: New American Library, 1974).
32. For a discussion of these Christian critiques of Jews, see Julliann Vitullo and Diane Wolfthal, eds, *Money, Morality, and Culture in Late Medieval and Early Modern Europe* (Burlington, VT: Ashgate Publishing, 2010), 2.
33. Shell, 'The Wether and the Ewe', 64.
34. Jyotsna Singh, 'Gendered "Gifts" in Shakespeare's Belmont', in *A Feminist Companion to Shakespeare*, ed. Dympna Callaghan (Oxford: Blackwell, 2001), 144–59, esp. 149.

35. For *Merchant*'s engagement with miscegenation in the context of overseas trade, see Kim F. Hall, 'Guess Who's Coming to Dinner? Colonization and Miscegenation in *The Merchant of Venice*', *Renaissance Drama* 23 (1992): 87–111; Daryl Palmer, 'Merchants and Miscegenation: *The Three Ladies of London, The Jew of Malta*, and *The Merchant of Venice*', in *Race, Ethnicity, Power in the Renaissance*, ed. Joyce Green MacDonald (New Brunswick, NJ: Associated University Press, 1997), 36–66, and Elizabeth Spiller, 'From Imagination to Miscegenation: Race and Romance in Shakespeare *The Merchant of Venice*', *Renaissance Drama* 29 (1998): 137–64.
36. de Sousa, '"My hopes abroad"', 37.
37. Craig Muldrew, '"Hard Food for Midas": Cash and Its Social Value in Early Modern England', *Past and Present* 170 (2001): 78–120, esp. 116. Singh makes the related argument that the casket test 'establishes a non-commercial value structure' which 'obfuscates the forces of demand and supply that bring the worlds of Venice and Belmont close together' ('Gendered "Gifts"', 152).
38. For more on Africans' presumed inability to assess value, see Natasha Korda, *Shakespeare's Domestic Economics: Gender and Property in Early Modern England* (Philadelphia: University of Pennsylvania Press, 2002), 113.
39. Elizabeth Valdez Acosta compares the casket test to the United States' Diversity Visa Immigration Program in claiming to promote equal access but ultimately preferring those who exhibit similarity to the dominant culture ('Open Doors, Secure Borders: The Paradoxical Immigration Policy of Belmont in *The Merchant of Venice*', in *Shakespeare and Immigration*, ed. Espinosa and Ruiter, 176–98).
40. Kim Hall, '"These bastard signs of fair": Literary Whiteness in Shakespeare's Sonnets', in *Post-Colonial Shakespeares*, ed. Ania Loomba and Martin Orkin (New York: Routledge, 1998), 64–83, esp. 78–9.
41. Kim Hall, *Things of Darkness: Economies of Race and Gender in Early Modern England* (Ithaca, NY: Cornell University Press, 1995), 10.

42. Hall, *Things of Darkness*, 9.
43. Noting the conditional nature of the proposal, Natasha Korda associates Portia with the female moneylender ('Dame Usury: Gender, Credit, and (Ac)counting in the Sonnets and *The Merchant of Venice*', *Shakespeare Quarterly* 60.2 [2009]: 129–53, esp. 151).
44. Ann Christensen, '"Because their business still lies out a' door": Resisting the Separation of the Spheres in Shakespeare's *The Comedy of Errors*', *Literature and History* 5.1 (1996): 19–37, esp. 19.
45. For the complicated reality of domestic life and work that was occluded by this ideal, see Wendy Wall, *Staging Domesticity: Household Work and English Identity in Early Modern England* (New York: Cambridge University Press, 2002); Michelle Dowd, *Women's Work in Early Modern English Literature and Culture* (New York: Palgrave, 2009); and Ariane M. Balizet, *Blood and Home in Early Modern Drama: Domestic Identity on the Renaissance Stage* (New York: Routledge, 2014).
46. Wendy Brown, *States of Injury: Power and Freedom in Late Modernity* (Princeton: Princeton University Press, 1995), 144.
47. Brown, *States of Injury*, 149.
48. For further discussions of the Protestant domestic sphere, see Lena Cowen Orlin, *Private Matters and Public Culture in Post-Reformation England* (Ithaca, NY: Cornell University Press, 1994); Diana E. Henderson, 'The Theater and Domestic Culture', in *A New History of Early English Drama*, ed. John D. Cox, David Scott Kastan and Stephen J. Greenblatt (New York: Columbia University Press, 1997), 173–94; Michael McKeon, *The Secret History of Domesticity: Public, Private and the Division of Knowledge* (Baltimore: Johns Hopkins University Press, 2005); and Frances Dolan, *Marriage and Violence: The Early Modern Legacy* (Philadelphia: University of Pennsylvania Press, 2008).
49. Ann Christensen, 'Words about Women's Work: The Case of Housewifery in Early Modern England', *Early Modern Studies Journal* 6 (2014): 1–28, esp. 5.

50. For more on *Merchant*'s engagement with the universalism of the marketplace, see Phyllis Rackin, 'The Impact of Global Trade in *The Merchant of Venice*', *Shakespeare Jahrbuch* 138 (2002): 73–88, esp. 78.
51. Vitkus, *Turning Turk*, 9. See also Britton, *Becoming Christian*, 12.
52. For a reading of Shylock as the money form, or general equivalent, see Richard Halpern, 'The Jewish Question: Shakespeare and Anti-Semitism', in *Shakespeare Among the Moderns* (Ithaca, NY: Cornell University Press, 1997), 159–226.
53. For more on conflicts between heterosexual and homoerotic bonds in the play, see Coppélia Kahn, 'The Cuckoo's Note: Male Friendships and Cuckoldry in *The Merchant of Venice*', in *Rough Magic: Renaissance Essays in Honor of C. L. Barber*, ed. Peter Erickson and Coppélia Kahn (Newark: University of Delaware Press, 1985), 104–12; and Steve Patterson, 'The Bankruptcy of Homoerotic Amity in Shakespeare's *Merchant of Venice*', *Shakespeare Quarterly* 50.1 (1999): 9–32.
54. Drew Daniel reads Antonio's desire for punishment as a masochistic manifestation of the early modern subject's general subjection to laws and to the economy ('"Let me have judgment, and the Jew his will": Melancholy Epistemology and Masochistic Fantasy in *The Merchant of Venice*', *Shakespeare Quarterly* 61.2 [2010]: 206–34).
55. For the association of Italians with sodomy, see James L. O'Rourke, 'Racism and Homophobia in *The Merchant of Venice*', *English Literary History* 70.2 (2003): 375–97, esp. 377–9, and Anthony G. Barthelemy, '"What news on the Rialto": Luxury, Sodomy, and Miscegenation in *The Merchant of Venice*', in *Shakespeare, Italy, and Intertextuality*, ed. Marrapodi, 132–44.
56. Ferguson, *Aberrations in Black*, 17–20.
57. M. Lindsay Kaplan, 'Others and Lovers in *The Merchant of Venice*', in *A Feminist Companion to Shakespeare*, ed. Callaghan, 341–57, esp. 349.
58. Britton, *Becoming Christian*, 4.
59. Britton, *Becoming Christian*, 27.

60. Mary Janell Metzger argues that 'the connection between blacks and Jews as alien others helped construct the racialized notion of Englishness' and that the categorisation of some Jews as 'deserving' and others as alien influenced the development of British imperialism and racialism ('"Now by My Hood, A Gentle and No Jew": Jessica, *The Merchant of Venice*, and the Discourse of Early Modern English Identity', *PMLA* 113.1 [1998]: 52–63, esp. 55).
61. For a discussion of this proverb in relation to blackness as a sign of the unalterable, see Britton, *Becoming Christian*, 1–5.
62. Janet Adelman, *Blood Relations: Christian and Jew in The Merchant of Venice* (Chicago: University of Chicago Press, 2008), 15.
63. Mark Netzloff, 'The Lead Casket: Capital, Mercantilism, and *The Merchant of Venice*', in *Money in the Age of Shakespeare*, ed. Linda Woodbridge (New York: Palgrave Macmillan, 2003), 159–76, esp. 171–2.
64. Singh, 'Gendered "Gifts"', 150.
65. For the argument that we should read the play against the backdrop of Barbary slavery, see Bindu Malieckal, '"Wanton Irreligious Madness": Conversion and Castration in Massinger's *The Renegado*', *Essays in Arts and Sciences* 31 (2002): 25–43.
66. Following Michael Neill, I use the early modern terms 'Mahomet' and 'Mahometan' to distinguish the play's representation of the Muslim world from the historical realities of Islam. See Neill, Introduction to *The Renegado*, Arden Early Modern Drama (London: Methuen, 2010), 1–71, esp. 2n.1.
67. *The Renegado*, Arden Early Modern Drama, ed. Michael Neill (London: Methuen, 2010), I, i, 46, hereafter cited parenthetically.
68. Vitkus, *Turning Turk*, 195.
69. Barbara Fuchs, 'Faithless Empires: Pirates, Renegados, and the English Nation', *English Literary History* 67.1 (2000): 45–69, esp. 63; Vitkus, *Turning Turk*, 63.
70. Jonathan Gil Harris, *Sick Economies: Drama, Mercantilism, and Disease in Shakespeare's England* (Philadelphia: University of Pennsylvania Press, 2004), 149.

71. Jane Hwang Degenhardt, 'Catholic Prophylactics and Islam's Sexual Threat: Preventing and Undoing Sexual Defilement in *The Renegado*', *The Journal for Early Modern Cultural Studies* 9.1 (2009): 62–92, esp. 65.
72. Degenhardt, 'Catholic Prophylactics', 66.
73. Britton, *Becoming Christian*, 171, 144. Britton reads the baptism as more theologically Protestant, suggesting that its Catholic elements are undermined and that the scene is marked by a 'figurative disunity' that is 'inherent to Protestant sacraments' (166).
74. Burton, *Traffic and Turning*, 94.
75. Britton, *Becoming Christian*, 149.
76. Harris, *Sick Economies*, 159.
77. Forman, *Tragicomic Redemptions*, 181.
78. Carol Pateman, *The Sexual Contract* (Stanford: Stanford University Press, 1988); Charles Mills, *The Racial Contract* (Ithaca, NY: Cornell University Press, 1997); Brown, *States of Injury*.
79. Brown, *States of Injury*, 142.
80. David R. Roediger, *The Wages of Whiteness: Race and the Marking of the American Working Class*, rev. edn (New York: Verso, 2007), 13.
81. Warren Montag, 'The Universalization of Whiteness: Racism and Enlightenment', in *Whiteness: A Critical Reader* (New York: New York University Press, 1997), 281–93, esp. 285.
82. Mary Floyd-Wilson, *English Ethnicity and Race in Early Modern Drama* (New York: Cambridge University Press, 2003); Jean E. Feerick, *Strangers in Blood: Relocating Race in the Renaissance* (Toronto: University of Toronto Press, 2010).

CHAPTER 6

CHASTE TREASURE AND NATIONAL IDENTITY IN *THE RAPE OF LUCRECE* AND *CYMBELINE*

In her foundational study, *Chaste Thinking: The Rape of Lucretia and the Birth of Humanism*, Stephanie Jed argues that the rape sacrifice at the heart of the Lucretia myth promotes the fantasy that a purified, 'chaste' condition can be restored both to the female body and to the body politic once corrupting forces have been expelled. Jed notes that the myth employs a series of words related to the Latin *tangere*, 'to touch', and *carere*, 'to be cut off from, to lack'.[1] The most central of these words is *chastity*, which connotes the 'quality of being cut off from contact or contamination'.[2] Such cutting off is manifested not only in Lucretia's resistance to Tarquin but also in her suicide, which divorces her pure spirit from her contaminated body, as well as in Brutus's insistence that Lucretia's kinsmen redirect their mourning toward political rebellion. The freedom of the Roman Republic thus arises from the suppression of both body and emotion, with the figure of the sacrificed woman emblematising the righteousness of the cause and diverting attention from more morally ambiguous aspects of the revolution. The legend therefore encourages what Jed calls 'chaste thinking', a mode of thought that divorces a concept from the ideological messiness that undergirds it.[3] In addition to providing the foundation for national origin stories, Jed contends, chaste thinking proves central to the humanist tradition that continually reproduces the Lucretia myth and that defines its literary and cultural value in contrast to more quotidian forms of expression, mercantile writing in particular.[4]

This republican model of subject formation was adapted to the monarchical context of early modern England, where Elizabeth I's chaste body served as an analogue to the alternately vulnerable and impenetrable boundaries of the nation state and promoted an idealised – and pure – notion of English national identity. According to Arthur Little, Lucretia's sexual purity is associated with whiteness that is then conferred upon the state.[5] As England expands its mercantile and colonial reach, therefore, the chaste thinking implicit in the Lucretia myth becomes 'one of early modern England's most imaginative models for defining and negotiating its national and imperial self'.[6] William Shakespeare's *The Rape of Lucrece* (1594) and *Cymbeline* (1611) are two of the many texts that explore the relevance of chaste thinking for early modern England. In particular, these works suggest that chaste thinking must be adapted for an aspiringly imperial and increasingly mercantile nation.

Conceptions of chastity as a commodity disrupt the humanist logic of chaste thinking that Jed identifies as well as the Elizabethan model in which the queen's body represents the body politic. The disconcerting commodity potential of Elizabeth I's chastity is brought to light, for example, in a marriage proposal from Archduke Charles of Austria in which he asked her to relinquish her ruby ring as a sign of her favour.[7] Elizabeth predictably refused his request, but the Archduke's association of her person with a jewel troubles the alignment of royal chastity with the nation, suggesting either that the queen is ultimately no different from any other woman or that the nation itself may be bought and sold. Concurrent developments within Protestantism – namely the downplaying of bodily virginity in favour of a more spiritual understanding of chastity that could be preserved within marriage – also problematised the chastity-nation homology. Protestantism's anti-material orientation paradoxically emphasises chastity's commodity status, as it abstracts chastity's physical essence so that it can survive the transaction of marriage. This paradox is reflected, for example, in Robert Greene's *Penelope's Web*, which terms chastity a woman's richest jewel, calling it 'an ornament ... that adorneth a woman which maketh her more honorable', and insisting that 'this is not done by jewels of golde, emeralds, precious stones, or sumptuous attyre, but by every thing that causeth her to be accounted honest, wise, humble, and chast'.[8] Greene adapts longstanding imagery of chastity as an inestimable jewel, what Juan Luis Vives calls 'a treasure without comparison' that is transferred from a woman's father and 'betaken unto [her] kepyng by [her] husbande'.[9] As with the Archduke's request for Elizabeth I's ruby, Greene's and Vives's understanding of chastity as an incomparable treasure falls short of purified chaste thinking; even as it ostensibly denies chastity's economic and material valences, it recalls chastity's function within the traffic in women.

Shakespeare's *Rape of Lucrece* and *Cymbeline* employ chastity-as-treasure discourse to interrogate the challenges that changing economic, religious and political ideologies pose to dominant models of national identity. *The Rape of Lucrece* exposes the ways in which chastity's commodity status invites sexual violence, and it illuminates the conceptual and ethical problems involved in converting commoditised personal chastity into a symbol of national integrity. A tragicomic retelling of the Lucretia myth written during the reign of James I, *Cymbeline* resolves the crisis arising from chastity's commoditisation by emphasising the potential of symbols to operate as signs of national chastity in the absence of a physical female body. As such, *Cymbeline* turns to a discourse of currency, which, as Stephen Deng has argued, was central to early modern state formation, to articulate a revised mode of chaste thinking suitable for a capitalist nation headed by a male monarch that sought to define itself through its expanding mercantile empire.[10] The reification of Innogen's chastity into her ring and bracelet, which circulate apart from her body, averts the violence of rape and suicide, but it also relegates Innogen to the domestic sphere where her body no longer functions as a metonym for the state. Innogen instead takes on the responsibility of reproducing British subjects, while her chaste essence is imbued within the nation's currency, legitimating its mercantile and imperial projects.

Chastity as National Treasure in The Rape of Lucrece

The opening Argument in Shakespeare's *The Rape of Lucrece* follows Livy in situating Lucrece's rape and suicide within its larger political context. Tarquin's acquisitive ravishment of Lucrece aligns with his father's 'excessive pride' and with the tyrannous manner in which he 'had possessed himself of the kingdom' and planned to lay siege to Ardea.[11] As such, Tarquin's rape of Lucrece inspires a rebellion against such tyranny. In the aftermath of Lucrece's death, her supporters 'vowed to root out the whole hated family of the Tarquins; and bearing the dead body to Rome, Brutus acquainted the people with the doer and manner of the vile deed, with a bitter invective against the tyranny of the king' (Arg. ll. 30–3). The spectacle of Lucrece's violated body inspires the Roman public to rise up, so that 'the Tarquins were all exiled, and the state government changed from kings to consuls' (Arg. ll. 35–6). With this framing, the Argument points toward the political stakes of the poem's exploration of chastity and the consequences of rape. Although Shakespeare emphasises the psychological effects of rape, his poem also conforms to the early modern tendency to present rape as a political allegory.[12] Throughout the poem, Lucrece's body is associated with the body politic. As Melissa E. Sanchez argues, 'The female body that can be contaminated against its will – penetrated, impregnated, infected – figures a body politic that may be similarly compromised by abusive and violent rule.'[13] Lucrece is described as a 'never-conquered fort' (l. 482) and a city with an 'ivory wall' (l. 464), while her contemplation of the tapestry depicting 'strong-besiegèd Troy' (l. 1429), a city destroyed as a result of Helen's rape (l. 1369), connects her fate to broader political events. Such images reflect the poem's engagement with the chaste thinking inherent in Lucretia myth as well as with Elizabethan ideologies that map the chaste body onto the contours of the state.

The poem's persistent economic imagery, pertaining both to mercantile and colonial conquest and to questions of possession and commoditisation, complicates this conventional alignment of chastity with the nation. While the poem's economic imagery has been discussed by feminist critics interested in unpacking Lucrece's status as a possession, it is often considered out of place in the poem's ethical exploration of chastity, rape and suicide.[14] Ian Donaldson, for example, expresses some puzzlement at Lucrece's lament, 'Poor helpless help, the treasure stol'n away, / To burn the guiltless casket where it lay!' (ll. 1056–7). To Donaldson, this reference to chastity as a pilfered treasure is anachronistic and 'morally speaking, less sophisticated' than other images Lucrece uses, as it fails to account for the Christian position promoted by St Augustine that a rape violates the body but not the soul.[15] Augustine specifically states that chastity 'is not a treasure which can be stolen without the mind's consent', yet Shakespeare persists in employing this construct.[16] This treasure imagery can partially be explained in terms of Shakespeare's vacillation between Roman and Christian value systems, reflecting what Donaldson terms 'a basic indecisiveness over the story's central moral issues', but it also reflects his concern with the ways in which chastity's status as a potentially commoditised possession complicates its prominent place within national ideologies.[17]

By the late sixteenth century, references to treasure were increasingly embedded within commercial discourses, as English venturers sought riches to be traded on international markets. Though *treasure* is a romantic term, evocative of limitless expanses of unquantifiable wealth, part of treasure's allure rests in the profits that could be gained from quantifying it, divvying it up, and submitting it to mechanisms of exchange. This tension within treasure discourse is evident in the correspondence of Sir Thomas Roe, James I's ambassador to the Ottoman Empire. Although Roe marvels at the incredible, seemingly infinite Eastern treasure he encounters, he dedicates a great deal of time in his letters to how he might purchase and sell 'esteemed jewells', that are 'most rare in the world'.[18] His language suggests an underlying appreciation for treasure's market value. Describing a convoy transporting the possessions of an Egyptian ruler, for instance, Roe remarks on the 'chests 80 of gold, in every chest 40000 checquins; besides his jewells, and the moveables of infinite valew'.[19] Although Roe emphasises the singularity of certain 'unparalleled' jewels that he might give as gifts, he remains oriented toward the monetary worth of treasures such as the gold, coins and movables.[20]

A similar ambiguity persists in depictions of women and their chastity as jewels and treasure. Mercantile thinking consistently undermines protestations that such treasure cannot be quantified. Such thinking, Shakespeare suggests, threatens dominant renderings of Lucretia's chastity as the Roman jewel. Coincidentally, Roe points to the dilemma of depicting Lucretia in terms of monetised jewels when he discovers a medal featuring 'Lucretius, the consul, of that famous chastetye which gave Rome her libertye'.[21] One of the 'few medals or coyness [one] may fynd rarely' in an Eastern context in which 'barbarism hath spitefully trodden out all worthy relicques of antiquitye', the medal (Roe believes it is a medal rather than a coin but is not certain) belongs to a substratum of Eastern treasure, and is thus an artefact that can be plundered by Westerners.[22]

The chastity invoked by the coin is honoured properly only by English merchants, yoking England and Rome in their common love of 'libertye' and cutting out those living currently in the Mediterranean. Roe's reference to Lucretia's chastity, then, in response to a medal containing her father's portrait, not only obliquely points to longstanding links between chastity and treasure but also underscores the significance of the Lucretia myth within English appropriations of Roman culture.

References to treasure first appear in *The Rape of Lucrece* when Collatine 'extol[s] the incomparable chastity of his wife' (Arg. ll. 9–10). When Collatine 'Unlock[s] the treasure of his happy state' (l. 16), he advertises the 'rich jewel he should keep unknown / From thievish ears, because it is his own' (ll. 34–5). These images of treasure encompass both Collatine's happy state and Lucrece herself, recalling common depictions of Lucrece as the jewel of Rome. Collatine boasts of

> What priceless wealth the heavens had him lent
> In the possession of his beauteous mate;
> Reck'ning his fortune at such high proud rate
>   That kings might be espousèd to more fame,
>   But king nor peer to such a peerless dame.   (ll. 17–21)

Collatine's language uncomfortably blurs the distinction that Renaissance moralists sought to maintain between the purportedly inestimable value of women, which belonged to the sphere of affective relations, and the quantifiable value of commodities.[23] He views both his fortune and wife in terms of treasure; his 'priceless wealth' refers to Lucrece as well as to the great honour of possessing her. As he reckons his fortune, he implicitly reckons Lucrece as well; even as he deems her 'peerless', he compares her to other women. This tension adheres as well in the Argument's description of Lucrece's chastity as 'incomparable', a slippery adjective suggesting an inability to be compared as well as superiority when compared to others.

Although Collatine considers his wife a possession, he stops short of commoditising her. Nonetheless, as with Roe's jewels, his treasure imagery signals her potential commoditisation. The prospect that Collatine's wife and, by extension, his fortune might be alienated from him inflames Tarquin's acquisitive desire.

Jed contends that 'the ideology of chastity and the separate, cut-off spaces it creates invite violation and corruption and the violent reestablishment of more chaste and cut-off spaces'.[24] In *The Rape of Lucrece*, economic thinking drives the violation of the chastity that Collatine seeks to protect. As Katharine Eisaman Maus notes, characters in the poem interpret tropes literally, construing them 'in their strong form' rather than recognising them as figurative.[25] Tarquin follows the implications of Collatine's boast and regards Lucrece as an object to be stolen. He quickly incorporates her into a discourse of mercantile exploration and colonial conquest. He imagines himself as a seafaring merchant adventurer, averring that the worth of an object obscures the dangers of its pursuit: 'when great treasure is the meed proposèd, / Though death be adjunct, there's no death supposèd' (ll. 132–3). A treasure so great, according to Tarquin's logic, justifies otherwise immoral actions. In other words, Tarquin transforms Lucrece into an 'economic object', a category of object that, for Arjun Appadurai, 'exist[s] in the space between pure desire and immediate enjoyment, with some distance between [it] and the person who desires [it]'.[26] This distance is typically overcome through economic exchange, a possibility foreclosed by Collatine's possessive protection of his wife's virtue and, though Tarquin does not realise it, by chastity's limited exchange potential. Because he cannot pursue this commercial form of acquisition, Tarquin turns to the language of theft, specifically colonial theft, employing imperialist imagery to depict Lucrece's chastity as an entity that can be alienated from Collatine's possession.

Tarquin uses conventional associations between women and land to verbally transform Lucrece's body into a New World landscape replete with riches to be acquired.[27] Weaving themes of commerce and conquest into the Petrarchan blazon, Tarquin represents Lucrece's body as uncharted territory:

> Her breasts like ivory globes circled with blue,
> A pair of maiden worlds unconquerèd,
> Save of their lord no bearing yoke they knew,
> And him by oath they truly honourèd.
> These worlds in Tarquin new ambition bred,
>   Who like a foul usurper went about
>   From this fair throne to heave the owner out.
>
>   (ll. 407–13)

This reference to Tarquin as a 'foul usurper', as Donaldson contends, recalls his father's unlawful seizure of the kingdom, further linking Lucrece to Rome.[28] In addition, the discourse of colonial exploration permits Tarquin to imagine Lucrece as a (nearly) virginal landscape that he is the first to (truly) discover. Adopting the Protestant view that marriage does not substantially alter a woman's purity, and conflating this vision with a colonial imaginary in which indigenous Americans laid no claim to their land, Tarquin depicts Lucrece as 'untouched' property, capable of being alienated from its current possessor. Her breasts are like 'maiden worlds', yet they have been 'yoked' and 'owned' by their lord, whom Tarquin wishes to vanquish. As such, Lucrece resembles Sir Walter Raleigh's depiction of Guiana as 'a Country that hath yet her Maydenhead, never sackt, turned, nor wrought, the face of the earth hath not been torne, nor the vertue and salt of the soyle spent by manurance, the graves have not been opened for gold, the mines not broken with sledges, nor their Images puld down out of their temples'.[29] This depiction of Lucrece as ostensibly virgin land ready to be plundered perversely transforms the poem's idealisation of Lucrece's chastity in such a way that effaces married sexuality. As Coppélia Kahn writes,

'Lucrece's chastity is emphatically that of the wife who has dedicated her body to her husband. This dedication has so rarefied and sanctified her sexuality that she seems virginal or even unsexual.'[30] As such, Tarquin incorrectly assumes that he could appropriate such a sanctified treasure for himself without compromising its purity.

Mercantile imagery obscures the cultural reality that chastity does not function like other commodities by creating the impression that, if Lucrece were stolen from Collatine, her chastity would nonetheless remain intact throughout this transaction, as it did in the exchange from her father to her husband. Yet, as the narrator's comments suggest, such assessments are misguided, and Tarquin's rapacious desire for treasure leads him to destroy the 'maiden' landscape he covets, leaving him 'bankrupt in this poor rich gain' (l. 140). Treasure discourse, Tarquin soon finds, applies only catachrestically to the possession of women and their chastity. Lucrece's chastity cannot be circulated among many owners but instead is depleted by rape. This failure of treasure discourse to accommodate chastity also points to the ways in which early capitalist commercial thinking may compromise ideologies that evoke chastity as the jewel of the nation.

Tarquin's distorted thinking raises anxieties about the consequences of mercantile expansion. In particular, his inability to distinguish properly between the commoditisable and the inestimable aligns him with Easterners in travel tracts by Englishmen such as Roe who fail to properly value items of sacred or cultural import, such as the relics from antiquity.[31] This tendency to commoditise items that should be revered dovetails with Little's contention that Tarquin shares much in common with depictions of dark-skinned, foreign rapists and that his expulsion whitens Rome as it purifies it.[32] Tarquin represents not only a dark outsider threatening to pollute the body politic with miscegenational rape but also the threat that commercial ideologies – imposed from the inside as well as the outside – posed to conceptions of national integrity. These commercial imperatives are racialised in contrast to Lucrece's pure, white virgin-like chastity that steadfastly resists circulation.

Treasure imagery – and the questions of materiality, possession and commoditisation that it raises – informs the remainder of the poem, particularly its assessment of the nature of Lucrece's chastity. The narrator simultaneously recalls and critiques the chastity-as-jewel image when recounting the rape, stating that Lucrece 'hath lost a dearer thing than life' (l. 687), and that 'Pure Chastity is rifled of her store, / And Lust the thief far poorer than before' (ll. 692–3). The narrator accepts the premise that chastity is a treasure trove that can be plundered. Nonetheless, the use of 'pure' as a modifier suggests that this chastity has an abstract quality and cannot adequately be equated with the material treasures of Tarquin's fantasies. Therefore, while chastity has been plundered in the manner foreshadowed by Tarquin's imperialist imagery, the plunderer is left with nothing, having 'won what he would lose again' (l. 688).

Lucrece complicates this question of the materiality and possessibility of her chastity as she ruminates on the effects of her rape. Her response to her violation hinges largely on her analysis of the relations among her chastity, her body and Collatine's honour. When she imagines her chastity as honey that has been stolen, she captures the nature of an entity that can be mutually owned.[33] She elaborates:

> If, Collatine, thine honour lay in me,
> From me by strong assault it is bereft;
> My honey lost, and I a drone-like bee,
> Have no perfection of my summer left,
> But robbed and ransacked by injurious theft.
> In thy weak hive a wandering wasp hath crept,
> And sucked the honey which thy chaste bee kept.
>
> (ll. 834–40)

In this image, Collatine's honour and Lucrece's chastity are one, each residing within Lucrece's chaste hive, which is curiously distinct from Lucrece who figures herself as a 'drone-like bee'. Her hive ransacked by the wasp, the bee can no longer produce chaste honey; she is therefore incapable of redeeming either her chastity or Collatine's honour. Instead, their joint possession has been stolen, leaving the possessors sullied. Although Lucrece confirms readings of her chastity as both a possession and a desirable commodity, it is one that is depleted through consumption and cannot be endlessly circulated as Tarquin assumes. The loss thus cannot be recuperated. Yet its effect on Lucrece remains ambiguous: with Lucrece's body, or more precisely her womb, symbolised by the hive but her person also figured by the bee, it appears as though Lucrece could continue living independent of her chastity, depleted but not irreparably polluted. Collatine remains bereft of honour, however; that is, as the conditional mode of the passages indicates, if one accepts the patriarchal premise that '[his] honour lay in' Lucrece and, by extension, that her honour lay in her chastity.

Whereas the men tend to think of Lucrece herself as a possession, Lucrece deploys chastity-as-treasure discourse to develop the possibility that the treasure is her chastity, a simple possession that she could potentially live without. In her lament, 'Poor helpless help, the treasure stol'n away, / To burn the guiltless casket where it lay' (ll. 1056–7), which Donaldson finds anachronistic, she inverts conventional Augustinian thinking that the body is defiled by rape while the mind remains pure. Conceiving of her chastity as treasure permits Lucrece to entertain the possibility that the rape has not corrupted her body but instead has left her bereft of a possession, something partially alienated from her even before the rape. She brings into relief her limited ownership of her chastity when she calls her husband the 'Dear lord of that dear jewel I have lost' (l. 1191), and when she insists to him that, 'thou shalt know thy int'rest was not bought / Basely with gold, but stol'n from forth thy gate' (ll. 1067–8). Viewing chastity as both treasure and potential commodity, liable to be stolen or sold, Lucrece carves out a space in patriarchal chastity-as-treasure discourse to imagine that the rape might not signify more strongly than the loss of any other possession and therefore might not compromise her honour.

This idea of chastity as a potentially alienable possession conflicts with Lucrece's alternate emphasis on the pollutive effects of the rape. Turning her attention to a potential pregnancy, Lucrece laments that her body has been contaminated: in place of her chastity, she 'bears the load of lust [Tarquin] left behind' (l. 734). Now the rape signifies not simply the loss of a possession, the treasure she had dedicated herself to guarding, but rather the forceful replacement of chastity with Tarquin's seed. Reflecting the Roman idea of *strumpum*, or dishonour, this physical violation brings shame to Lucrece and her family. In a more Augustinian vein, Lucrece insists that her mind remains 'Immaculate and spotless' although '[her] gross blood be stained with this abuse' (ll. 1655–6). Nonetheless, she finally concludes that her soul cannot continue to exist undefiled within the 'poisoned closet' of her body (l. 1659). Like a tree whose bark has been stripped away, her soul is left to 'wither' and 'decay' (l. 1168). Lucrece therefore decides that suicide will 'bail' her soul from the 'polluted prison' of her body (ll. 1725–6). Although it contravenes Augustinian precepts, Lucrece's conclusion accords with dominant Roman and Elizabethan sexual ideologies in which moral and physical integrity were intertwined. The divided blood that streams from Lucrece's wounds after the suicide – some 'still pure and red remained, / And some looked black, and that false Tarquin stained' (ll. 1742–3) – attests to the ambiguous nature of chastity in the poem, where the material and spiritual effects of rape are ostensibly distinguished from one another, yet are simultaneously present in the physical blood. Read in more racial, nationalistic terms, Lucrece's suicide purifies her body, cleansing it of Tarquin's blackness and allowing her sacrifice to similarly cleanse the body politic of corrupting influences.[34] In this way, Lucrece reclaims her chaste subjecthood when she kills herself.[35]

Although Lucrece's kinsman respond with horror to her death, standing 'Stone-still, astonished with this deadly deed' (l. 1730), they quickly incorporate Lucrece and her chastity into a patriarchal logic in which women function as objects of homosocial competition. The inadequacy of viewing women as possessions is highlighted in the squabble between Collatine and Lucretius. Both claim the sole right to mourn Lucrece, the one having given her life and the other having 'owed' her in marriage, 'Yet neither may possess the claim they lay' (ll. 1803, 1794). The men's possessiveness is presented as futile in the wake of Lucrece's death; their cries of 'my daughter' and 'my wife' echo around them, alienating them from their claims (l. 1806). Moreover, the men's acquisitive desire underscores the patriarchal dynamics that inspired the rape in the first place. Such individual possessiveness leads to the violation of women and, from the men's perspective, to the loss of value.

Intervening in the argument, Brutus amends Collatine and Lucretius's view of Lucrece as a personal treasure and thus transforms her from an object of male rivalry to a national treasure of the Roman state. Brutus, as Jed proposes, plays a pivotal role in the establishment of chaste thinking when he redirects the men's lamentations, depicting it as 'childish humour from weak minds' (l. 1825) and cutting off affective considerations in favour of the violence of revolution. His actions also reflect awareness that mercantile conceptions of women and their chastity as treasure undermine national ideologies that rely on the physically intact female form to represent both the body politic and the bodies of male subjects. Conceptions of chastity as treasure, when placed within commercial contexts, not only inspire sexual aggression but also distract men from the public good, as they are focused on their own personal proprietorship. Brutus reasserts the political dimensions of Lucrece's rape, conflating it with treason against the state. He asserts that 'Rome herself in [these abominations] doth stand disgracèd' and swears 'To show her bleeding body thorough Rome, / And so to publish Tarquin's foul offence' (l. 1833, ll. 1851–2). As Sanchez writes, 'to "publish" a tyrant's offence is to oppose it, so this move from private secrecy to public revelation of Lucrece's bleeding body – a mirror of the Roman body politic – is itself a form of rebellion'.[36] In this rebellion, Lucrece functions not simply as a possession usurped by the tyrant, but as a metonym for the state. Her self-inflicted wounds are presented to the public both as signs of the oppressive violence inflicted by the Tarquins and as evidence of the nation's preserved, exemplary virtue. Formerly a privately owned treasure that provoked rivalry, theft and rape, Lucrece's body becomes the collective possession of Rome, a commonwealth in which men share interest. Only with a dead woman is such collective ownership possible: freed from the responsibility of ensuring patriarchal reproduction, Lucrece becomes a national symbol. As such, *The Rape of Lucrece* participates in what Jed calls a 'search for idealized origins', not only for Rome but also for England.[37] By expelling Tarquin, the avengers chasten Rome, purging it of corrupting influences; this purification in turn enables Rome to become the cultural and intellectual progenitor of early modern England, as it encourages the sort of chaste thinking that elides complicating factors such as the presence of modern day Italians and England's own hybrid ethnic and cultural composition.

Despite adhering to the received contours of the Lucretia myth, Shakespeare's poem evinces some discomfort with the dynamics of chaste thinking embedded within it. At points, the poem strains against a narrative logic in which the establishment of national stability and liberty depends upon the rape and suicide of a chaste woman. Even Brutus, the architect of the rebellion, criticises Lucrece's decision to kill herself, stating that she 'mistook the matter so, / To slay herself that should have slain her foe' (ll. 1826–7). His call for revenge, moreover, is complicated by his question to Collatine, 'is woe the cure for woe? / Do wounds help wounds, or grief help grievous deeds?' (ll. 1821–2). This sentiment, as Donaldson contends, may point toward a more Christian ethic suggesting that 'there are other ways of dealing with grief than through violent retribution and blood vengeance'.[38] In addition to this ethical concern, *The Rape of Lucrece* questions of the efficacy of ideologies, such as those employed by Elizabeth I, that place chastity at the heart of national identity. Such ideologies not only fetishise chastity and in doing so invite violence against a sanctified female body, but they also accord imperfectly with Protestant understandings of chastity as a spiritual treasure belonging to a woman and her husband. While Protestant marriage discourse largely accommodates the language of commodity, which was increasingly common in early capitalist England, such commercial discourses challenge the idealisation of chastity upon which chaste national thinking depends. As such, the narrative arc of the Lucretia myth reconciles commercial impulses only with great difficulty. Even though Brutus succeeds in transforming Lucrece from a personal into a national treasure, this treasure and the body politic it represents seem insecure, susceptible to assault – or theft – from the outside.

The tragic structure of the Lucretia myth, however, constrains Shakespeare's critique of chaste national thinking. The exigencies of the plot require that Lucrece die and become a corporeal symbol of Rome, analogous in many ways to Elizabeth I's portrayal in national iconography. Shakespeare returns to this topic, however, in *Cymbeline*, where the theatrical medium and the genre of tragicomedy permit a revised understanding of chaste thinking more suitable for England's increasingly mercantile national identity and for a country no longer headed by a female monarch.

Chaste Currency and the Construction of an Imperial Economy in Cymbeline

Cymbeline reformulates the Lucretia story in the context of Roman Britain, where it informs a larger exploration of Britain's national identity and its place on Europe's expanding imperial stage.[39] *Cymbeline* reflects James I's attempts to unify Great Britain, while also looking beyond Wales and Scotland to imperial vistas in Ireland and the Americas.[40] Paul Innes has demonstrated that *Cymbeline*'s depiction of 'the progression from Roman Empire to British Empire as natural, continuous and unproblematic' works to bring about 'the creation of the new British Empire as it looks to the west'.[41] The Lucretia myth proves central to this project, as Shakespeare transposes it into an English tragicomedy, where it comingles with elements from Britain's ancient past and mercantile present and where it is marshalled in the service of the state's imperial aspirations. The empire *Cymbeline* calls into being is distinctly mercantile, and Shakespeare revises his rendering of the Lucretia myth accordingly.[42] As in *The Rape of Lucrece*, commercial modes of thinking initially prove violently disruptive. However, the generic conventions of tragicomedy work to recuperate commercial discourse while the semiotics of currency provide a mechanism for averting tragedy by abstracting the signs of Innogen's chastity – her ring and bracelet – from her physical body. The reification of chastity into jewels – which function as a sort of currency – obviates the need to physically rape Innogen as well as the imperative for a chaste female body to visibly represent the body politic. Although Innogen initially functions as a metonym for the state, referring to herself as 'Britain', she is relegated to the domestic sphere by the end of the play, where she is responsible for reproducing British subjects.[43] Her chastity, meanwhile, infuses the nation's currency, legitimating Britain's expanding economic sphere.

As in *The Rape of Lucrece*, *Cymbeline* evinces anxiety about the effects of commercial ideologies on assessments of personal value. In particular, *Cymbeline* suggests that such ideologies objectify men as well as women, reducing them to external markers such as wealth, clothes and class status and depleting them of intrinsic personal value. The opening scenes of the play are specifically concerned with the objectification of male value and the ways in which men's value can be augmented by women. The courtiers debate Posthumous's worth, observing that Innogen's

>   own price
> Proclaims how she esteemed him; and his virtue
> By her election may be truly read,
> What kind of man he is.   (I, i, 51–4)

In the courtiers' view, Posthumous's social status and moral worth are defined – and augmented – by his association with Innogen. His value relies on the 'price' of Innogen herself, which is determined largely by her chastity and by her status as heir to the throne. For King Cymbeline, Posthumous's value is reduced to his social class, as his common blood will allegedly turn the throne into a 'seat for baseness' (I, i, 142). In either case, any personal or moral qualities Posthumous may possess are disregarded in favour of external signifiers such as his wealth or Innogen's admiration for him.

Although Posthumous internalises this mode of assessing people in terms of calculable and transferable worth, Innogen considers Posthumous to be intrinsically valuable for his own unique qualities. She views him in terms of the inestimable value generally reserved for women, calling him 'a jewel' (I, I, 91) that she cannot live without, who will add 'lustre' (I, i, 143) to the throne. In contrast to the common perception that Posthumous must compensate for his low class status, Innogen asserts that he 'is / A man worth any woman, over-buys me /

Almost the sum he pays' (I, i, 145–7), suggesting that, because the lovers are of equal value, any trouble Posthumous endures on her behalf causes him extra, unnecessary exertion. Despite her anti-commercial orientation, however, Innogen persists in using economic figures of speech, a tendency which, as in *The Rape of Lucrece*, signals impending danger.

In place of the strong tropes of narrative poetry deployed in *The Rape of Lucrece*, *Cymbeline* invokes chastity-as-treasure discourse primarily through the props of the ring and the bracelet that Posthumous and Innogen exchange in the quasi-marriage ceremony that establishes their fidelity.[44] These tokens give rise to debates over the nature of value, and their initial exchange reflects Innogen's and Posthumous's divergent attitudes toward economic and personal value. Throughout this scene, Innogen works to shelter the jewels – and the lovers – from the logic of commoditisation. Imbuing her ring with sentimental, familial value, Innogen explains, 'This diamond was my mother's. Take it, heart, / But keep it till you woo another wife, / When Innogen is dead' (I, i, 112–14).[45] Like Portia in *The Merchant of Venice*, Innogen imbues her ring with a singularity incommensurate with logics of commoditisation, showing it instead to be, in Igor Kopytoff's terms, 'uncommon, incomparable, unique, singular, and therefore not exchangeable for anything else'.[46] The ring binds Posthumous to Innogen and to her maternal heritage, which is unsullied by the corrupting influence of her conniving stepmother. Presented in this way, the ring functions as an inalienable extension of the woman it signifies, and it therefore cannot be given away until the woman dies or until her chastity is compromised, a point Innogen does not countenance. Rejecting Innogen's focus on affective and intrinsic value, Posthumous initially correlates the jewels with the unequal worth of the respective givers: 'As I my poor self did exchange for you / To your so infinite loss, so in our trifles / I still win of you' (I, i, 119–21). The context of marriage highlights the commodity potential of women and, in this case, of Posthumous as well. Posthumous understands the marriage as an exchange in which he must compensate for perceived inadequacies. To him, Innogen not only loses personal value by marrying him but also makes an unprofitable trade when she exchanges her precious diamond for his less costly bracelet. Whereas Innogen uses jewel imagery to refer to abstract, inestimable value, Posthumous insists on a quantitative analysis that weighs the lovers' respective value in terms of class status and that considers the tokens to be symbolic of their respective givers' unequal worth.

Perhaps attempting to erase these inequalities, Posthumous gradually turns the bracelet from a representation of his own low value into a 'manacle of love' (I, i, 122) symbolising the marriage and, in turn, Innogen's chastity. Posthumous's verbal shift reflects the dynamics of marriage, in which female chastity functions as a jointly owned and prized possession, leaving male fidelity tangential. Where Innogen had hoped for a fair exchange of inestimable and therefore equal jewels, she is instead given a binding manacle symbolic not of Posthumous's value but of the joint ownership of her chastity. Posthumous, by contrast, has gained: his person is now augmented by the 'jewel' of his wife's chastity. It is Innogen's fidelity rather than Posthumous's that becomes integral to the marriage contract and that comes to be represented by both the ring and the bracelet. The prominence of the ring and bracelet in this scene highlights the possessive dynamics of Protestant marriage: even as it abstracts chastity from the body, Protestant marriage involves a symbolic commodity exchange. Furthermore, as in *The Rape of Lucrece*, the presumption that chastity is retained, rather than lost, in marriage opens space for it to be viewed as a commodity that can potentially be lost, stolen or sold.

In contrast to Portia's successful assertion of the link between her ring and her singular chastity in *Merchant*, Innogen's jewels – and the people and relationships they represent – are subject to contested evaluations throughout the play. The ramifications of Posthumous's commercial logic of love are exposed when he wagers on his wife's chastity, submitting it to an overtly economic contract. Like Collatine's wager, the contest is inspired by homosocial competition, as Posthumous's boasts tempt other men to usurp the prized female jewel. In the Italian setting, European men assess Posthumous's worth – and by extension English masculinity – in economic terms. The scene's mercantile language perhaps reflects Shakespeare's source in the *Decameron* in which the men are merchants rather than aristocrats.[47] As Innes argues, the presence of a Frenchman, a Dutchman and a Spaniard in this international scene speaks to contemporary concerns over Britain's role in the European economy, 'condens[ing] the associations of emerging empire and competition between nation states in the representative persons of the figures on stage'.[48] In this competitive atmosphere, Iachimo calls attention to Posthumous's contingent class status, in which 'he must be weighed rather by [Innogen's] value than his own' (I, iv, 10–11). Cognisant that he is being judged in relation to his lover, Posthumous appeals to Innogen's chastity, boasting that he has 'abate[d] her nothing' (I, iv, 54–5) since his youthful claim that her chastity surpassed that of the women of other countries. Iachimo, who also recognises that Posthumous's value rests in his possession of Innogen, sets out to deflate or appropriate her value, thus demoting Posthumous himself.

Iachimo baits Posthumous into the wager by focusing on the relationship between the ring and Innogen's chastity, insisting that her chastity can be treated in the same manner as the material property: like the ring, it could be lost, stolen, rated, sold or wagered. He exploits the ambiguities in Posthumous's defense of Innogen: 'I praised her as I rated her; so do I my stone' (I, iv, 62). Questioning the worth of the diamond, Iachimo observes that, it 'outlustres many I have beheld ... but I have not seen the most precious diamond that is, nor you the lady' (I, iv, 59–61). He draws out the unsavoury connotations of comparing Innogen to a trinket that could easily be sold on the market, noting, for instance, that Posthumous's lady is 'outprized by a trifle' (I, iv, 65–6). Whereas Tarquin focuses on Lucrece's physical body as treasure, Iachimo dwells on jewellery, commoditised treasure that stands in for Innogen's chastity. Even when Posthumous distinguishes between Innogen and the ring, protesting that 'The one may be sold or given ... The other is not a thing for sale, and only the gift of the gods' (I, iv, 67–9), Iachimo returns to the equivalence between the two. Recalling Iago's deployment of the handkerchief in *Othello*, Iachimo compares the ring with Innogen's genitalia and taunts Posthumous by saying, 'Your ring may be stolen too, so your brace of unprizable estimations, the one is but frail and the other casual. A cunning thief or a that way accomplished courtier would hazard the winning both of first and last' (I, iv, 73–6). Contrary to Posthumous's protestations, Iachimo maintains that both the diamond ring and Innogen's body are 'prizable' and therefore can be integrated into market exchange. Iachimo's language indicates that Innogen's chastity is not unique, as Posthumous wishes to assert, but instead has entered what Arjun Appadurai terms the 'commodity state', in which an item's 'exchangeability ... for some other thing is its socially relevant feature'.[49] Iachimo's logic, then, raises the threatening possibility that, like the material ring, Innogen's chastity may be alienated from Posthumous, becoming the property of another through exchange or theft.

The terms of the wager even more fully incorporate Innogen's chastity into an economic logic of commensurability. Iachimo offers to 'pawn the moiety of [his] estate to [the] ring' (I, iv, 88), betting both on Innogen's chastity. If Innogen proves chaste, Posthumous wins the ring and the estate; if unchaste, the two go to Iachimo, who would have also 'won' Innogen in the process of testing her chastity. Posthumous's contract with Iachimo, which symbolically replaces his marriage contract with Innogen, codifies the logic of exchange value, equating Innogen's chastity with the ring. As Iachimo states,

> If I bring you no sufficient testimony that I have enjoyed the dearest bodily part of your mistress, my ten thousand ducats are yours, so is your diamond too. If I come off, and leave her in such honour as you have trust in, she your jewel, this your jewel, and my gold are yours – provided I have your commendation for my more free entertainment. (I, iv, 121–6)

Iachimo asserts not only the equivalence of the diamond and the ducats but also their joint equivalence with Innogen's chastity, resulting in a triple equivalence syntactically reiterated in Iachimo's list 'she your jewel, this your jewel, and my gold'. The bracelet, which Iachimo later uses as proof that he has succeeded in seducing Innogen, becomes a secondary symbol of her chastity. Although Posthumous initially resists the commoditisation of both Innogen and the ring, which he holds 'dear as [his] finger' (I, iv, 107–8) and rates at 'More than the world enjoys' (I, iv, 64), he ultimately accepts the wager and its economic assessments of human value, as he had previously shown a propensity to do.

Iachimo's attempted sexual violation of Innogen is inspired by a commoditising discourse indicating that chastity can be transferred among men or usurped by interlopers. The wager's emphasis on symbols of chastity, and the attendant abstraction of chastity away from the physical female body, averts the tragic outcome of the Lucretia myth. Despite drawing explicit parallels to 'Our Tarquin' who 'thus / Did softly press the rushes, ere he wakened / The chastity he wounded' (II, ii, 12–14), Iachimo uses specular violation and theft as mercantile substitutes for rape. Rather than physically violate Innogen, Iachimo surveys her body and records details such as the 'cinque-spotted' (II, ii, 38) mole on her left breast, which could later be relayed as proof to Posthumous. As Patricia Parker notes, this inventory of Innogen's body and chamber resembles mercantile reports of foreign lands to be plundered, and Iachimo's fabrication of a trunk full of 'plate of rare device, and jewels / Of rich and exquisite form' (I, vi, 189–90) recalls Tarquin's imperialist conflation of rape and mercantile conquest.[50] This conflation is particularly evident in Iachimo's seizure of the bracelet. Punning lasciviously, Iachimo whispers, 'Come off, come off – / As slippery as the Gordian knot was hard! / 'Tis mine' (II, ii, 33–5). Iachimo's sexual satisfaction arises from stealing the bracelet, which becomes a fourth term in the equivalences established by the wager. Due to the wager's commoditisation of Innogen's chastity, Iachimo is content to steal an object equivalent to her chastity rather than to physically rape her. The bracelet, he believes 'will witness outwardly, / As strongly as the conscience does within, / To th'madding of her lord' (II, ii, 35–7). As he gloats, Iachimo insists on the equivalences of the wager, stating, 'If I had lost [the ring], / I should have lost the worth of it in gold (II, iv, 41–2) and thus reminding Posthumous that he conceded to defining Innogen's chastity as a fungible commodity.

Nonetheless, Iachimo's case against Innogen is incomplete without reference to her body. If the bracelet does not fully convince Posthumous of Innogen's infidelity, Iachimo's description of Innogen's mole acts as 'a voucher, / Stronger than ever law could make', proving that Iachimo has 'picked the lock and ta'en / The treasure of her honour' (II, ii, 39–42). Although Posthumous initially defends Innogen through reference to ring, stating, 'All is well yet. / Sparkles this stone as it was wont' (II, iv, 39–40), he becomes incensed by the combination of the bracelet and Iachimo's corporeal evidence, expressing the cuckold's desire to 'tear [Innogen] limb-meal' (II, iv, 147) and focusing on the mole as a sign that 'confirm[s] / Another stain, as big as hell can hold' (II, iv, 139–40). Abandoning the abstract focus on theft, Posthumous returns to a Roman conception of rape or unchastity as bodily contamination. This ideological reversion, however, transpires largely because he has been convinced that the ring and the bracelet are in some sense equal to Innogen's physical chastity. Although this conflation of Innogen's body and her jewels nearly results in tragedy, the play's tragicomic trajectory works to replace Iachimo's presentation of Innogen's chastity as a fungible commodity, equivalent to her jewels, with an alternate model in which the jewels simply represent, but do not replace, Innogen's value.

Cymbeline's discussion of the representative function of the jewels finds a parallel in early modern debates about currency, which centred on the question of whether coins embodied or simply represented value. Bradley Ryner observes that *Cymbeline* engages with mercantilist concerns that English currency remain stable in order to promote an equal balance of trade, noting that Posthumous's experience reflects 'the difficulty of determining a coin's value as it traveled from country to country'.[51] The anxiety that English currency may be abused in foreign contexts and may fail to accurately represent English value further registers in Iachimo's misrepresentation of the jewellery. As Stephen Deng has demonstrated, the production of coinage was a primary function of the state and played a central role in early modern state formation.[52] Coins possessed a political as well as an economic function; stamped with the royal seal, they 'emanated state authority and so were sometimes perceived as representations of the state'.[53] Material properties of coins, such as mottoes, portraits of monarchs and other royal iconography, served a propagandistic function and reminded subjects that, by enacting transactions with currency, they implicitly supported the state's authority to create and regulate value.[54]

Given Innogen's metonymic association with the state, the threats faced by her representative jewels reflect the fear that foreign manipulation of currency may damage the reputation of the sovereign, whose image or seal is imprinted on coins. Coins, as Deng notes, were not simply instruments of unidirectional state power; instead, their meaning could be interpreted and manipulated by subjects. As Roy Strong notes, for example, rebels often defaced portraits of Elizabeth I, including those on coins.[55] As such, the state had an interest in asserting the intrinsic value of English coinage and in yoking this value to the inviolable and divinely sanctioned authority of the sovereign.

In response to these anxieties about symbolising English value, *Cymbeline* turns to a discourse of chastity, with its associations of representational stability. The trope of chaste currency is most dramatically rendered in Gerard de Malynes's *Saint George for England, Allegorically Described* (1601), which figures the national treasure as the king's virgin daughter besieged by the Dragon of International Usury. As chaste treasure, the nation's currency is miraculously stable but also paradoxically in need of chivalric protection from policy makers. Elizabeth I's regime promoted a similar ideological message by adorning coins with idealised images of the queen's famously virginal body.[56] This association of coinage with the queen's authority and chastity was complicated, however, both by the national recoinages that occurred during Elizabeth's reign, which called into question the specie value of the currency, and by the unseemliness of metaphorically submitting the queen's virginal body to circulation.[57] Like Malynes's *Saint George*, *Cymbeline* deploys the representational strategies of romance to surmount these practical obstacles, drawing on generic conventions to suggest both that Innogen is preternaturally chaste and that her essence has been reified within her jewels. In its movement away from the material properties of the ring and bracelet and toward their symbolic value as signs of chastity, *Cymbeline* mirrors what Karl Marx calls the 'idealization of money', a process in which currency's representational value subsumes the value of its specie content.[58] This abstracting process, which as Deng maintains remained incomplete in the early modern period, provides Shakespeare with a narrative means of circumventing the rape and suicide of a chaste woman as well as a political means of reconfiguring national ideologies of chastity to suit an increasingly mercantile nation headed by a male monarch.

Critics often claim that Innogen's trials – Iachimo's assault on her chastity, her failed suicide attempt in the forest, and her near death by sleeping potion – serve virtually the same function as a literal rape and death, marginalising her from political power and relegating her to the domestic sphere. As Karen Bamford argues, for instance, Innogen mirrors Lucrece in becoming a national martyr, 'redeeming both family and country' with her 'wounded chastity'.[59] The abstraction of Innogen's symbolic jewels from her physical body, however, enables the tragicomic trajectory in which Innogen's person is discursively extracted from the economic sphere. As a result, Innogen evades a fate of true Lucretian martyrdom and instead survives to live as a private woman, albeit one whose chastity retains great national significance.

The romance setting of Milford Haven, to which Innogen travels after she has been divorced from her representative jewels, affirms Innogen's intrinsic value, which had been threatened by market logic in the wager scene. As Ellen Spolsky contends, Shakespeare mobilises tragicomedy's conventional depiction of transparent moral value to resolve the problem of chastity's unknowable nature.[60] In Milford Haven, Innogen's body assumes a nearly transparent, semi-divine state, inspiring the servant Pisanio to describe her as 'More goddess-like than wife-like' (III, ii, 8). Upon meeting her, Innogen's long-lost brothers Guiderius and Arviragus and their guardian Belarius fawn over her, with Belarius exclaiming, 'By Jupiter, an angel – or, if not, / An earthly paragon. Behold divineness / No elder than a boy!' (III, vi, 42–4). Innogen's virtue is evident despite her disguise as a boy, a disguise that temporarily removes her from the sexual marketplace that had compromised her chastity. The romance world, which Belarius depicts as an escape from 'the city's usuries' (III, iii, 45), is characterised by the absence of the court's market-driven estimations of character and of misleading forms of representation. It is for this reason that the brothers immediately vanquish Innogen's stepbrother Cloten, who, like Iachimo, substitutes signs for value itself, believing that clothing and other external signifiers of status constitute a person's identity. Divorced from her representative jewellery, Innogen's chastity speaks for itself, proving that she cannot be reduced to a catalogue of physical attributes, to her social status, or to men's boasts of ownership. In Milford Haven, identities cannot be obscured despite disguises: not Cloten's perfidy, not the brothers' nobility, and not Innogen's chaste virtue, which shines through her male garments, nearly inspiring her brothers to fall in love with her. Away from court, Innogen's chastity is no longer conceived of as a jewel to be appropriated and exchanged by men and instead becomes what Appadurai calls an 'enclaved' commodity, a special category of commodity that is, for the most part, protected from the market.[61] As a result of this transition, Innogen and her chastity are endowed with intrinsic, singular value that later grounds the 'currency' that circulates in her name.

In the final acts of the play, the intrinsic virtue of Innogen and her brothers serves as a purifying force that counteracts the court's corruption and the objectifying demands of the international economy. The men's valour, like Innogen's chastity, shines through their beggar's weeds, and they courageously lead the Britons to triumph over the Romans. Guilt over Innogen's supposed death inspires Posthumous to reject his earlier economic thinking and to cultivate his own internal value: 'To shame the guise o'th'world, I will begin / The fashion – less without, and more within' (V, i, 32–3). Altering his orientation toward human value, he abandons the perspective that allowed him to treat his wife and her ring as commodities and instead adopts Innogen's emphasis on intrinsic and unique human value. These demonstrations of intrinsic virtue persuade even Iachimo to renounce his former economic logic and to admit to the emptiness of his status symbols, conceding that 'Knighthoods and honours borne / As I wear mine are titles but of scorn' (V, ii, 6–7). By this point, the emphasis on extrinsic signs of value that characterised the homosocial competition of the wager has been replaced by a respect for intrinsic national and sexual virtue.

The personal virtue demonstrated by Innogen and her brothers is distinctly British, and it carries with it the potential to reform men from other countries and to incorporate them into a British sphere of influence. As both Jean Feerick and Mary Floyd-Wilson have argued, *Cymbeline*'s imperial ideologies are crafted in relation to anxieties about racial purity, as the English sought to revise Classical geo-humoral models that positioned them as northern barbarians.[62] In *Cymbeline*, Shakespeare redeems this supposed barbarity, as the influence of the rugged Welsh countryside remediates a court that has fallen prey to the seductions of commodity consumption and a preoccupation with social status. In addition to cultivating a Northern hardiness, Milford Haven also enhances Innogen's and her brothers' claims to whiteness as a sign of virtue. As Feerick contends, 'Their exposure to British topography ... imprints their bodies with northern features, whitening and strengthening their bodies beyond compare.'[63] Though the brothers are described as 'hot summer's tanlings' (IV, iv, 29), Posthumous also notes that they are 'fairer / Than those for preservation cased' (V, iii, 21–2), and their acquired tans contribute to an impression of their essential fairness. Innogen, whose intrinsic chastity is associated with whiteness, similarly emphasises her fair skin in Milford Haven when she marks her face with blood from Cloten's corpse, asking it to 'Give colour to my pale cheek' (IV, ii, 329). Associating Guiderius and Arviragus with the Anglo-Saxons rather than with early Britons, Mary Floyd-Wilson argues that 'genealogy, environment, and providence have come together to produce a race of Anglo "Angels" who will resist the cycle of degeneration implicit in the translation of empires'.[64]

Britishness thus comes further into alignment with whiteness, as the spirit of the Welsh hinterland is incorporated into Englishness, forming a national identity defined in large part against 'yellow' Iachimo's racialised Italianness (II, v, 14).[65] By divorcing early modern Italians from their Roman roots, *Cymbeline* carves out space in which to assert Britain's own Roman heritage and connects this heritage to Wales, the fabled birthplace of King Arthur and origin of the Tudor/Stuart line. As Ian Smith contends, this linkage of a recuperated Celtic past to Roman civilisation shaped emerging ideologies of whiteness, as whiteness is 'detached from savagery and primitivism and reformulated as the distinct, esteemed ethnic feature of the new national historiography'.[66] In addition, Wales functions within the play's emerging imperial imaginary as a symbol of England's ability to incorporate those at its margins, thus providing ideological support for the Act of Union.[67] *Cymbeline* further suggests that English national identity – comprised of Roman civility, Celtic strength and Anglo-Saxon purity – can survive in colonial outposts, not only within Britain but also in New World colonies to which ships from Milford Haven historically set sail.[68] In this way, *Cymbeline* dramatises the process of *translatio imperii*: having inherited from the Romans the mantle of cosmopolitan imperialism, the British are poised to enact 'the westward translation of Rome's imperial tradition to the nascent European empires'.[69]

King Cymbeline's voluntary agreement to pay tribute to Rome befits a nation seeking to ground its imperial ambitions in international trade. He suggests that Britain will no longer exist as a political and economic island – the policy stance held by the xenophobic Cloten and the queen – but will instead claim a place as part of a larger empire. As Innogen had previously wished, the country will become a page 'I'th'world's volume', recognising that 'There's livers out of Britain' (III, iv, 136, 139) and engaging in ostensibly cooperative interchange with other nations. Cymbeline's gesture places Britain on more equal footing with Rome and depicts Britain as a nation fuelled by peaceful exchange in contrast to the martial domination of the Romans. The king implies a parallel between this commercial exchange and the affective exchange of family members. Describing the reunion of the siblings and lovers at the play's conclusion, Cymbeline expounds:

> Posthumous anchors upon Innogen,
> And she, like harmless lightning, throws her eye
> On him, her brothers, me, her master, hitting
> Each object with a joy; the counterchange
> Is severally in all.   (V, iv, 393–7)

Such 'counterchange' becomes the hallmark of the peace that Cymbeline inaugurates by agreeing to pay the tribute to Rome, thus 'Let[ting] / A Roman and a British ensign wave / Friendly together' (V, iv, 477–9). Just as Cymbeline's affective language of gifts and friendship obscures the competitive and proto-imperialist realities of early seventeenth-century trade, it also elides the possessive dynamics of Protestant marriage, as Posthumous and Innogen's relationship is now ostensibly marked by joyous exchange, seemingly free of coercion and objectification.

As King Cymbeline gestures toward international trade, the reunion of Innogen with her jewels works to allay anxieties about the loss of British bullion and about the connection between coins and their royal referents.[70] The events of the play have exposed the threatening nature of the European economic sphere, both to British masculinity and to signs of British value such as Innogen's ring. Mitigating these concerns, Innogen and her signifying jewels, like coins invested in foreign ventures, return to court, this time with the added value of her brothers in tow. Furthermore, the conclusion's emphasis on intrinsic value reduces anxieties about the fate of English travellers, commodities and coins: English people and products, the play suggests, are inherently valuable, even when compared to others or exchanged in market transactions. In the context of the lovers' reunion, the jewels regain the singular, affective value that Innogen initially attributed to them. Like the currency whose intrinsic value mercantilists hoped to validate, the jewels have (at least temporarily) been distinguished from common commodities. Having preserved her own value, therefore, Innogen implicitly helps to secure the worth of her representative signs, endowing them with a stable value that can survive the vicissitudes of circulation.

The closing of the play thus articulates a revised function for female chastity within England's emerging economic empire.[71] As in *The Merchant of Venice*, the extraction of chastity from the overtly economic realm results in a clearer delineation between a feminine domestic sphere charged with protecting intrinsic value and a masculine public sphere fuelled by exchange and circulation. Innogen's status is lowered after the discovery of her brothers, leaving her to forge a more egalitarian marriage with Posthumous since her 'price' is now 'less, and so more equal ballasting' (III, vi, 74–5). Now officially married and poised to become a mother but not a queen, Innogen brings the intrinsic and transparent virtue of Milford Haven with her to the private realm. As Jodi Mikalachki observes, moreover, *Cymbeline* anticipates the later model in which a pure woman reflects the respectability of the nation, with Innogen, 'so beloved by the Victorians for her wifely devotion and forbearance', serving as an alternative to the militant queen.[72] Harnessing the ethic of the romance world, the feminised domestic sphere becomes a redemptive and restorative 'haven' from life in the early capitalist economy, all while mirroring the supposed respectability of the nation's economic practices. Despite the spiritualising discourses surrounding the Protestant family, Innogen's bodily chastity remains central to the national project, as she is charged with reproducing noble, legitimate Britains whose intrinsic virtue will enhance the nation's prosperity.[73] In contrast to the Elizabethan model in which the female body functions as a metonym for the nation, *Cymbeline* concludes by emphasising chastity's sexual function within Protestant marriage ideologies, where it provides the domestic sphere with its spiritual foundations and serves as a safeguard of British identity.

Calling attention to the dual meanings of *domestic*, Wendy Wall demonstrates that dramatic representations of domesticity constitute a 'nostalgic return to national origins' and function to solidify a sense of English national identity.[74] '[T]hese dramatic scenes', she argues, 'insist that English citizens are bound by the seemingly primal scene of home, with its vexed cultural and economic concerns.'[75] Though Wall is primarily interested in more realistic theatrical depictions of household labour, *Cymbeline*'s closing affirmation of the sexual ideologies of an emerging domestic sphere similarly illuminates the connection between the home and the nation, as Innogen's chastity ensures the reproduction of Englishness. Innogen's chaste body, moreover, remains the referent for the 'jewels' – coins and commodities – that circulate in Britain's name. British currency is legitimised by the power of the king and by the transparent, intrinsic value of the idealised domestic sphere. Stabilised by its chaste referent, British coins can be handled by many men as they circulate throughout the international economy. Earlier in the play, believing that Innogen had betrayed him, Posthumous wished for a method of human reproduction that bypassed women:

> Is there no way for men to be, but women
> Must be half-workers? We are all bastards,
> And that most venerable man which I
> Did call my father was I know not where
> When I was stamped. Some coiner with his tools
> Made me a counterfeit.   (II, v, 1–6)

It is, of course, impossible to banish women from reproductive responsibilities; nonetheless, Posthumous's image of all men as counterfeit coins stamped outside of wedlock gestures toward the play's resolution to the problem of unstable female value. Coins, in contrast to men, can be produced without the help of women. By the end of *Cymbeline*, women have been largely exiled from the political and economic realms – realms in which women's chastity played a central, if problematic, role in both republican Rome and Elizabethan England.

Nonetheless, chastity's symbolic value remains a potent ideological means of asserting the stability of English currency in increasingly distant and volatile markets. Authenticated by but distinguished from her physical chastity, Innogen's jewellery becomes a sort of currency that can pass through the hands of many men without losing value and without damaging the physical body of the woman whose value it signifies. The reification of Innogen's chastity into jewellery thus permits the plot's tragicomic transcendence of the tensions encapsulated in *The Rape of Lucrece*'s treasure tropes: that bodily chastity can be stolen but never repossessed and that chastity's status as a private possession often conflicts with its function within national ideologies. In this way, *Cymbeline* modifies chaste thinking for the Jacobean era, mobilising aspects of Elizabeth I's chaste authority while downplaying the metonymic power of the physical female body. Chastity nonetheless appears in

Cymbeline as a valuable tool of empire, serving to link the nation's commercial activity to the reproduction of a purer, superior manifestation of English identity. Reified within Innogen's jewels, this sanctified national identity infuses England's commercial endeavours and circulates throughout its aspirational empire. The spectre of Lucrece's violated body underlies this imperial economy, however, reminding audiences of the violence of mercantile conquest and the injustice of national ideologies that mobilise the symbols of female chastity without granting full subjecthood to women.

Notes

1. Stephanie H. Jed, *Chaste Thinking: The Rape of Lucretia and the Birth of Humanism* (Bloomington: Indiana University Press, 1989), 8.
2. Jed, *Chaste Thinking*, 12.
3. Jed, *Chaste Thinking*, 2.
4. Jed, *Chaste Thinking*, 7–14.
5. Arthur L. Little Jr., *Shakespeare Jungle Fever: National-Imperial Re-Visions of Race, Rape, and Sacrifice* (Stanford: Stanford University Press, 2000), 2.
6. Little, *Shakespeare Jungle Fever*, 1–2.
7. For a fuller telling of this story and a discussion of Elizabeth I's strategic use of jewels, see Cassandra Auble, 'Bejeweled Majesty: Queen Elizabeth I, Precious Stones, and Statecraft', in *The Emblematic Queen: Extra-Literary Representations of Early Modern Queenship*, ed. Debra Barrett-Graves (New York: Palgrave, 2013), 35–51, esp. 39.
8. Robert Greene, *Penelope's Web* (London: Printed [by E. Allde] for John Hodgets, 1601), E2v, reproduction of the Huntington Copy, EEBO.
9. Juan Luis Vives, *The Instruction of a Christian Woman*, trans. Richard Hyrde (1529), ed. Virginia Walcott Beauchamp, Elizabeth H. Hageman and Margaret Mikesell (Urbana: University of Illinois Press, 2002), 28, 91.

10. Stephen Deng, *Coinage and State Formation in Early Modern English Literature* (New York: Palgrave, 2008).
11. William Shakespeare, *The Rape of Lucrece*, in *The Poems*, ed. John Roe (New York: Cambridge University Press, 2006), 148–238, esp. Argument ll. 1–6, hereafter cited parenthetically.
12. See Jocelyn Catty, *Writing Rape, Writing Women in Early Modern England: Unbridled Speech* (London: MacMillan Press, 1999).
13. Melissa E. Sanchez, *Erotic Subjects: The Sexuality of Politics in Early Modern English Literature* (New York: Oxford University Press, 2011), 88. For other aspects of the play's political allegory, see Michael Platt, 'The Rape of Lucrece and the Republic for which it Stands', *Centennial Review* 19 (1975): 59–79.
14. For discussion of Lucrece as a possession, see Oliver Arnold, '"Their tribute and their trust": Political Representation, Property, and Rape in *Titus Andronicus* and *The Rape of Lucrece*', in *The Third Citizen: Shakespeare's Theatre and the Early Modern House of Commons* (Baltimore: Johns Hopkins University Press, 2007), 101–39; Catherine Belsey, 'Tarquin Dispossessed: Expropriation and Consent in *The Rape of Lucrece*', *Shakespeare Quarterly* 52.3 (2001): 315–35; Coppélia Kahn, 'Publishing Shame: *The Rape of Lucrece*', in *A Companion to Shakespeare's Works, Volume IV: The Poems, Problem Comedies, Late Plays*, ed. Richard Dutton and Jean E. Howard (Malden, MA: Blackwell, 2003), 259–74; and Jennifer Laws, 'Paradoxes of Possession in Shakespeare's *Lucrece*', *Bulletin of the Australian National Association for Medieval and Early Modern Studies* 31.1 (1995): 53–68.
15. Ian Donaldson, *The Rapes of Lucretia: A Myth and its Transformations* (Oxford: Clarendon Press, 1982), 49.
16. Augustine, *City of God*, trans. Henry Betteson, ed. David Knowles, 1:29, 40, quoted in Donaldson, *The Rapes of Lucretia*, 49.
17. Donaldson, *The Rapes of Lucretia*, 49.

18. Sir Thomas Roe, *Letter To the Queen of Bohemia: With Relations*, No. CCXXIV, November 1624, Constantinople, in *The Negotiations of Sir Thomas Roe in his Embassy to the Ottoman Porte, from the Year 1621 to 1628* (London: Samuel Richardson, 1740), Folger Collection, 313.
19. Roe, *Letter To Sir Edward Conway*, 1625, No. CCXCIX, in *The Negotiations of Sir Thomas Roe in his Embassy to the Ottoman Porte*, Folger Collection, 430.
20. Roe, *Letter To My Lorde Admiral*, Two Letters, the first in Character 9/19 March 1621, No. XXI, in *The Negotiations of Sir Thomas Roe in his Embassy to the Ottoman Porte*, Folger Collection, 27.
21. Roe, *Letter* No. CDXXVIII, in *The Negotiations of Sir Thomas Roe in his Embassy to the Ottoman Porte*, Folger Collection, 584.
22. Roe, *Letter* No. CCVLI, May 1623, in *The Negotiations of Sir Thomas Roe in his Embassy to the Ottoman Porte*, Folger Collection, 334.
23. For this distinction, see Barbara Sebek, '"By gift of my chaste body": Female Chastity and Exchange Value in *Measure for Measure* and *A Woman Killed with Kindness*', *Journal of Culture and Criticism* 5.1–2 (2001): 51–85, esp. 52, 60–1.
24. Jed, *Chaste Thinking*, 45.
25. Katharine Eisaman Maus, 'Taking Tropes Seriously: Language and Violence in Shakespeare's *Rape of Lucrece*', *Shakespeare Quarterly* 37.1 (1986): 66–82, esp. 76.
26. Arjun Appadurai, 'Introduction: Commodities and the Politics of Value', in *The Social Life of Things* (New York: Cambridge University Press, 1986), 3–63, esp. 3.
27. This trope is not unique to Shakespeare and is present in Edmund Spenser's *Amoretti*, Sonnet 15 and John Donne's 'Elegy XX: To His Mistress Going to Bed'. For more on imperial uses of the blazon, see Roland Greene, *Unrequited Contests: Conquest and Empire in the Colonial Americas* (Chicago: University of Chicago Press, 1999) and Louis Montrose, 'The Work of Gender in the Discourse of Discovery', *Representations* 33 (Winter 1991): 1–41.

28. Donaldson, *The Rapes of Lucretia*, 52.
29. Walter Raleigh, *The Discouerie of the Large, Rich and Bevvtiful Empire of Guiana* (London: Printed by Robert Robinson, 1596), 196, Folger Copy.
30. Coppélia Kahn, 'The Rape in Shakespeare's *Lucrece*', *Shakespeare Studies* 9 (1976): 45–72, 49.
31. For more on Easterners' purported failure to assess items of cultural value, see Chapter 5 in this book.
32. Little, *Shakespeare Jungle Fever*, 44–8.
33. For an extended analysis of this conceit, see Sarah Plant, 'Shakespeare's Lucrece as Chaste Bee', *Cahiers Elisabéthains* 49 (1996): 51–7.
34. For an extended reading along these lines, see Little, *Jungle Fever*, 46–7.
35. Critical views vary regarding Lucrece's level of agency at the end of the poem. Catherine Belsey argues that Lucrece transcends her status as a possession with her suicide, showing herself to be a subject with agency. Coppélia Kahn maintains in '*Lucrece:* The Sexual Politics of Subjectivity' that Lucrece's suicide reinscribes the violence of the rape, signalling her complicity with patriarchal Roman codes of honour, but she revises this argument in 'Publishing Shame' to draw it more in line with Belsey's position. Alternately, Maus contends that Lucrece obscures questions of agency, positioning herself as both guilty and innocent, and Lynn Enterline suggests that Lucrece possesses partial and fragmentary agency. See Belsey, 'Tarqin Dispossessed'; Kahn, '*Lucrece*: The Sexual Politics of Subjectivity', in *Rape and Representation*, ed. Lynn A. Higgins and Brenda R. Silver (New York: Columbia University Press, 1991), 141–61; Kahn, 'Publishing Shame'; Maus, 'Taking Tropes Seriously'; Enterline, '"Poor Instruments" and Unspeakable Events in *The Rape of Lucrece*', in *The Rhetoric of the Body from Ovid to Shakespeare* (New York: Cambridge University Press, 2000), 152–97.
36. Sanchez, *Erotic Subjects*, 104.
37. Jed, *Chaste Thinking*, 123.
38. Donaldson, *The Rapes of Lucretia*, 55.

39. For connections between Shakespeare's *The Rape of Lucrece* and *Cymbeline*, see Georgianna Ziegler, 'My Lady's Chamber: Female Space, Female Chastity in Shakespeare', *Textual Practice* 4.1 (1990): 73–90; Karen Bamford, 'Imogen's Wounded Chastity', *Studies in Theatre* 12.1 (1993): 51–61; and Ellen Spolsky, 'Women's Work is Chastity: Lucretia, Cymbeline, and Cognitive Impenetrability', in *The Work of Fiction: Cognition, Culture, and Complexity*, ed. Alan Richardson and Ellen Spolsky (Burlington, VT: Ashgate, 2004), 51–84.
40. For analyses of *Cymbeline*'s engagement with James I's plans to unify Britain, see David Bergeron, 'Images of Rule in *Cymbeline*', *Journal of Dramatic Theory and Criticism* 1.2 (1987): 31–7; Leah Marcus, '*Cymbeline* and the Unease of Topicality', in *New Essays on Tudor and Stuart Literature and Culture*, ed. Heather Dubrow and Richard Strier (Chicago: University of Chicago Press, 1988), 134–68; and Jonathan Goldberg, *James I and the Politics of Literature* (Baltimore: Johns Hopkins University Press, 1989). For broader discussions of *Cymbeline*'s engagement with questions of empire, see Patricia Parker, 'Romance and Empire: Anachronistic *Cymbeline*', in *Unfolded Tales: Essays on Renaissance Romance*, ed. George M. Logan and Gordon Teskey (Ithaca, NY: Cornell University Press, 1989), 198–207; Willy Maley, 'Postcolonial Shakespeare: British Identity Formation and *Cymbeline*', in *Shakespeare's Late Plays: New Readings*, ed. J. Richards and J. Knowles (Edinburgh: Edinburgh University Press, 1999), 145–57; and Andrew Escobedo, 'From Britannia to England: *Cymbeline* and the Beginning of Nations', *Shakespeare Quarterly* 59.1 (2008): 60–87.
41. Paul Innes, '*Cymbeline* and Empire', *Critical Survey* 19.2 (2007): 1–18, esp. 9, 12.
42. For *Cymbeline*'s interest in asserting Britain's status in the European economy, see Bradley D. Ryner, 'The Panoramic View in Mercantile Thought: Or, A Merchants Map of *Cymbeline*', in *Global Traffic: Discourses and Practices of Trade in English Literature and Culture from 1550 to 1700*, ed. Barbara Sebek and Stephen Deng (New York: Palgrave, 2008), 77–94. Innes also briefly addresses the mercantile aspect of empire in '*Cymbeline* and Empire', 14–15.

43. William Shakespeare, *Cymbeline*, ed. Martin Butler (Cambridge: Cambridge University Press, 2005), I, vi, 113, hereafter cited parenthetically.
44. There has been much debate over the precise nature of Innogen and Posthumous's relationship, with critics disagreeing as to whether they are actually married and whether the contract has been consummated. See Anne Barton, '"Wrying but a little": Marriage, Law and Sexuality in the Plays of Shakespeare', in *Essays, Mainly Shakespearean* (Cambridge: Cambridge University Press, 1994), 3–30, and Martin Butler, Introduction to *Cymbeline* (Cambridge: Cambridge University Press, 2005), 1–74.
45. For an alternate discussion of the shifting significance of the ring and the bracelet, see Valerie Wayne 'The Career of *Cymbeline*'s Manacle', *Early Modern Culture* 1 (2000): 1–21.
46. Igor Kopytoff, 'The Cultural Biography of Things', in *The Social Life of Things*, ed. Arjun Appadurai (New York: Cambridge University Press, 1986), 64–91, esp. 69.
47. See William Lawrence, 'The Wager in *Cymbeline*', PMLA 35.4 (1920): 391–431.
48. Innes, '*Cymbeline* and Empire', 16.
49. Arjun Appadurai, 'Introduction: Commodities and the Politics of Value', in *The Social Life of Things* (New York: Cambridge University Press, 1986), 3–63, 16.
50. Patricia Parker, 'Rhetorics of Property: Exploration, Inventory, Blazon', in *Literary Fat Ladies: Rhetoric, Gender, Property* (New York: Methuen, 1987), 126–54.
51. Ryner, 'The Panoramic View in Mercantile Thought', 78.
52. Deng, *Coinage and State Formation*, 1. For other studies of links between currency and sovereign power, see Marc Shell, Art and Money (Chicago: University of Chicago Press, 1995), and Jotham Parsons, 'Money and Sovereignty in Early Modern France', *Journal of the History of Ideas* 62.1 (2001): 59–79.
53. Deng, *Coinage and State Formation*, 2.
54. Deng, *Coinage and State Formation*, 2–4.
55. Roy Strong, *Portraits of Queen Elizabeth I* (Oxford: The Clarendon Press, 1963), 40.

56. For Elizabeth I's propagandistic use of coinage, see Clifton W. Potter Jr., 'Images of Majesty: Money as Propaganda in Elizabethan England', in *Money: Lure, Lore, and Literature*, ed. John Louis DiGaetani (Westport, CT: Greenwood Press, 1994), 69–85. For more on Elizabeth's strategies of self-presentation, see Louis Montrose, *The Subject of Elizabeth: Authority, Gender, and Representation* (Chicago: University of Chicago Press, 2006).
57. Catherine Loomis notes that this anxiety was highlighted in the public reception of coins depicting Elizabeth posing in the open-kneed manner of the male sovereign ('"Bear Your Body More Seeming": Open-Kneed Portraits of Elizabeth I', in *The Emblematic Queen: Extra-Literary Representations of Early Modern Queenship*, ed. Debra Barrett-Graves [New York: Palgrave, 2013], 53–68).
58. Karl Marx, *A Contribution to Political Economy*, ed. Maurice Dobb (New York: International Publishers, 1970), 110.
59. Bamford, 'Innogen's Wounded Chastity', 57. For a variant of this argument, see Laura Di Michele, 'Shakespeare's Writing of Rome in *Cymbeline*', in *Identity, Otherness, and Empire in Shakespeare's Rome*, ed. Maria Del Sapio Garbio (Burlington, VT: Ashgate, 2009), 157–74.
60. Spolsky, 'Women's Work is Chastity', 71–8.
61. Appadurai, 'Commodities and the Politics of Value', 16.
62. Jean Feerick, 'A "Nation . . . Now Degenerate": Shakespeare's *Cymbeline*, Nova Britania, and the Role of Diet and Climate in Reproducing Races', *Early American Studies* 1.2 (2003): 30–71, 40, and Mary Floyd-Wilson, '*Cymbeline*'s Angels', in *English Ethnicity and Race in Early Modern Drama* (New York: Cambridge University Press, 2003), 161–83.
63. Feerick, 'A "Nation . . . Now Degenerate"', 57.
64. Floyd-Wilson, '*Cymbeline*'s Angels', 169.
65. For more on anti-Italian stereotypes in the play, see Thomas G. Olsen, 'Iachimo's "Drug-Damn'd Italy" and the Problem of British National Character in *Cymbeline*', *Shakespeare Yearbook* 10 (1999): 269–96.
66. Ian Smith, *Race and Rhetoric in the Renaissance: Barbarian Errors* (New York: Palgrave, 2009), 6.
67. There has been a great deal written on the significance of Wales in *Cymbeline*'s presentation of British national identity.

For the fullest treatment of this subject, see Ronald J. Boling, 'Anglo-Welsh Relations in *Cymbeline*', *Shakespeare Quarterly* 51.1 (2000): 33–66.

68. For Milford Haven's role as a colonial port, see Feerick, 'A "Nation ... Now Degenerate"', 59–71.
69. Innes, '*Cymbeline* and Empire', 9. Critics disagree about the play's attitude toward Rome. Robert S. Miola argues that Shakespeare sought to differentiate Britain from Roman barbarism, positing Britain as more civilised and Christian than Rome. Other critics, such as David Bergeron have focused on the play's recuperation of Augustan Rome in the service of James I's conception of himself as inaugurating a Pax Britannica. See Miola, '*Cymbeline*: Shakespeare's Valediction to Rome', in *Roman Images: Selected Papers from the English Institute, 1982*, ed. Annabel Patterson (Baltimore: Johns Hopkins University Press, 1984), 51–62; Bergeron, '*Cymbeline*: Shakespeare's Last Roman Play', *Shakespeare Quarterly* 31.1 (1980): 31–41.
70. For an analysis of how tragicomedies quell economic concerns about bullion leaving the realm by reframing loss in terms of potential gains, see Valerie Forman, *Tragicomic Redemptions: Global Economics and the Early Modern Stage* (Philadelphia: University of Pennsylvania Press, 2008).
71. There is some debate as to the gender coding of Britain at the end of the play, Janet Adelman argues that the infusion of the masculine sphere of Milford Haven allows Britain to form a fully male-dominated public sphere that no longer relies on women such as Innogen or the evil queen. Differing slightly from Adelman, Jodi Mikalachki contends that Shakespeare feels the need to repudiate the violent, autonomous nationalism associated with ancient queens such as Boadicea (and perhaps more modern queens like Elizabeth I). Alternately Laura Di Michele examines Innogen's cross-dressing to argue that 'Roman Britain (and James I's Britain as well) is neither a "feminine" society subject to the danger of invasions as Elizabethan England usually conceptualized itself, nor a "masculine" society as Imperial Rome was in the collective imagination of the British. The new Britain (like Innogen) is both feminine and masculine.' In keeping with this view,

Valerie Wayne suggests that the presence of the bracelet and ring mitigates the excision of women from the ending, serving as a visible 'mark of their commodification, containment, devaluation and circulation through exchange'. See Adelman, *Suffocating Mothers: Fantasies of Maternal Origin in Shakespeare's Plays* (New York: Routledge, 1992); Mikalachki, '*Cymbeline* and the Masculine Romance of Roman Britain', in *The Legacy of Boadicea: Gender and Nation in Early Modern England* (New York: Routledge, 1998), 96–114; Di Michele, 'Shakespeare's Writing of Rome in *Cymbeline*', 171; and Wayne, 'The Career of *Cymbeline's* Manacle', 21.

72. Mikalachki, '*Cymbeline* and the Masculine Romance of Roman Britain', 100.
73. Ariane M. Balizet contends that the bloody cloth Posthumous carries with him, supposed to symbolise Innogen's death, 'reassert[s] the necessity of blood, bodies, and sex in the marriage contract' and is 'a testament to the gradual and uneven absorption of reform in the performance of marriage and domesticity' (*Blood and Home in Early Modern Drama: Domestic Identity on the Renaissance Stage* [New York: Routledge, 2014], 52).
74. Wendy Wall, *Staging Domesticity: Household Work and English Identity in Early Modern Drama* (New York: Cambridge University Press, 2002), 11. For other discussions that touch on the national implications of domestic drama, see Diana E. Henderson, 'The Theater and Domestic Culture', in *A New History of Early English Drama*, ed. John D. Cox, David Scott Kastan and Stephen J. Greenblatt (New York: Columbia University Press, 1997), 173–94, and Catherine Richardson, 'Tragedy, Family and Household', in *The Cambridge Companion to English Renaissance Tragedy*, ed. Emma Smith and Garrett A. Sullivan Jr. (New York: Cambridge University Press, 2010), 17–29.
75. Wall, *Staging Domesticity*, 10.

CODA: APPROACHING CAPITALIST MODERNITY

The plays discussed in *Chaste Value* respond to a sense that early capitalist forces destabilise the primacy of intrinsic personal value, which was fundamental to the aristocratic order. Tragedies such as *The Revenger's Tragedy*, *The White Devil* and *The Changeling* underscore capitalism's disruptive power, suggesting that shifting social hierarchies and commercial modes of evaluation engender both sin and personal fragmentation. A fully performative self emerges from this context, yet proves incapable of ethical action. Plays such as *Othello* draw out the racial implications of this commoditised performativity. Iago's proclamation 'I am not what I am' (I, i, 64) signals the alienation and emptiness of the commoditised self; when he displaces these characteristics onto Othello, he paints black bodies as susceptible to a particularly abject form of commoditisation that involves objectification rather than performativity. City comedies, by contrast, work to accommodate new capitalist realities, acknowledging overlapping sexual and commercial economies and drawing on female chastity to articulate new modes of selfhood. Rather than embracing this constructed selfhood, tragicomic romances such as *The Merchant of Venice*, *The Renegado* and *Cymbeline* recuperate intrinsic personal value from market-based logics, in part as a means of restricting the exchange of women in multicultural environments. Such intrinsic value, however, is largely reserved for middle- and upper-class white Christians and is not extended to workers, the poor, racial and religious others, or those marked by non-normative sexual identities.

In their use of chastity to explore questions of value, subjectivity and commoditisation, early modern plays register many of modernity's foundational social and epistemological trends. They contribute to the development of *homo economicus*, the economic subject who must balance an interior reality against a host of external markers, including wealth, status and appearance. The viable economic subject, a play such as *Bartholomew Fair* indicates, must learn to live with his or her commodity potential and conform to the transactional nature of urban, capitalist life. The drama's exploration of economic selfhood also informs the rise of possessive individualism. Plays ranging from *Troilus and Cressida* to *The Fair Maid of the West, Part I* suggest that some people are capable of managing or possessing themselves, while some are depicted as possessions or must accept that their labour power, sexuality and other attributes effectively belong to others. Whiteness is similarly transformed into property, with many plays presenting it as an embodied sign of Christian, English, or even human value.

These articulations of economic subjectivity, possessive individualism and white supremacy point toward the drama's anticipation of the emerging liberal paradigm attending the rise of capitalism. Not fully developed until the Enlightenment, liberalism endows subjects with formal equality – a formulation that accords with the commercial understanding of people as fungible – while also sustaining oppressive hierarchies of gender, race, class and nationality. As Wendy Brown argues, 'the autonomous subject of liberalism requires a large population of nonautonomous subjects, a population that generates, tends, and avows the bonds, relations, dependencies and connections that sustain and nourish human life'.[1] The emergence of the autonomous white male subject depends upon the subjugation of women, the working class, and racial others. Liberalism, as Brown's analysis suggests, also necessitates a realignment of the private and public realms, in which the feminised home accrues the affective, relational aspects of life that are increasingly expunged from the capitalist economy. The plays discussed in *Chaste Value* engage with these developments, illuminating the ways in which concerns about personal commoditisation and exchange shape emerging liberal epistemologies.

The theatre's response, then, to early capitalism's crisis of value contributes to an oppressive modern episteme in which performative selfhood is accessible only to a select few and in which gendered, racial and class-based value is reified, paradoxically endowed with essential qualities even in a capitalist world characterised by the primacy of exchange value. This trajectory is by no means absolute, however. Rather, the stage – with its embodied, cross-dressed, spectacular and mimetic modes of representation – repeatedly and intensively interrogates the nature of personal value. In doing so, it demystifies forces of value creation and imagines new ways of conceiving of selfhood, personal value and social difference. At times, these alternatives break free from the omnipresent dichotomy of intrinsic and extrinsic value, providing fruitful means of thinking through the challenges of capitalist modernity.

One compelling alterative can be found in Shakespeare and Wilkins's *Pericles*. When Marina transforms the brothel from a bawdy house to an 'honest house' for the teaching of creative and domestic arts, she indicates that chastity rests not so much in intrinsic sexual purity as in ethical, socially valuable labour. Labour figures prominently in *Pericles*'s defence of the theatre, complicating the intrinsic-extrinsic value binary and proffering a revised interpretive schema in which a production's worth is assessed in terms of the ethical orientation of its producer and the collective response of audience members. Labour may be inevitably alienated in the early capitalist economy – Marina still works for a wage – but *Pericles* maintains that labour can nonetheless create value that surpasses the price for which it is exchanged. *Pericles* thus mobilises the public theatre's artisanal roots to reject capitalist epistemologies. In so doing, it provides us with a means of legitimising noneconomic forms of value without receding into essentialism and of conceptualising the collective construction of value beyond the reductive model of supply and demand.

Although Marina's chastity retains its function as both symbol of representative authenticity and object of exchange, *Pericles* gestures toward a world in which the social fabric coheres not though the sexual purity of women but through collective ethical action and interpretation. In Marina's creative labour (and behind it the labour of the fishermen who aid Pericles on his journey and the labour of the actors themselves), we see a social vision with the potential to affirm those marginal figures who are excluded from the rise of the possessive individual but who provide its affective and material sustenance. While *Pericles* focuses on respectable, white, English workers, its conception of labour value may also extend to the prostitutes who previously occupied the brothel and to the immigrants and workers of colour who were increasingly central to the early capitalist economy. Even as early modern drama anticipates Western capitalist regimes of value, then, it also offers a means of validating, rather than demeaning, those who must sell their labour – and often their bodies – to survive in a market economy.

Note

1. Wendy Brown, *States of Injury: Power and Freedom in Late Modernity* (Princeton: Princeton University Press, 1995), 157.

INDEX

abstraction, 129, 192
   Cymbeline, 270, 273, 276, 280
   The Merchant of Venice, 221, 225, 227
Acosta, Elizabeth Valdez, 249n
Adelman, Janet, 182, 225, 295n
Aebischer, Pascale, 81n
affectivity, 35, 211, 299
   The Changeling, 115, 116
   Cymbeline, 272, 284, 285
   The Merchant of Venice, 212–13, 219, 220–1, 222, 226, 227
   Othello, 186
   Pericles, 57
   The Rape of Lucrece, 260, 267
Africans, 180, 202n, 214–15, 217–18; *see also* slavery
Agnew, Jean-Christophe, 15, 19, 66, 72, 145, 152–3
alienation, 149, 154, 217
   of commodities, 114, 182, 185–7, 194–5, 202n, 231
   and labour, 52, 60, 110, 116
   of property, 261, 262–3, 265, 266, 267, 275
   self-, 182, 234, 297
allegory, 60, 72–3, 129, 137–8; *see also* Malynes, Gerard de, *Saint George for England*. . .; rape: as political allegory
anti-Semitism *see* racism
antitheatricalism, 20, 33–5, 36–7, 75, 79n, 90
   Pericles, 49, 51, 54, 57, 61
   The Revenger's Tragedy, 62, 64

Appadurai, Arjun, 24n, 205, 261, 275, 281
appearance and essence, 12–13, 14, 15, 21, 34, 36, 88–9
   The Changeling, 111–13
   Cymbeline, 281
   Jonson and, 143, 153
   Measure for Measure, 38–9, 46
   The Merchant of Venice, 215, 217
   Othello, 181, 182, 187–90, 191, 192–4, 196
   Pericles, 50–1, 53, 54–5, 58
   The Renegado, 238
   The White Devil, 103–4
   see also false representation
appetite, 3, 9, 95, 130, 133, 232
aristocracy
   disruption by capitalism, 3, 5, 87, 297
   male integrity, 111, 119, 154
   male personal value, 90, 91, 95
   male selfhood, 21, 88, 100
   threats to, 101–2, 117, 140
   values of, 18, 53, 98, 129–30, 174
   see also court life
Aristotle, 63, 88, 211
audiences
   antitheatricalism and, 33, 35
   Bartholomew Fair, 159, 160–1
   Measure for Measure, 46
   Othello, 192, 197
   Pericles, 54, 57, 58, 59, 61, 75, 299–300
   The Rape of Lucrece, 288
   The Roaring Girl, 158

Augustine of Hippo, St, 158, 258, 265, 266
autonomy, virgins'
  Bartholomew Fair, 144, 146, 149, 154
  The Fair Maid of the West, Part I, 173–4
  Jonson and, 127–8, 137, 152
  Measure for Measure, 48
  Pericles, 61
  The Renegado, 232–3
  The Roaring Girl, 135, 137, 150
  Volpone, 139

Bacon, Francis, 46
Bailey, Amanda, 7, 210
Balizet, Ariane M., 296n
Bamford, Karen, 280
Bartels, Emily C., 200n, 201n
Barthelemy, Anthony Gerard, 200n, 223
bastardy, 3, 39, 43–4, 64, 65–6, 287
Belsey, Catherine, 291n
Bergeron, David, 295n
black men, 173, 176, 178, 225, 252n, 263
  excluded from full subjecthood, 168, 179, 180, 239–40, 243–4
  Othello, 181, 190–2, 193–4, 196
Boose, Lynda, 202n
Bovilsky, Lara, 169
Brathwaite, Richard
  The English Gentleman, 129, 130
  The English Gentlewoman. . ., 36, 88, 89, 94–5, 102, 121n
Breitenberg, Mark, 3–4
Britton, Dennis Austin, 224, 239, 240, 253n
brothels, 49, 51, 53–6, 146, 300
  theatres as, 20–1, 33–5, 48, 57, 61, 75
  see also prostitution
Brown, Wendy, 220, 243, 298–9
Bruster, Douglas, 8, 15–16, 163n
Burton, Jonathan, 209, 210, 240
Butler, Judith, 17, 18, 19–20, 32n

Callaghan, Dympna, 102, 123–4n, 204n
castration, 178, 201n, 207, 208, 222–3, 230–1
Catholicism, 5, 79n, 99, 224
  The Merchant of Venice, 228
  Pericles, 56, 83n

The Renegado, 238–9, 240–1, 243, 253n
  see also relics, Catholic
centredness, 100, 127, 139, 140, 143, 155
chaste thinking
  Cymbeline, 24, 256–7, 287
  Lucretia myth, 254–5, 258
  The Rape of Lucrece, 267, 268–9
chorus figure, 49, 51, 58, 59, 61
Christensen, Ann, 219–20
Christianity
  and intrinsic value, 19, 23, 209–10, 215–16, 298
  racial whiteness, 227, 244, 245
  value systems, 41–2, 211–12, 213–14, 221–2, 258, 269, 295n
  and virtue, 235–6
  see also Catholicism; conversion, religious; slavery: Mediterranean trade
city comedies, 19, 21–2, 22–3, 128–9, 231, 297
  and chaste women, 137, 157–8
  and male commoditisation, 120–1, 130–1
class
  hierarchies, 2, 19, 51–2, 231
  middle-, 146–7, 210, 227
  and personal value, 8, 174–5, 271–2, 273, 274, 298
  race and, 169, 182
  structures disrupted, 65, 115, 116, 117
  theatre and, 18, 20
  see also aristocracy; social difference
Coddon, Karin S., 70
coinage, 36, 278–80, 284–5, 286–7, 294n
  counterfeit, 1, 38–9, 67, 79n, 101
  intrinsic value, 10–11, 12, 29n, 63, 181
  see also usury
colonialism *see* imperialism
conduct books, 12, 88–90, 94, 129–30, 148, 153
consumption, material, 2, 130, 132, 140–1
  aristocratic, 52, 65, 282
contingency, 19, 274
  Bartholomew Fair, 131, 144–5, 149, 151, 154, 158
  early capitalist, 22, 46, 100

conversion, religious, 191, 206–7
  The Fair Maid of the West, Part I, 177
  The Merchant of Venice, 221, 223, 224–5
  The Renegado, 228–31, 233, 234, 237–41, 242, 243
  The White Devil, 106
Correll, Barbara, 7
court life
  The Changeling, 115
  Cymbeline, 271, 281, 282
  The Fair Maid of the West, Part I, 200n
  Jonson and, 144, 160, 167n
  Pericles, 49, 51, 52
  The Renegado, 230
  The Revenger's Tragedy, 62, 64–5, 67–8
  The White Devil, 107–8, 109
  see also masques
cross-dressing *see* transvestism
cuckoldry, 65–6, 114, 226, 277–8
  willing, 132–3, 138, 163n
currency *see* coinage

Daniel, Drew, 251n
de Sousa, Geraldo U., 210, 215
death and chaste women, 39–40, 43, 67–71, 74–5, 192, 193
  fake, 134
  see also suicide after rape
debt bondage, 7, 14, 210–11, 213, 222–3
Degenhardt, Jane Hwang, 234, 236
Dekker, Thomas, 14–15; *see also* Middleton, Thomas and Thomas Dekker, *The Roaring Girl*
Deng, Stephen, 7, 29n, 79n, 256–7, 278–9, 280
Di Michele, Laura, 295n
Diehl, Huston, 35, 79n
dissimulation *see* false representation
Dollimore, Jonathan, 72, 117
Donaldson, Ian, 258, 262, 265, 269
Douglas, Mary, 4
Dowd, Michelle M., 115
Dyer, Richard, 192, 193

East, the, 23, 175, 178, 200n, 227, 241–2;
  see also Mahometans; Muslims; slavery: Mediterranean trade; Turks

Elizabeth I, 48, 67, 71, 135, 287, 295n
  body/state analogy, 4, 24, 130, 255–6, 258, 269
  and coinage, 11, 279, 294n
  The Fair Maid of the West, Part I, 172, 174, 176, 177
  and slave trade, 168, 169–70, 180, 200n
Engels, Friedrich, *The Origin of the Family*, 25–6n
Engle, Lars, 16, 61
Enterline, Lynn, 291n
Erikson, Peter, 203n
eunuchs *see* castration
exchange, 2, 14–16, 19–20, 35–6, 75, 88–9, 259, 299
  Bartholomew Fair, 146, 148–9
  The Changeling, 110, 112, 113–14
  A Chaste Maid in Cheapside, 132–3
  city comedies, 128–9, 131, 152, 157
  Cymbeline, 272–3, 275–6, 281, 284, 285, 296n
  The Fair Maid of the West, Part I, 175, 177, 179
  Measure for Measure, 37–8, 40–2, 43, 44–9
  The Merchant of Venice, 214, 215, 217, 218–19, 220–1, 222, 223–4, 225–7
  Othello, 182–3, 186, 187, 196
  Pericles, 49–50, 51–2, 52–3, 56–7, 59–62, 300
  The Rape of Lucrece, 261, 263
  The Renegado, 228, 230, 236–7, 238, 241, 243
  The Revenger's Tragedy, 62–3, 64, 69–70, 70–1
  The Roaring Girl, 136, 137
  Troilus and Cressida, 96
  Volpone, 139
  The White Devil, 100
  see also regimes of value; trade, English/British overseas

Fair Maid of the Exchange, The (anon.), 21, 128, 131, 132, 134–5
false representation, 66–7, 68–9, 72, 117–18, 153–4, 216, 230
Feerick, Jean E., 182, 245, 282
Ferguson, Roderick A., 208, 223

fetishisation, 70, 136, 186–7, 197
  of chastity, 42, 142, 174, 243, 269
  see also relics, Catholic
Finin-Farber, Kathryn R., 102
Finkelstein, Richard, 54–5
Fischer, Sandra, 2–3, 7, 181
Floyd-Wilson, Mary, 202n, 245, 282, 283
Forman, Valerie, 242
Friedlander, Ari, 142
Friedman, Michael D., 80n
Fuchs, Barbara, 230
fungibility, 9, 66, 206, 298
  Bartholomew Fair, 149–50
  Cymbeline, 277, 278
  Measure for Measure, 40, 44–5

gender, 8, 17–18, 32n, 89
  The Changeling, 114, 119
  Cymbeline, 295n
  hierarchies, 2, 19, 20, 298, 299
  Jonson and, 141–2, 156, 165n
  in patriarchal systems, 5, 62
  and race, 171, 196, 197, 208, 232, 240
  The Renegado, 236
  The Roaring Girl, 136
  The White Devil, 102, 108, 109
gift giving
  Cymbeline, 275, 284–5
  Measure for Measure, 42, 46–8
  The Merchant of Venice, 227
  Pericles, 60–1, 84n
Glancy, Jennifer, 191
Gossett, Suzanne, 60, 84n
Gosson, Stephen
  Plays Confuted in Five Actions, 34
  The Schoole of Abuse, 33–4, 35, 50–1, 57
Gottlieb, Christine M., 70
Goux, Jean-Joseph, 7, 9, 35
Gower, John, *Confessio Amantis*, 49
Grady, Hugh, 96
Graeber, David, 199n
Greene, Robert, *Penelope's Web*, 130, 256
Greene, Thomas, 127
Greenstadt, Amy, 17, 158
Guillory, John, 6

Habib, Imtiaz, 168, 180, 201n

Hakluyt, Richard, *The Principal Navigations, Voyages, Traffiques and Discoveries of the English Nation*, 200n, 206
Hall, Kim, 171–2, 217–18
Hanson, Elizabeth, 129
Harris, Jonathan Gil, 29n, 136
  on *The Fair Maid of the West*, 200n, 201n
  on *The Renegado*, 230, 242
  on *Troilus and Cressida*, 122n
Hawkes, David
  The Culture of Usury in Renaissance England, 8
  Idols of the Marketplace: Idolatry and Commodity Fetishism in English Literature: 1580–1680, 27–8n, 72
  Shakespeare and Economic Theory, 12, 14, 63, 77n, 171, 187, 199n
  'Sodomy, Usury, and the Narrative of Shakespeare's Sonnets', 8
Hawkins, John (slave trader), 168, 169–70, 198n
Henslowe, Philip, 34
Heywood, Thomas
  The Fair Maid of the West, Part I, 22–3, 172–3, 173–9, 180, 195, 196, 200n, 201n
  The Fair Maid of the West, Part II, 178
Higgins, John C., 45
Hobbes, Thomas, 94–5, 122n, 243
homoeroticism, 206, 209, 222–3; see also castration
homosociality
  The Changeling, 116, 118, 119
  Cymbeline, 274, 282
  Jonson and, 131, 143–4, 151, 155–6, 160
  The Merchant of Venice, 219
  The Rape of Lucrece, 267
  The Renegado, 240
Howard, Frances (1590–1632), 125n
Howard, Jean E., 8, 128, 174, 175, 200n, 201n
hypocrisy, 38, 39, 51, 155, 156, 211

idolatry, 55, 72, 155, 156
imperialism, 7, 208, 290n
  Cymbeline, 270, 282, 283–4, 288, 292n

English, 171–2, 252n, 255, 257
European, 219
The Rape of Lucrece, 24, 258, 261–2
The Renegado, 228, 229, 237, 243
incest, 43, 50, 53, 58, 60
individualism, 135, 171, 213, 229, 243;
  see also possessive individualism
inner essence *see* appearance and essence
Innes, Paul, 270, 274, 292n
interiority, 12–13, 18, 191
  The Changeling, 126n
  The Fair Maid of the West, Part I, 196
  Othello, 173, 194
  The White Devil, 104, 111
international trade, 11–12, 110, 214–15, 217, 218, 219
  free, 242
  threats from, 220, 221, 222, 229–30, 245
  see also slavery; trade, English/British overseas
intrinsic personal value, 2, 18, 129, 244–5, 297–8, 299
  The Changeling, 117, 118–19
  Cymbeline, 271–2, 273, 280–2, 285
  Measure for Measure, 44
  The Merchant of Venice, 214, 215–16, 218, 219, 225–6, 227
  Othello, 173, 181, 184, 191–2
  and public exchange value, 15, 87, 88, 89
  recuperated and reallocated, 19, 20
  The Renegado, 235–6, 237–8, 239, 241, 243
  Troilus and Cressida, 91, 94–6, 97–9, 103
  The White Devil, 102, 104–5, 106, 108–10
  see also value creation
Irigaray, Luce, 4–5, 148–9

James I, 4, 48, 127, 207, 259
  Cymbeline and, 256, 270, 295n
Jed, Stephanie H., 4, 23–4, 254–5, 261, 267, 268
jewel analogies, 5, 255, 256
  The Changeling, 113, 114–15
  Cymbeline, 24, 270, 271–4, 274–8, 279–80, 281, 284–5, 287–8
  Othello, 184

The Renegado, 230, 235, 236, 239
The White Devil, 100, 104–5, 106
  see also treasure analogies
Jews, 210, 212, 213, 222, 225, 252n
Jonson, Ben
  Bartholomew Fair, 22, 128, 131, 138, 144–57, 158–61
  Epicoene, or the Silent Woman, 22, 128, 131, 137–8, 139–44, 165n
  Hymenaei, or the Solemnities of Masque Barriers at a Marriage, 127–8, 131, 139, 144
  Volpone, 128, 131, 138–9
Jowitt, Claire, 200–1n

Kahn, Coppélia, 262–3, 291n
Kahn, Victoria, 128
Kaplan, M. Lindsay, 223
Kelso, Ruth, 5
Kendrick, Matthew, 31n, 52
Kopytoff, Igor, 211, 272
Korda, Natasha, 7, 186, 250n
Kyd, Thomas, *The Spanish Tragedy*, 73

labour
  artisanal, 37, 52–3, 56–7, 60, 61
  black men's, 179, 180, 196
  capitalism and, 8, 110, 119–20, 149, 208
  theatrical, 15–16, 31n, 35, 52, 54–6, 58
  see also wage labour
Landreth, David, 7, 11
language
  economic, 2–3, 6–7
  economic in *Cymbeline*, 272, 274
  economic in *Othello*, 182, 185
  economic in *The Merchant of Venice*, 218–19
  economic in *The Rape of Lucrece*, 260–1, 269
  as exchange, 36
  and race, 169
  of temperance, 129
  usurious, 8, 63
Lenz, Joseph, 9, 34
Levant Company, 205, 210
liberalism, 243–4, 298–9
  The Fair Maid of the West, Part I, 173, 179, 298

liberalism (cont.)
  The Renegado, 229, 233
Little, Arthur L., 190, 204n, 255, 263
Loomis, Catherine, 294n
Luckyj, Christina, 17
Lupton, Donald, *London and the Country carbonadoed and quartered into several characters*, 34, 174
Lupton, Julia Reinhard, 52

Mahometans, 228, 230, 232–3, 240–1, 252n; *see also* Muslims; Turks; turning Turk
male commoditisation, 5, 14, 23, 177, 209–10, 273
  black, 172, 179, 297
  The Changeling, 110, 115, 119, 120
  city comedies, 120–1, 130–1
  The Merchant of Venice, 221, 222, 227
  playwrights, 22
  see also wage labour
Malynes, Gerard de, *Saint George for England, Allegorically Described*, 10, 11, 29n, 71, 279
Marcus, Leah, 203n
Mardock, James, 151
market activity
  Bartholomew Fair and, 145, 147, 154, 159
  A Chaste Maid in Cheapside, 132, 133–4
  city comedies, 128, 129, 130–1
  Epicoene, 140
  The Renegado, 231–2, 233
  The Roaring Girl, 136
market forces, 3, 22, 87, 91–4, 110, 235, 237
marriage
  in city comedies, 132, 133–4, 135, 136, 137, 157
  commoditisation of women, 36, 88, 182–5, 214–15
  companionate, 37, 133–4, 217, 220
  and equality, 218–19, 273
  Jonson and, 138, 139, 143–4, 149–53, 156, 157
  as legitimate exchange, 47–8, 60–1, 61–2, 75, 129, 223–4
  subject/state analogy, 128, 145, 152–3
  as unsatisfactory resolution, 80–1n
  see also Protestantism: and marriage

Marx, Karl, 8, 10–11, 280
masques, 49, 59, 72–4; *see also* Jonson, Ben: *Hymenaei, or the Solemnities of Masque and Barriers at a Marriage*
Massinger, Philip, *The Renegado; or The Gentleman of Venice*, 23, 208–10, 228–42, 242–5, 297–8
Matar, Nabil, 207
Maus, Katharine Eisaman, 13, 89, 261, 291n
mercantilism, 3, 12–13, 16, 30n, 172, 255
  Cymbeline, 24, 257, 270, 274, 276–7, 285, 288
  The Rape of Lucrece, 24, 258, 259–60, 261, 263–4, 267–8
  The Renegado, 242
  Troilus Cressida, 90–1, 93–5, 120, 122n
  The White Devil, 100, 120
  see also international trade; Malynes, Gerard de, *Saint George for England, Allegorically Described*; trade, English/British overseas
metatheatricality, 37, 62, 71–2, 73–4, 124n
Metzger, Mary Janell, 252n
Middleton, Thomas
  A Chaste Maid in Cheapside, 21, 128, 131, 132–4
  The Revenger's Tragedy, 1, 20, 21, 37, 62–75, 297
  Women Beware Women, 1
Middleton, Thomas and Thomas Dekker, *The Roaring Girl*, 21, 128, 131, 132, 135–7, 158, 164n
Middleton, Thomas and William Rowley, *The Changeling*, 21, 87–8, 90, 110–21, 297
Mikalachki, Jodi, 285–6, 295n
Miller, Shannon, 129
Miola, Robert S., 295n
miscegenation, 23, 180, 204n, 214, 216, 249n, 263
misogyny
  Jonson and, 141, 161n
  Othello, 182
  The Revenger's Tragedy, 74, 75
  The White Devil, 103, 108–9
Moore, John, 171
Moors *see* Africans

Moulton, Ian, 14
Muldrew, Craig, 2, 215
Muslims, 177, 244; *see also* Mahometans; slavery: Mediterranean trade; Turks

national identity, 209
    Cymbeline, 270, 286, 288
    The Fair Maid of the West, Part I, 175–7
    The Rape of Lucrece, 23–4, 254–5, 256, 258, 269
national integrity, 4, 24, 177, 207, 256, 263–4; *see also* personal integrity
nationality, 2, 8, 18, 19, 169, 298
    stereotypes, 217–18
Neill, Michael, 64, 252n
Netzloff, Mark, 226–7
Newman, Karen, 129, 133
Nocentelli, Carmen, 208
Northbrooke, John, 57

objectification, 3, 18–19, 23
    Bartholomew Fair, 152
    The Changeling, 110, 111, 114, 115
    Cymbeline, 271, 281, 284
    Epicoene, 142
    Measure for Measure, 48–9
    The Merchant of Venice, 219
    Othello, 297
    Pericles, 57
    Troilus and Cressida, 91
    see also slavery
O'Rourke, James L., 223
Ottoman Empire, 210, 259; *see also* Turks

Parker, Patricia, 277
patriarchy, 4, 36, 128
    Bartholomew Fair, 145, 148–9, 153
    The Changeling, 111, 114, 116
    A Chaste Maid in Cheapside, 132–3
    Measure for Measure, 44, 48
    The Merchant of Venice, 217, 223, 225
    Pericles, 61–2
    The Rape of Lucrece, 265–6, 267
    The Renegado, 232, 243
    The Roaring Girl, 136
    Troilus and Cressida, 100
    The White Devil, 102–3, 106–7, 108, 109
Peacham, Henry, *The Complete Gentleman*, 111, 129–30

performativity
    authorial, 159
    of chastity, 13, 36, 88–90
    of chastity in *Bartholomew Fair*, 154
    of chastity *in Measure for Measure*, 39
    of chastity in *The Changeling*, 116–18
    commoditised, 169, 191, 194, 221, 297
    and gender, 17–18, 32n
    and selfhood, 15
    of selfhood, 14, 19, 21, 299
    of selfhood in *Bartholomew Fair*, 148
    of selfhood in *Epicoene*, 140, 143
    of selfhood in *Pericles*, 53
    of selfhood in *The White Devil*, 99–100, 103, 108–9
    of subjectivity, 18, 156–7
    of temperance, 153–4
    theatrical, 157
    of virtue in *The Renegado*, 237
personal autonomy, 135, 145, 243–4, 298–9
    Jonson and, 140, 147, 153; *see also* autonomy, virgins'
personal integrity, 36, 206
    The Changeling, 111, 119
    city comedies, 132, 134, 135, 136, 137, 157
    The Fair Maid of the West, Part I, 172–3, 175, 177, 178
    Jonson and, 22, 127, 129, 131, 155
    Measure for Measure, 40
    Othello, 189
    The Rape of Lucrece, 266
    The Renegado, 209, 228, 229–30, 231, 233–4, 236–7, 242
    The White Devil, 106, 108
    see also temperance
piracy, 176, 200n, 201n, 207, 210, 230
Polanyi, Karl, 3, 5
possessive individualism, 7, 298
    Othello, 186, 195
    Pericles, 300
    The Rape of Lucrece, 267
    The Renegado, 233, 244
prostitution, 8–9, 20, 63, 128, 142
    A Chaste Maid in Cheapside, 133, 134
    Measure for Measure, 37–8, 43–4, 75
    Othello, 196–7
    The Revenger's Tragedy, 62, 66, 70–1
    theatre as, 20–1, 33–5, 36–7

prostitution (*cont.*)
  Volpone, 138, 139
  The White Devil, 101, 107
  see also brothels
Protestantism, 54–5, 56
  and Catholic signifiers, 234, 239, 253n
  and interiority, 12–13, 18
  and marriage, 5, 9–10, 262, 269, 273, 284, 286
  and virginity, 38, 75, 255–6
  see also antitheatricalism
Prynne, William, 67

queerness, 17, 18, 131, 132, 208
  The Fair Maid of the Exchange, 135
  Jonson and, 22, 128
  The Roaring Girl, 135, 137

race, 169, 182, 203n, 282
  and abjection, 181, 188
  and difference, 171, 192, 208, 217–18, 298
  and identity, 44, 169, 209
  interracial relationships, 171–2, 177, 180–1, 209, 226–7, 233–4
  and personal value, 2, 8, 22–3, 299
  and religious conversion, 224–5, 242
  and sex, 204n, 208, 223
  theatrical presentation, 18, 19, 20
  see also black men; slavery
racism, 177, 213, 216, 222, 240, 243
  Othello, 180, 182, 192, 194
  and slavery, 169, 170, 172
Rainolds, John, 33
Raleigh, Sir Walter, 262
rape, 17
  and commoditisation, 256, 263–4
  and honour, 260, 264–5, 266
  law as, 105
  marriage as, 81
  misrepresented, 183, 193
  as political allegory, 257–8, 267–8, 268–9
  and race, 204n
  The Revenger's Tragedy, 65
  St Augustine and, 158, 258, 265, 266
  and suicide see suicide after rape
  symbolic, 270, 276–8, 280
  as theft, 264–5, 265–6, 269
  threat of, 55, 135
  Troilus and Cressida, 92, 258

Rawlins, John, *The Famous and Wonderful Recovery of a Ship of Bristol. . .*, 206–7
redemption, theatre's, 37, 75
  Measure for Measure, 46, 48
  Pericles, 49–50, 54, 56, 57, 61
regimes of value, 205, 208, 300
  The Merchant of Venice, 211–12, 213–14, 221, 226
relics, Catholic
  The Renegado, 229, 234–6, 237, 239, 242, 245
  The Revenger's Tragedy, 70
representational authenticity, 9–10, 36, 37, 88
  Cymbeline, 287
  Measure for Measure, 39
  Pericles, 54, 56, 57, 300
Rich, Barnabe, *The Excellency of Good Women. . .*, 12–13, 88, 102, 103, 121n
Roe, Sir Thomas (ambassador of James I), 259–60, 263, 290n
Roediger, David R., 244
Roman value systems, 258, 260, 266, 278
romance conventions, 50, 55, 60, 224, 240, 281, 286
Rowley, William see Middleton, Thomas and William Rowley, *The Changeling*
Rubin, Gayle, 4
Ryner, Bradley, 16, 110, 113, 278

Sanchez, Melissa E., 128, 257–8, 268
Sandys, George, *Relation of a Journey begun an: Dom: 1610. . .*, 206, 207, 211–12
Schwarz, Kathryn, 16–17, 145, 152
Scott, William, *An Essay of Drapery: or The Compleate Citizen. . .*, 130, 153–4
Sebek, Barbara, 7, 47, 177
selfhood, 297–9
  aristocratic, 18, 21, 87–8
  authorial, 157–61
  Bartholomew Fair, 144, 147, 148
  chastity and, 2, 17, 175
  Christian, 229
  city comedies, 128, 131
  commoditised, 19
  Epicoene, 140, 143

Hymenaei, 139
Othello, 191
performative, 19
The Renegado, 229
The White Devil, 100, 109
Shakespeare, William
   All's Well That Ends Well, 1, 134
   Cymbeline, 23–4, 256–7, 270–88, 293n, 295–6n
   Measure for Measure, 20, 21, 37–49, 74–5
   The Merchant of Venice, 23, 208–10, 210–27, 228, 242–5
   Much Ado About Nothing, 134
   Othello, 22–3, 172, 173, 179, 180–97
   The Rape of Lucrece, 23–4, 254–5, 256, 257–69, 288
   Troilus and Cressida, 21, 87–8, 90–9
Shakespeare, William and George Wilkins, *Pericles*, 20, 21, 37, 49–62, 74–5, 299–300
   authorship, 81n
Shannon, Laurie, 155
Shell, Marc, 6, 7, 35–6, 63, 213
Singh, Jyotsna G., 214, 227, 249n
slavery, 19, 20, 191
   African, 168–71, 172, 175, 210
   Mediterranean trade, 205–7, 208, 209
   The Merchant of Venice, 210–11, 213, 221, 222, 227
   Othello, 182, 184–5, 186, 189, 194–5, 196–7
   The Renegado, 228, 229, 235, 240, 241
   and wage labour, 13–14, 171, 172, 199n, 244
Smith, Ian, 169, 202n, 283
social construct, chastity as, 21, 71, 87
social contract, 145, 243
social difference, 7, 229, 299
social order, 3–5, 6–7, 9, 10, 21, 87, 297
   Bartholomew Fair, 147, 150, 154, 159
   A Chaste Maid in Cheapside, 133
   Epicoene, 140, 143
   Othello, 197
   Pericles, 52, 60, 300
   The Revenger's Tragedy, 64, 65, 67–8, 69, 74
   Troilus Cressida, 95–6
   The White Devil, 101–2, 110
   see also class; homosociality

spheres, private and public, 19, 243, 244, 270
   Cymbeline, 257, 270, 280, 285–6, 287, 295n
   The Fair Maid of the West, Part I, 174
   The Merchant of Venice, 209, 219–21, 222, 223, 225–6, 227, 244
Spolsky, Ellen, 280
Stallybrass, Peter, 75, 90, 158–9
Stevenson, Sheryle A., 106
Stone, Lawrence, 3
subjecthood, 20, 168–9, 170, 172, 243–4, 255, 298–9
   The Fair Maid of the West, Part I, 173, 179
   The Merchant of Venice, 219, 221, 251n
   Othello, 180, 184–5, 195
   The Rape of Lucrece, 267
   The Renegado, 229, 239–40, 243
subjectivity, 7–8, 17, 18, 175, 180, 298
   aristocratic, 119
   Bartholomew Fair, 138, 144–5, 149, 152, 154, 155–7, 158–9, 160–1
   black male, 182, 187, 196
   bourgeois, 120–1, 138
   capitalist, 14
   commercial, 128–9, 132, 155
   commoditised, 2, 22, 191, 196, 221
   Epicoene, 139, 140, 141–2, 144
   Jonson and, 21, 131
   male, 130–1, 135, 178, 187–8, 229
   racial, 169, 173, 179, 243
   threatened, 44
   The White Devil, 100, 107–8
suicide after rape, 69, 254, 266–7, 268–9, 280, 291n

temperance, 129–31, 153–4
   A Chaste Maid in Cheapside, 134
   The Fair Maid of the West, Part I, 174–5
   Jonson and, 137, 138, 139, 143, 144, 148
   lack of, 132–3
   The Renegado, 231, 232–3, 237
Timberlake, Henry, *A true and strange discourse of the travailes of two English pilgrimes...*, 207

trade, English/British overseas, 205, 210, 259, 278, 284
  The Fair Maid of the West, Part I, 172, 173, 175–7, 177–8, 179
  Mediterranean, 200n, 207–8
  see also international trade; slavery
transvestism, 17–18, 135, 156, 299
  Cymbeline, 281, 295n
  Epicoene, 131, 139, 141–2, 143
travel narratives, 206–9, 211, 227, 229
treasure analogies, 1, 24, 256, 269
  The Changeling, 110, 113
  A Chaste Maid in Cheapside, 133
  Measure for Measure, 41, 42
  The Merchant of Venice, 214
  The Rape of Lucrece, 258–61, 263–4, 265–6, 267–8
  Troilus Cressida, 96
  see also jewel analogies
Tuke, Thomas, *A Treatise Against Painting*, 89
Turks, 176, 206, 207, 208, 209, 211–12; *see also* Mahometans; Muslims
turning Turk, 228, 229, 239

usury, 1, 8, 10, 36, 44, 279
  The Merchant of Venice, 211, 212, 222
  The Revenger's Tragedy, 62, 63, 65–7, 68, 71–2, 74

value creation, 299
  The Changeling, 110–11, 113
  Cymbeline, 274, 285
  The Fair Maid of the West, Part I, 176
  The Merchant of Venice, 212–13, 220–1, 226
  Othello, 180–1, 191–2, 195–6, 197
  Troilus Cressida, 91–4, 96–8
  The White Devil, 100
virginity, militant, 75
  The Fair Maid of the West, Part I, 178
  Measure for Measure, 37, 38, 39–40, 42–3
  Pericles, 55–7
  The Revenger's Tragedy, 62, 69–70
  The Roaring Girl, 135–6, 137

virginity, proofs of, 88, 117–18, 125n
Vitkus, Daniel J., 177, 207–8, 209, 210, 221, 230
Vives, Juan Luis, 256

wage labour, 2, 20, 115–16, 120, 199n, 299–300
  military, 182, 194
  prostitution as stand-in, 8, 54, 196–7
  and slavery, 13–14, 169, 170, 171, 172, 244
Wall, Wendy, 286
Waswo, Richard, 166n
Wayne, Valerie, 296n
Webster, John, *The White Devil*, 1, 21, 87–8, 90, 99–110
  compared with *The Changeling*, 111, 117–18, 120
Wheeler, John, *A Treatise of Commerce*, 13–14, 207
White, Allon, 158–9
whiteness, 171–2, 204n, 210, 244–5, 298–9
  Cymbeline, 24, 282–3
  The Fair Maid of the West, Part I, 172–3, 177, 179
  The Merchant of Venice, 211, 215, 216, 217–18, 219, 223, 224–5, 227
  Othello, 173, 182, 185, 187–8, 191–3, 196, 197
  The Rape of Lucrece, 255, 263–4
  The Renegado, 229, 238, 240, 242, 243
  see also slavery: Mediterranean trade
Wilkins, George *see* Shakespeare, William and George Wilkins, *Pericles*
will, female, 17, 114, 152, 158, 184, 219
  subordinated, 150, 244
Wilson, Thomas, *A Discourse Upon Usury*, 63, 66

Yachnin, Paul, 16, 35, 61

Zucker, Adam, 150

EU representative:
Easy Access System Europe
Mustamäe tee 50, 10621 Tallinn, Estonia
Gpsr.requests@easproject.com